New Woman Plays

Between 1890 and 1914, the British feminist movement, which included the new militancy of the suffragettes, encouraged an increasing number of women to use theatre to explore women's experience. These are not the idealised portraits of the 'New Women' of male playwrights such as Shaw, but realistic pictures of women's problematic lives. Florence Bell's and Elizabeth Robins's *Alan's Wife*, which created a scandal when first performed in 1893, treats the killing of a handicapped child by his widowed mother not as polemic nor sensation, but with insight into the woman's situation. *Diana of Dobson's* by Cicely Hamilton was a popular success in 1908, with its realistic picture of women's work in a drapery store and its examination of the economic motives for marriage. Elizabeth Baker's *Chains* (1909) and Githa Sowerby's *Rutherford and Son* (1912) both expose the tyranny of family and labour. The former deals with the claustrophobia of suburban life, the latter with the oppressive patriarchal system operating in the industrial North.

Linda Fitzsimmons teaches in the Department of Drama: Theatre, Film, Television at the University of Bristol.
Viv Gardner teaches in the Department of Drama at the University of Manchester.

D0743577

Love and Thunder. Plays by Women in the Age of Queen Anne (*Love at a Loss* by Catharine Trotter; *The Spanish Wives* by Mary Pix; *The Adventures of Venice* by Susanna Centlivre; *Antiochus the Great* by Jane Wiseman) Selected and introduced by Kendall

Plays by Women Volume One (*Vinegar Tom* by Caryl Churchill; *Dusa, Fish, Stas and Vi* by Pam Gems; *Tissue* by Louise Page; *Aurora Leigh* by Michelene Wandor) Introduced and edited by Michelene Wandor

Plays by Women Volume Two (*Rites* by Maureen Duffy; *Letters Home* by Rose Leiman Goldemberg; *Trafford Tanzi* by Claire Luckham; *Find Me* by Olwen Wymark) Introduced and edited by Michelene Wandor

Plays by Women Volume Three (*Aunt Mary* by Pam Gems; *Red Devils* by Debbie Horsfield; *Blood Relations* by Sharon Pollock; *Time Pieces* by Lou Wakefield and The Women's Theatre Group) Introduced and edited by Michelene Wandor

Plays by Women Volume Four (*Objections to Sex and Violence* by Caryl Churchill; *Rose's Story* by Grace Dayley; *Blood and Ice* by Liz Lochhead; *Pinball* by Alison Lyssa) Introduced and edited by Michelene Wandor

Plays by Women Volume Five (*Queen Christina* by Pam Gems; *A Raisin in the Sun* by Lorraine Hansberry; *Piper's Cave* by Rosa Munro; *Money To Live* by Jacqueline Rudet) Introduced and edited by Mary Remnant

Plays by Women Volume Six (*About Face* by Cordelia Ditton and Maggie Ford; *More* by Maro Green and Caroline Griffin; *Origin of the Species* by Bryony Lavery; *Ficky Stingers* by Eve Lewis) Introduced and edited by Mary Remnant

Plays by Women Volume Seven (*Thatcher's Women* by Kay Adshead; *Adult Child/Dead Child* by Claire Dowie; *Stamping, Shouting and Singing Home* by Lisa Evans; *Night* by Marie Laberge, Rita Fraticelli; *Effie's Burning* by Valerie Windsor) Introduced and edited by Mary Remnant

Plays by Women Volume Eight (*Ironmistress* by April De Angelis; *Heartgame* by Mary Cooper; *The One-Sided Wall* by Janet Cresswell and Niki Johnson; *Caving In* by Ayshe Raif; *Towards Evening* and *Walkies Times* by Ena Lamont Stewart; *Motherlove* by Joan Wolton) Introduced and edited by Mary Remnant

Gay Plays: Volume One (*Submariners* by Tom McClenaghan; *The Green Bay Tree* by Mordaunt Shairp; *Passing By* by Martin Sherman; *Accounts* by Michael Wilcox) Introduced and edited by Michael Wilcox

Gay Plays: Volume Two (*Quaint Honour* by Roger Gellert; *Bearclaw* by Timothy Mason; *Cracks* by Martin Sherman; *Lies About Vietnam* by C. P. Taylor) Introduced and edited by Michael Wilcox

Gay Plays: Volume Three (*Cock & Bull Story* by Richard Crowe and Richard Zajdlic; *Terminal Bar* by Paul Selig; *Levitation* by Timothy Mason; *The Prisoners of War* by J. R. Ackerly)

Gay Plays: Volume Four (*A Vision of Love Revealed in Sleep* by Neil Bartlett; *Days of Cavafy* by Ray Killingworth; *Round Two* by Eric Bentley; *Wild Blue* by Joseph Pintauro) Introduced and edited by Michael Wilcox

Lesbian Plays: Volume One (*Any Woman Can* by Jill Posener; *Double Vision* by Women's Theatre Group; *Chiaroscuro* by Jackie Kay; *The Rug of Identity* by Jill Fleming) Introduced and edited by Jill Davis

Lesbian Plays: Volume Two (*Coming Soon* by Debby Klein; *Julie* by Catherine Kilcoyne; *Supporting Roles* by Sandra Freeman; *The Housetrample* by Sue Frumin; *Cinderella, The Real True Story* by Cheryl Moch) Introduced and edited by Jill Davies

Black Plays: Volume One (*Chameleon* by Michael Ellis; *Lonely Cowboy* by Alfred Fagon; *The Lower Depths* by Tunde Ikoli; *Basin* by Jacqueline Rudet) Introduced and edited by Yvonne Brewster

Black Plays: Volume Two (*Job Rocking* by Benjamin Zephaniah; *The Dragon Can't Dance* by Earl Lovelace; *A Rock in Water* by Winsome Pinnock; *Blood, Sweat and Fears* by Marie Oshodi)

New Woman Plays

Alan's Wife
Florence Bell and Elizabeth Robins

Diana of Dobson's
Cicely Hamilton

Chains
Elizabeth Baker

Rutherford and Son
Githa Sowerby

Edited and introduced by Linda Fitzsimmons and Viv Gardner

Methuen Drama

A METHUEN NEW THEATRESCRIPT

This volume first published in Great Britain as a Methuen Paperback
original in 1991 by Methuen Drama, Michelin House, 81 Fulham Road,
London SW3 6RB and distributed in the United States of America by HEB Inc.,
361 Hanover Street, Portsmouth, New Hampshire 03801, USA

The picture on the front cover shows Lena Ashwell as Diana with other cast members in
Diana of Dobson's, Kingsway Theatre, 1908. (By courtesy of the Trustees of the Theatre
Museum, Victoria and Albert Museum.)

A CIP catalogue record for this book is available from the British Library

ISBN 0 413 64200 3

Printed in Great Britain
by Clays Ltd, St Ives Plc

Contents

Introduction

The New Woman

Life has taken on a strange unloveliness, and the least beautiful thing therein is the New Woman.[1]

The four plays in this volume, Florence Bell and Elizabeth Robins's *Alan's Wife* (1894), Cicely Hamilton's *Diana of Dobson's* (1908), Elizabeth Baker's *Chains* (1909) and Githa Sowerby's *Rutherford and Son* (1912), have been brought together under the title of *New Woman Plays*. It is not a label that any of the writers would necessarily have chosen for their work, but it is a description they would certainly have recognised. 'The New Woman', in the period between 1894 and 1914, was a term broadly synonymous with our contemporary 'feminist' – for some a tag of contumely and contempt, for others a rallying cry. The women who wrote these plays were each in their way New Women, and were writing of, and for, the New Women of their generation.

The term was reputedly first used by the radical novelist, Sarah Grand, in an article in the *North American Review* of May 1894. The image of the New Woman rapidly became fixed in the press of the period. *Punch* could not go through an edition without a couple of satirical references to, and the odd cartoon of, this apparently new phenomenon. By September of that year the popular comic dramatist, Sydney Grundy, had produced a play of that name at the Comedy Theatre, in the knowledge that his public would instantly recognise The New Woman.

The image of the New Woman is best exemplified by one of those *Punch* cartoons entitled 'Donna Quixote'. She sits, plain and bespectacled, in an armchair, in her sensible, 'hygienic' or 'rational' dress, book in one hand and latchkey held aloft in the other. She is surrounded by images of the 'disorderly notions' that crowd her imagination and the sources of those notions – the works of Mona Caird, Ibsen and *The Yellow Book*. Behind her there is the Amazon holding aloft the flag of the divided skirt, another fighting the dragon of Decorum and a third tilting at the windmill of Marriage Laws. The decapitated head of 'Tyrant Man' sits by one foot, her new 'Mrs' Cerberus, with the three heads of Mrs Grundy, Chaperone and Mamma, 'keeping the portals of that Home Elysian/That cranks now call a Hades', by the other. The accompanying poem has her cry:

> . . . In spite of babies, bonnets, tea,
> Creation's Heir, I must, I will be – Free! . . .
>
> Nay, 'tis a gaol to those who long to roam,
> Unchaperoned, emancipate, and free,
> With the large Liberty of the Latch-key![2]

The poet then warns Donna that despite the '*Doll's House* delirium that sets your nerves a-thrill' she should ignore all 'the cants/ Of culture's cranks' for these will never produce true emancipation, and she is exhorted by *Punch*:

> . . . dear Donna Quixote, be not stupid,
> Fight not with Hymen and war not with Cupid,
> Run not amuck 'gainst Mother Nature's plan,
> Nor make a monster of your mate, poor Man,
> Or like La Mancha's cracked, though noble knight,
> You'll find blank failure in mistaken fight.[3]

The New Woman, then, was typically seen as young, middle-class and single on principle. She eschewed the fripperies of fashion in favour of more masculine dress and severe coiffure. She had probably been educated to a standard unknown to previous generations of women and was certainly a devotee of Ibsen and given to reading 'advanced' books. She was financially independent of father or husband, often through earning her own living in one of the careers opening up to women at the time like journalism and teaching. She affected emancipated habits, like smoking, riding a bicycle, using bold language and taking the omnibus or train unescorted. She belonged to all-female clubs, like Mrs Massingberd's Pioneer Club, or societies where like-minded individuals met and ideas and sexes mixed freely. She sought freedom from, and equality with, men. In the process she was prepared to overturn all convention and all accepted notions of femininity. She presented a challenge to established thinking and as such she also presented a threat – to be ridiculed and contained.

Naturally, this two-dimensional New Woman did not exist outside the pages of *Punch* and other fictions. But the ideas that she stood for did. The fight for women's emancipation had been in existence for decades, if not centuries. The pace had quickened during the 1880s and by the 1890s there was a burgeoning of radical activity in the women's movement. It was not at this stage focused on the franchise, though that was necessarily one plank of the platform. The freedoms sought by the real New Women of the 1890s were more personal, and these preoccupations did not cease to exist in the more politically-oriented and militant 1900s. The struggle centred on the need to determine their own lives, whether in relation to education, work, men or even the apparently trivial details of women's lives. It is easy at a century's distance to smile at the New Woman's insistence on her right to smoke or to wear a divided skirt and play tennis or golf. But each of these activities represented a small victory over the dictates of society on the acceptable norm of female behaviour. They undermined the passivity, physical, mental and emotional, expected of women in the typical middle-class Victorian household – decorative but useless, inactive but subservient to father, brother or husband.

The reality of the lives of the New Women of the period 1890–1914 is, of course, more complex. Many women had begun to break the straitjacket of middle-class conformity – the path for working-class women was usually different – through education and work. The fruits of the improvements in girls' education were maturing by the 1890s. Since Miss Buss had established the first girls' day or 'high' school, the North London Collegiate, in 1850, the day school and girls' public school movement had expanded rapidly. Over ninety girls' schools alone were created under the 1869 Endowed School Act. Access to Higher Education was also well established by the 1890s – though not to all faculties and not always to degree level as at Oxford and Cambridge. There was then by 1890 a generation of reasonably educated girls who looked for some continuing fulfilment through work. Many went into teaching, some into journalism, typewriting and other 'white collar' occupations; some went into the theatre.

The Theatre

They were years during which I realised the truth of the many warnings I had received concerning the difficulty of making a living by the art of the theatre. . . . [It] was a life of many disadvantages, badly paid and uncertain; a life where long periods of unemployment were taken as a matter of course. But it had its compensations; and for all its disappointments and often squalid hardship, I am more than glad to have lived it.[4]

In addition to the warnings that Cicely Hamilton received about the theatre there was, of course, the age-old prejudice against it as a fit place for respectable women to be – on either side of the curtain. Despite a gradual change in the public attitude towards the profession, best exemplified by the knighting of Henry Irving in 1895, few of the women who entered the theatre did so with the unconditional blessing of their families. And yet many of the so-called New Women looked to the theatre for a career. Its unconventionality may have been part of the attraction for these unconventional women. Certainly in moving into that 'nether world' they were 'to lose caste'[5], but in doing so they were to achieve a degree of autonomy in their lives and an opportunity for creative fulfilment. The irony was that this 'uncoventional' world was the purveyor of some of the most conventional – not to say reactionary – attitudes towards women in the period. True, productions of Ibsen had been known since 1880, but these were all at private performances and had been met with howls of derision by many critics and incomprehension and indifference by the greater public. The dominant popular theatrical genres in the 1890s and even into the 1900s were melodrama and society dramas. Both Cicely Hamilton and Elizabeth Robins, who worked as actresses before writing plays, spent many years playing in melodrama.

Whilst there is little evidence that many actresses began their careers with a radical view of the repertoire, it is clear that some were radicalised by the frustrations of playing parts that were not only far from representing their – or any other woman's – experience of life but also presented images of women that ran counter to their personal politics. An example of this can be found in the cast of Grundy's antagonistic comedy of *The New Woman*, where one of the caricatured New Women, Victoria Vivash, was played by Gertrude Warden who was Mrs Linden in the first London production of *A Doll's House* – not an enterprise that the uncommitted lent their name to – and Alma Murray, another 'Ibsenite', played the destructive New Woman of the title. The actresses were also frustrated by the domination of the profession by men at the expense of their equally talented female colleagues; the tradition of the actor-manager had only infrequently been challenged by an actress-manager.

The period from 1890 up to the First World War saw some changes in this situation, many initiated by women themselves. The key production of the radical theatre movement of the 1880s had been Janet Achurch and her husband Charles Charrington's production of *A Doll's House*. This, and J. T. Grein's Independent Theatre which opened in 1891, offered a model which some women performers were able to follow. Actresses like Achurch, Florence Farr, Elizabeth Robins and Marion Lea set up their own companies to perform the plays of Ibsen; Lena Ashwell took over the Kingsway Theatre in 1907, successfully premiering Cicely Hamilton's *Diana of Dobson's*, amongst other plays. Olga Nethersole, Lillah McCarthy and Gertrude Kingston were but three of the actresses known to have been involved in the women's movement at this time, who ran so-called 'little theatres' committed to a more adventurous repertoire. Emma Cons and subsequently her niece, Lilian Baylis, managed the Old Vic, producing 'cheap and decent amusement along temperance lines'. Other women were involved in more strictly commercial managements. In 1907, Annie Horniman, who had financed Florence Farr's 1894 management venture at the Avenue, established Britain's first provincial repertory theatre at the Gaiety in Manchester.

Actresses seized the opportunities offered by these institutions, but they were too few and too unstable to offer hope of permanent employment in a 'women-oriented' theatre. Even some of the most successful, like Elizabeth Robins, were eventually forced out of management and performing texts that they chose, and into writing, because of the uncertainty of income from experimental theatre work. The most consistent feminist work emerged, for a limited period, from the founding of the Actresses' Franchise League in 1908, with its policy of performances in support of the campaign for votes for women. Out of the Actresses' Franchise League's work came Inez Bensusan's successful Woman's Theatre season at the Coronet Theatre in 1913 – a second season was unfortunately prevented by the outbreak of war – and Edy Craig's Pioneer Players which lasted into the 1920s. Craig's company, set up in 1911, though not exclusively female, was dominated by women in all areas of production and administration and was committed to experimental work, including, naturally, that by women. What was perhaps most important in these two decades was that the mould had been broken, and these New Women in theatre had effectively shown that there was an alternative.

The 'feminism' in theatre at this time was not confined to the activism of the performers and managers, it was also at work amongst the writers. Whilst Ibsen provided some of the most popular women's roles with these actresses, giving women a centrality, complexity and seriousness rarely found elsewhere, other writers, influenced by Ibsen and the changes in the social climate, were creating dramatic New Women. Not all of them were hostile like Grundy or Henry Arthur Jones in *The Case of Rebellious Susan*. Some, like Pinero in *The Notorious Mrs Ebbsmith*, were sympathetic, but were unable to see the New Woman as anything other than doomed. As Mrs Patrick Campbell, who created the role of Agnes Ebbsmith, wrote in her memoirs:

The role of Agnes Ebbsmith and the first three acts of the play filled me with ecstasy . . . but the last act broke my heart. I knew that such an Agnes in life could not have drifted into the Bible-reading inertia of the woman she became in the last act. . . . To me Agnes was a finer woman. In those days, not so long ago, she was a new and daring type, the woman agitator, the pessimist with original independent ideas – in revolt against sham morals.[6]

She goes on to ask whether 'Sir Arthur Pinero missed an opportunity or was the time not yet ripe? The suffragette, with her hammer in her muff, had not yet risen above the horizon'.[7] Some, like Shaw and Barker, created admirable, independent, self-determining women – Vivie Warren in *Mrs Warren's Profession* and Marion Yates in *The Madras House* – but denied them any sort of reality. It remained for the women writers to combine the new ideas and ideology emerging from the debate over the 'woman question' with a grasp of the reality of the lives of women in the period. In the four, representative, plays in this volume, you will not find idealised portraits of successfully 'new' New Women, but women struggling to control and improve their lives in an implacably male world. None of the women in the plays articulate any 'New' philosophy, they are shown living out the problems created by traditional views of women. Three preoccupations dominate the plays – marriage, motherhood and work. The theme that unites these plays is the question of choice.

Marriage

What I rebelled at chiefly was the dependence implied in the idea of 'destined' marriage, 'destined' motherhood – the identification of success with marriage, of failure with spinsterhood, the artificial concentration of the hopes of girlhood on sexual attraction and maternity.[8]

Whilst Cicely Hamilton was in revolt against the 'destiny' of the so-called normal women by repudiating marriage, others too were arguing for greater recognition of female sexuality, free liaisons, more liberal divorce laws. The majority of women, however, were not looking for lives without men or even marriage, but a greater equality within their relationships with men. However in an era in which women far outnumbered men in the population, many had no choice but to become one of the 'odd' or 'superfluous' women. Women dramatists, including Baker, Hamilton, Robins and Sowerby, tended to deal with the practicalities of marriage and motherhood, more than the ideologies of the sexual revolution in their plays. As Hamilton vigorously argues in her book, *Marriage as a Trade*, marriage for many women was the only economic alternative to the 'slave labour' in which many of them were engaged.

The female characters in the plays do not marry for love and romance. Even in Hamilton's 'romantic comedy', *Diana of Dobson's*, when Diana finally accepts Bretherton's proposal she does so pointing out the strain her unemployed poverty places on her 'disinterestedness' – 'I'm homeless and penniless – I haven't tasted food for nearly twelve hours – I've half starved for days'. In Baker's *Chains*, Maggie finally rejects a loveless marriage, recognising that she would just be swapping one cage (the shop) for another. Her future is uncertain, but it is her own. Maggie's sister, Lily, is used to show the other side of marriage. She is a woman trapped by the conventional attitude to marriage whose pursuit of respectability in her lower middle-class household, binds herself and her husband, Charley, tighter and tighter. Her final 'chain' – the news of her pregnancy – thwarts Charley's hopes of ever breaking out of the destructive suburban spiral that holds them both. Mary, in Sowerby's *Rutherford and Son*, states clearly that she has married to escape the drudgery of office life in London. The only free, 'romantic' marriage that is represented in these four plays is that of Jean Creyke in Bell and Robins's *Alan's Wife*. The unconventionality of this relationship is that it is a free choice, made in the face of opposition by her mother and against her upbringing. There is a frank acknowledgement of the sexual attraction that Alan has for Jean and it comes closest to the notorious writings of contemporary New Women novelists like George Egerton.

Motherhood

The various explanations which have been given for women's existence can be narrowed down to two – her husband and her child. Male humanity has wobbled between two convictions – the one that she exists for the entire benefit of contemporary mankind; the other, that she exists for the entire benefit of the next generation. The latter is at present the favourite. One consideration only male humanity has refused to entertain – that she exists in any degree whatsoever for the benefit of herself.[9]

Three of the plays also deal, in three completely different ways, with the question of motherhood. In the earliest play, *Alan's Wife*, Jean Creyke kills her handicapped child. In the last act, she finally and simply defends her action as her one act of courage – 'I showed him the only true mercy' – and believes that she will find him 'up yonder made straight and fair and happy'. She kills from love for the child and her dead husband. In a lengthy introduction to the published edition of the play, William Archer defends the play against its critics but also undermines Robins's handling of the killing. He, had he written the scene, would have turned the play into a polemic – a eugenic defence of the killing of the handicapped, in a dialogue between Jean and the doctor which would have been 'a subtle piece of intellectual as opposed to merely emotional, drama'.[10] The emotional truth of Jean's matricidal act was something that the male rationalist and ideologist, Archer, would not and could not have written. This rational attitude permeates many of the plays written by the male writers of the period. Emancipation for women is often equated with freedom from conventional relationships with men, and particularly the principle of freedom to choose to bear a child outside marriage without stigma. Barker's Miss Yates in *The Madras House*, refuses to name the father of her child and is defiantly 'pleased and proud'. This is not an option for any of the women in these plays by women dramatists. In *Rutherford and Son*, it is quite clear that Mary's priority is to save her child from the type of poverty she – and all the other Miss Yateses in lower middle-class occupations – would be condemned to by remaining in her original position. She condemns her husband for his Nora-like abandonment of his child in pursuit of freedom:

Try and realise – we've no right to live as we like – we've had our day together, you and I – but it's past, and we know it. He's [their son] what matters now . . .[11]

This positive and responsible attitude to parenthood is far from the manipulative use of maternity shown by Lily in *Chains*. In Lily's mind motherhood is, as Hamilton indicates in *Marriage as a Trade*, merely part of women's conventional expectations of marriage.

Work

It's jolly hard though! I often think 'I'd rather be a kitten and cry mew' than a woman trying to earn a living. (Eleanor Marx to her sister, Laura Lafarge, 1889)[12]

As we have seen, for some women work was a considered choice, for others it was a necessity.

There was a small, but significant rise in the number of women employed in the United Kingdom in the period 1890–1914. The rise was concentrated amongst the middle classes, with a concomitant fall amongst female working-class employment. Between 1881 and 1911 there was an increase from 12.6 per cent to 23.7 per cent, in the number of middle class women in the total female workforce. This was accounted for by the Board of Trade correspondent on female employment, Clara Collet, in a report in 1894:

> In the middle class, therefore, a high standard of comfort, a smaller field of domestic usefulness, a diminished probability of marriage, apprehension with regard to the future, have all combined to encourage the entrance into the labour market of middle-class girls.[13]

No mention here of the idealistic search for work that was seen as part of the ethos of the New Woman. The reality was that, unless a woman had a private income to support her, the experience of the middle-class woman and work, whether in the theatre or shop, was likely to be hard and exploitative. Conditions for working-class women altered very little at this time, with scant attention paid to the specific needs of working women by the emergent unions.

Given their own experience it is not surprising that the women dramatists in this period should present the problems of working women rather than the idealised view of work found in, say, Shaw's New Woman, Vivie Warren who is happy to be 'a woman of business, permanently single and permanently unromantic'.[14] The three plays in this volume that depict the economic context of women's lives, *Chains*, *Diana of Dobson's* and *Rutherford and Son*, show how severe conditions were for working women. In both *Chains* and *Diana of Dobson's*, the drudgery and exploitation of shop life is clearly delineated. For both Maggie and the employees of Dobson's emporium, the only escape from the tyranny of the shop is marriage. Those of the 'superfluous' women who miss this opportunity are condemned, as Diana sees herself condemned, to a lifetime working in establishments similar to Dobson's:

> . . . cringing to be taken on at the same starvation salary – and then settle down in the same stuffy dormitory, with the same mean little rules to obey – I shall serve the same stream of intelligent customers – and bolt my dinner off the same tough meat in the same gloomy dining-room with the same mustard-coloured paper on the walls.[15]

A later play by Elizabeth Baker, *Miss Tassey*, is also set in the living-in accommodation of a large drapery store. Its unseen eponymous heroine, a spinster of forty-five, having missed her opportunity of marriage and finding herself dismissed on account of her age and infirmity – itself a result of her work – commits suicide.

The reality of the world that Baker and Hamilton depict is not in doubt; Hamilton asked Margaret Bondfield, organiser of the Shop Assistants' Union, to read the play and check the facts before the play went into rehearsal. Only two minor changes were suggested.

Sowerby's play, *Rutherford and Son*, contrasts two women's experiences of class and work. Janet, the daughter of the *nouveau riche* Rutherford household, has been forced into idleness by her father's insistence that his daughter should not 'do things like a servant'. As a consequence, Janet has become frustrated, isolated and embittered. Her sister-in-law, Mary, has chosen the opposite path. She has, like Kitty in *Diana of Dobson's*, married to escape work:

> Day after day in an office. The crowded train morning and night – bad light – bad food . . . It's been nothing else all along – the bare struggle for life.[16]

Mary is prepared to do anything to protect her son from that experience, even to the extent of 'selling' him to her father-in-law, Rutherford. Money means power, the power to make choices.

Conclusion

> Creation's Heir, I must, I will be – Free![17]

Punch's burlesque cry from the New Woman can in the light of these New Woman plays be seen to have some truth and genuine passion. Each of the dramas shows women struggling to find or create circumstances in which they can make decisions over their own lives – to take responsibility for their own actions. Each woman succeeds in different ways. Jean Creyke has chosen her own partner and assumes responsibility for the decision over her child's and her own death. Diana Massingberd, eschewing the sensible advice of her shop colleagues, chooses how to spend her small inheritance and hence her life. Janet Rutherford, having chosen 'her man' then chooses to leave him and her father, when she discovers that Martin's loyalty is more to her father than to her. Mary chooses to put her child before her marriage. And in *Chains* Maggie asserts her freedom to choose between the alternative cages of marriage or the shop.

All these freedoms are circumscribed by circumstances, but they are none the less significant and represent a realistic enactment of the philosophy of the New Woman.

Viv Gardner
Department of Drama
University of Manchester
September 1990

Notes

1. Mrs Roy Devereux, 'The Feminine Potential' in the *Saturday Review*, 22 June 1895, pp. 824–5.
2. 'Donna Quixote' in *Punch*, 28 April 1894, p. 195.
3. 'Donna Quixote', p. 195.
4. Cicely Hamilton, *Life Errant* (London, Dent, 1935) pp. 32–3.
5. Lena Ashwell, *Myself a Player* (London, Michael Joseph, 1936) p.46.
6. Mrs Patrick Campbell, *My Life and Some Letters* (London, Hutchinson, 1922) pp.98–9.
7. Campbell, pp. 99–100.
8. Hamilton, *Life Errant*, p. 65.
9. Cicely Hamilton, *Marriage as a Trade* (London, Chapman and Hall, 1909; reprinted, London, The Women's Press, 1981) pp. 24–5.
10. William Archer, Introduction to *Alan's Wife* (London, Henry and Co., 1893) p.xv.
11. Githa Sowerby, *Rutherford and Son* (London, Sidgwick and Jackson, 1912) p. 95.
12. Olga Meier (ed.), *The Daughters of Karl Marx: Family Correspondence 1866–1898* (London, Deutsch, 1982) p. 210.
13. A. L. Bowley, *Wages and Income in the United Kingdom since 1860* (Cambridge, Cambridge University Press, 1937), cited in David Rubinstein, *Before the Suffragettes* (Brighton, Harvester Press, 1986) p. 70.
14. Clare Collet, *Report by Miss Collet on the Statistics of Employment of Women and Girls*, cited in Rubinstein, p. 71.
15. G. B. Shaw, *Mrs Warren's Profession* in *Plays Unpleasant* (Harmondsworth, Penguin, 1981) p. 274.
16. Cicely Hamilton, *Diana of Dobson's* (London, Samuel French, 1925) p. 13.
17. 'Donna Quixote', p. 195.

Select Bibliography

Lena Ashwell, *Myself a Player* (London, Michael Joseph, 1936)

Mrs Patrick Campbell, *My Life and Some Letters* (London, Hutchinson, 1922)

Ian Clarke, *Edwardian Drama* (London, Faber and Faber, 1989)

Viv Gardner (ed.), *Sketches from the Actresses' Franchise League* (Nottingham, Nottingham Drama Texts, 1986)

Cicely Hamilton, *Marrige as a Trade* (London, Chapman and Hall, 1909, reprinted London, The Women's Press, 1981)

C. Hayman and D. Spender (eds.), *How the Vote was Won and Other Suffragette Plays* (London, Methuen, 1985)

Julie Holledge, *Innocent Flowers: Women in the Edwardian Theatre* (London, Virago, 1981)

Josephine Johnson, *Florence Farr: Bernard Shaw's 'New Woman'* (Totowa, N. J., Rowman and Littlefield, 1975)

Gertrude Kingston, *Curtsey While You're Thinking* . . . (London, Williams and Norgate, 1937)

Jane Lewis, *Women in England: Sexual Division and Social Change 1870–1950* (Brighton, Wheatsheaf Books, 1984)

Lillah McCarthy, *Myself and Friends* (London, Thornton Butterworth, 1933)

Jan McDonald, *The 'New Drama' 1900–1914* (Basingstoke, Macmillan, 1986)

Elizabeth Robins, *Ibsen and the Actress* (London, Hogarth Press, 1928)

—*Theatre and Friendship* (London, Cape, 1932)

—*Both Sides of the Curtain* (London, Heinemann, 1940)

David Rubinstein, *Before the Suffragettes* (Brighton, Harvester Press, 1986)

Lis Whitelaw, *The Life and Rebellious Times of Cicely Hamilton: Actress, Writer, Suffragist* (London, The Women's Press, 1990)

A Note on the Text

The texts have been prepared from the earliest published editions of the plays available in the British Library (see individual bibliographies). In the case of *Diana of Dobson's*, this is a French's Acting Edition, with additional stage directions.

Alan's Wife

Florence Bell and Elizabeth Robins

Florence Bell (1851–1930) and Elizabeth Robins (1862–1952)

Florence Bell is now best known for her book *At the Works: A Study of a Manufacturing Town* (1907), and it is likely that she provided some of the contextual detail of *Alan's Wife* from her first-hand observations of working-class domestic life in Middlesbrough. In her introduction to the Virago reprint of *At the Works*, Angela John writes, 'though not a feminist tract, Florence Bell's concern is essentially with and for the women of the community' (1985). She was to use her research again in her play *The Way the Money Goes*, produced by the Stage Society at the Shaftesbury and the Royalty in 1910, which examines the effects of gambling on working-class women and family life in an iron-manufacturing town. She wrote a number of other plays, as well as novels, essays and children's stories. Her pageant play, *The Heart of Yorkshire* (1923), written to help raise money for the preservation of the Five Sisters window in York Minster, dramatises the legend attributing the design of the window to tapestries worked by five sisters, and goes on to invent (as far as I can discover) the idea that the city archives were saved by a woman, Anne Fairfax, braving the royalist army occupying the city. Elizabeth Robins wrote in *The Times* of Bell's 'being the one person who, not of the theatre, yet loved and understood the theatre beyond any other I had known. . . . In those early days, to see her actually behind the scenes was to forget that she did not belong there – was to feel she did belong there' (17 May 1930).

Elizabeth Robins was a prominent feminist campaigner, furthering the feminist cause through her theatre work, her writing, and her political activities. In the 1890s she was instrumental in introducing Ibsen to Britain, not only acting many of his major characters, but also producing several of the plays, together with actress Marion Lea, and helping in their translation (she learnt Norwegian so she could read him in the original). She recognised the opportunities his work offered to women performers to take on exciting roles and her experience as producer left her even more dissatisfied with the actor-manager system that dominated the commercial theatre. She was an active and prominent member of the Actresses' Franchise League and of the Women Writers' Suffrage League, and from 1907 to 1912 was a member of the board of the Women's Social and Political Union. In 1907 her play *Votes for Women!* was performed at the Court Theatre, directed by Harley Granville Barker. The press acclaimed the second act – a suffrage rally in Trafalgar Square – for its realism and excitement, but the play takes on more than the suffrage in its insistence on women's right to self-determination and in its rejection of women's enforced dependency on and exploitation by men. In the same year she re-wrote the play as a novel, *The Convert*. After the war she was one of the three original directors of the feminist weekly periodical *Time and Tide*, was an active member of the 'Six Point Group', campaigning for equal opportunities for women, and published *Ancilla's Share: an Indictment of Sex Antagonism* (1924).

She was fully aware of the particular problems for women working in theatre. In *Theatre and Friendship* (1932), she wrote:

We had . . . seen how freedom in the practice of our art, how the bare opportunity to practise it at all, depended, for the actress, on considerations humiliatingly different from those that confronted the actor. The stage career of an actress was inextricably involved in the fact that she was a woman and that those who were masters of the Theatre were men. These considerations did not belong to art; they stultified art. (pp. 29–30)

She saw a patriarchal control of women's writing, too. In *Woman's Secret*, a pamphlet published by the Women's Social and Political Union in 1907, she wrote:

> Contrary to the popular impression, to say in print what she thinks is the last thing the woman-novelist or journalist is so rash as to attempt. Here even more than elsewhere (unless she is reckless) she must wear the aspect that shall have the best chance of pleasing her brothers. Her publishers are not women.

Her recognition of the power of male control of women's creativity led her and Florence Bell to have *Alan's Wife* appear anonymously, and to keep the authorship secret for many years.

Alan's Wife was first presented at a matinée on 28 April 1893, and again on 2 May, at Terry's Theatre, by the Independent Theatre Society, founded and run by J. T. Grein. Robins writes of the play in *Theatre and Friendship* that 'controversy raged round the question of authorship of the play, and ink continued to be spilt on the dreadfulness of the theme' (p. 118).

Grein was also responsible for publishing the play, which was based on a story by a Swedish writer, Elin Ameen. The playtext was published together with a brief editorial preface by Grein, in which he praises the play and quotes from his own review of it in the *Westminster Review*:

> For a long time no play has elicited so much comment, such high praise, and such virulent abuse, as this psychological and physical study of a woman's character. . . . What we admire so greatly in *Alan's Wife* is the utter simplicity, the wonderful mixture of light and shade. . . . If ever tragedy has been written by a modern Englishman, *Alan's Wife* has a right to claim that title. We know but one more powerful, modern play, equally sad and equally simple: Ibsen's *Ghosts* – that is all.

The edition has a lengthy introduction by William Archer, too, in which he defends the play, and uses it as the starting point for a discussion of the power of realism in the theatre and of 'the question whether art has limitations of subject'. But he also, at great length, claims credit for having originated the play – 'I am in great measure responsible for the existence of the play, and it is only right that I should put on record my complicity before the fact' – although Robins's writing on the play nowhere suggests that it was his idea. He goes on to describe some of the contemporary critical reactions to the play as 'almost inarticulate outcries of horror, contempt and reprobation'. The critic in the *Era* wrote that the character of Jean is that of 'a monster, with whom we can feel no sympathy whatsoever. . . . She is simply an ignorant, cruel, and presumptuous person' (6 May 1893), and A. B. Walkley, dramatic critic of *The Times* and the *Speaker*, declared that the play has 'no intellectual quality at all. It presents no ethical thesis, no *crux*, not even any development of character . . . I submit that this play ought never to have been written' (*Speaker*, 6 May 1893).

Although the reviewer in the *Athenaeum* (6 May 1893) complained that it 'does not pretend to be a play. It consists of three disconnected scenes, the links between which are easily supplied by the audience', most of the critics' objections were not to the form of the play so much as to its subject matter: it dared to present a woman as having physical desires – Jean speaks in Act One of physical attraction to her husband, Alan – and it showed a woman who commits Medea's crime: she kills her own child. By today's standards, there are problems with the play, such as Jean's delighting in Alan's being her 'master', and the suggestion that she kills the child out of some eugenicist notion that he is too imperfect to live. But her decision to smother the baby comes out of her love for him and her recognition that she will be unable always to protect and provide for him. The play shows that it is women who are left with the responsibility to provide, and asks what they can do with their guilt when they are unable to. Jean's killing her child, and silently accepting her death-sentence in punishment, are an indictment of an uncaring society. Jean accepts her responsibility and takes control in the only way she sees possible.

Linda Fitzsimmons
Department of Drama: Theatre, Film, Television
University of Bristol
September 1990

Select Bibliography

Lady Bell, *Alan's Wife*, with Elizabeth Robins, published anonymously (London, Henry and Co., 1893)

—*At the Works* (London, Edward Arnold, 1907; repr. London, Virago, 1985)

—*The Way the Money Goes* (London, Sidgwick and Jackson, 1910)

—*The Heart of Yorkshire* (London, A. L. Humphreys, 1923)

—*Landmarks: A Reprint of Some Essays and Other Pieces Published between the Years 1894 and 1922* (London, Ernest Benn, 1929) [includes an essay, 'Elizabeth Robins']

Elizabeth Robins, *The Convert* (London, Methuen, 1907; repr. London, The Women's Press, 1980, intro. Jane Marcus)

—*Votes for Women!* (London, Mills and Boon, 1909; repr. in *How the Vote Was Won and other Suffragette Plays*, ed. Dale Spender and Carole Hayman (London, Methuen, 1985)

—*Way Stations* (London, Woman's Press, 1913)

—*Ancilla's Share: an Indictment of Sex Antagonism* (London, Hutchinson, 1924)

—*Ibsen and the Actress* (London, Hogarth Press, 1928)

—*Both Sides of the Curtain* (London, Heinemann, 1940)

Alan's Wife was first performed by the Independent Theatre at Terry's Theatre, London, on 2 May 1893, with the following cast:

Jean Creyke	Miss Elizabeth Robins
Mrs Holroyd	Mrs E. H. Brooke
Mrs Ridley	Mrs Edmund Phelps
First Woman	Miss Mabel Hardy
Second Woman	Miss Annie Saker
Jamie Warren	Mr James Welch
Colonel Stuart	Mr Mervyn Herapath
Roberts (Chief Warder)	Mr Waler
First Warder	Mr Charles Greeven
Second Warder	Mr E. G. Waller

Produced by Mr H. de Lange

The ACTION of the Play takes place in a Village in the North of England, at the PRESENT DAY.

Scene One

A village street runs transversely from front corner, R, to back, L. At right angles to it, starting from front corner, L, the outside of a workman's cottage. Door leading to passage: a window on each side of it, through which glimpses can be obtained of cottage interior. The central portion of the stage, in the angle between the street and the cottage, represents the cottage garden, shut off from the street by a low fence with a gate in it. A bench runs along the cottage wall: by it a table, on which are piled up plates, knives, etc., ready for the table to be laid.

Mrs Holroyd *discovered sitting on bench outside house to the right of door, knitting. People passing along the street. Two men pass with a little child between them, then a little girl, then a woman carrying a child.*

Woman (*as she passes to* **Mrs Holroyd**) A fine day!

Mrs Holroyd (*nodding*) Ay, it's a fine day. (*The woman passes on.*)

Mrs Ridley (*comes along with a basket on her arm – she stops*) Good morning, Mrs Holroyd!

Mrs Holroyd Good morning to you, Mrs Ridley: it's a warm day!

Mrs Ridley And you look very comfortable there.

Mrs Holroyd Yes, it's nice out here – sit you down and rest a bit; you'll be tired after your marketing.

Mrs Ridley (*sitting down by her on the seat*) Well, I don't say I won't be glad of a rest.

It's fine to see you settled in your daughter's house for a bit, like this.

Mrs Holroyd It's the only place I do feel settled in, now she's married. I just feel lost in my own house without her.

Mrs Ridley Ay, you will that. It's bad when lassies take up with their husbands and leave their mothers alone.

Mrs Holroyd Ay, you may well say so! And Jean is all I have. I never had a lad of my own, or another lass either, and it's hard to be left when one is getting into years.

Mrs Ridley Still, you must be glad she has got a good husband, that can work hard and give her all she wants.

Mrs Holroyd Ay, Alan Creyke's a fine fellow, no doubt, and they say he'll soon be foreman. But I did think my Jean would have looked higher. I always thought she would marry a schoolmaster, as I did, or even a minister – seeing all the book-learning she got from her poor father. She knows as much as any lady, I do believe.

Mrs Ridley Ay, it's wonderful what the books'll do. They say young Mr Warren, that's just come to the chapel here, has got more book-learning than the schoolmaster himself, and can talk about it so as no one can understand him. Eh, but it's fine to know as much as that!

Mrs Holroyd (*with a sigh*) It is indeed! And, Mrs Ridley, as sure as you see me sitting here beside you, there was a time when that young man was after our Jean, and she might have been the mistress of yon pretty house near the chapel, instead of living in a cottage like this.

Mrs Ridley Dear, dear! To think of that! Ah well, it's no wonder you're put about at the way she chose.

Mrs Holroyd I don't say that Alan isn't a

good husband, mind you, and a good worker too – only I did hope to see my girl a bit grander than she is, as mothers will.

Mrs Ridley Ah well, young people will do their own way. You must just make up your mind to it, Mrs Holroyd. I fear the book-learning doesn't go for much with the lassies, where a fine fellow like Creyke is concerned – and after all, as to the cottage, it's a nice little place, and she keeps it beautiful!

Mrs Holroyd She does that – and she wouldn't be her mother's daughter if she didn't. And the pleasure she takes in it, too! keeping it as bright and shining as if there were five or six pair of hands to do it! She and Alan are nobbut two children about it, and their house is just like a new toy.

Mrs Ridley Well, that's right! let them be happy now, poor things; they'll leave it off soon enough.

Mrs Holroyd Eh, yes, I doubt they will, like other folk.

Mrs Ridley Where is Jean? I should like to wish her good morning. Is she in?

Mrs Holroyd Yes, she's in the kitchen, I believe. (*Calls.*) Jean, Jean! What are you doing, honey? Here's a neighbour come to see you.

Jean (*from within room to the* L) I'll come directly. I'm getting Alan's dinner ready. I can't leave the saucepan.

Mrs Ridley (*smiling*) Ay, getting Alan's dinner ready! That's the way of it.

Mrs Holroyd Yes, it's always Alan's dinner, or Alan's tea, or Alan's supper, or Alan's pipe. There isn't another man in the North gets waited on as he does.

Mrs Ridley Eh, but that's what he'll want to keep him in his home; they're bad to please, is the men, unless you spoil them.

(*Bell begins to ring outside.*) There's the midday bell from the works. Creyke'll soon be here now – I must be getting home too.

Mrs Holroyd Eh, now, but Jean would have liked to shake hands with ye. (*Calls.*) Jean! Jean! Be quick, child!

Jean (*from within*) Just ready, Mother – I'm lifting it off the fire.

Mrs Ridley (*looking along the street*) And in the nick of time too, for here are the men. (*Two or three men walk past.*) Yes, hurry up, Jean, or your man will be here before his dinner's ready.

Jean (*from within*) No, no, he won't. (*Appears in doorway of cottage.*) Here it is! (*Comes out carrying a large smoking dish in her hand, which she puts on the table.*) There! How are you, Mrs Ridley? (*Shakes hands with her.*)

Mrs Ridley Nicely, thank you. And are you going to get your dinner outside then?

Jean Yes, indeed; let's be in the air while we can – it's not often we have it as fine as this.

Mrs Holroyd I never saw such a lass for fresh air! and Alan is just as bad.

Mrs Ridley Well, they'll take no harm with it, I daresay; fresh air is bad for nowt but cobwebs, as the saying is.

Jean (*laughs*) Ah, that's true enough! (*Arranging table.*) Now then, if that isn't a dinner fit for a king!

Mrs Ridley And I'll be bound, if it is, you won't be thinking it too good for your husband.

Jean Too good! I should think not! Is anything too good for him? Is anything good enough?

Mrs Holroyd (*smiling*) Ah, Jean, Jean!

Jean Well, Mother, you know quite well

it's true! Isn't he the best husband a girl ever had? And the handsomest, and the strongest?

Mrs Holroyd Ah, yes, he's all that, I daresay.

Jean (*vigorously wiping tumblers*) Well, what more do you want?

Mrs Holroyd Ah, my dear, as I've often told you, I should like you to have looked higher.

Jean Looked higher! How could I have looked higher than Alan?

Mrs Holroyd I wanted to see you marry a scholar.

Jean We can't all marry scholars, Mother dear – some of us prefer marrying men instead. (*Goes into house.*)

Mrs Ridley The lass is right – there must be some of that sort that there may be some of all sorts, as the saying is; and, neighbour, you must just make the best of it, and be pleased with the man that's made her look so happy. (*Getting up.*)

Mrs Holroyd (*smiling*) Ay, she looks bright enough, in all conscience. (**Jean** *comes back with cheese and butter on a dish.*)

Mrs Ridley (*smiling at* **Jean**) She does that, indeed! Well, you won't have to wait long for him now, honey. Here they come down the road, and I must get back to my two lads. Good day to you both. (*Exit through garden gate and up street, to the* L, *exchanging greetings with passing workmen.*)

Jean (*cutting bread*) Scholar, indeed! Mother, how can you say such things before folks? I know what you mean when you say scholar – yon minister, poor little Jamie Warren.

Mrs Holroyd Ah, Jean, how can you speak so! He's a man who is looked up to

by everybody. Didn't he go up to the big house last Christmastide, to dinner with the gentry, just like one of themselves?

Jean Well, that's right enough if it pleased him, but I shouldn't care to go among folk who thought themselves my betters. (*Look from* **Mrs Holroyd**.) No, I shouldn't. I like Jamie, and have done ever since we were boy and girl together; but it's a far cry to think of taking him for my master! no, Mother, that's not my kind. (*Goes to tub under the window, wrings out tea cloths and hangs them on picket fence.*)

Mrs Holroyd Ah, Jean, what would your poor father have said! When you and Jamie used to play together on the village green and go to school together, and Jamie was minding his books and getting all the prizes, your father used to say, 'When that lad grows up, he'll be the husband for Jean – he's a good lad, he never gets into mischief; he's never without a book in his hand'.

Jean Ah, poor father! but what would *I* have done with a good boy who never got into mischief! (*Laughs.*) No, I always knew it wasn't to be Jamie. Why, I remember as far back as when Jamie and I used to come from school, and I'd rush on before and go flying up on the moors, to find the stags-horn moss, with the heathery wind in my face, and hear the whirring summer sounds around us, I used to want to shout aloud, just for the pleasure of being alive – and Jamie, poor little creature, used to come toiling up after me, and call out, 'Not so fast, Jean, I'm out of breath, wait for me!' And *I* used to have to help *him* up!

Mrs Holroyd Well, perhaps he couldn't run and jump as well as you, but he had read all about the flowers and plants in his book, and could tell you the names of every one of them.

Jean Ay, their names, perhaps; but he

couldn't swing himself up to the steep places where they grew to pull them for me. He was afraid – afraid! while I, a girl, didn't know what it was like to be afraid. I don't know now.

Mrs Holroyd Maybe – but he would have been a good husband for all that!

Jean Not for me. I want a husband who is brave and strong, a man who is my master as well as other folks'; who loves the hills and the heather, and loves to feel the strong wind blowing in his face and the blood rushing through his veins! Ah! to be happy – to be alive!

Mrs Holroyd Oh, Jean, you always were a strange girl! (*Two men pass.*)

Jean Ah, Mother, can't you see how fine it is to have life, and health, and strength! Jamie Warren, indeed! Think of the way he comes along, poor fellow, as though he were scared of coming into bits if he moved faster! And the way Alan comes striding and swinging down the street, with his head up, looking as if the world belonged to him! Ah! it's good to be as happy as I am!

Mrs Holroyd Well, you silly fondy! In the meantime, I wonder what Alan is doing this morning? Yon fine dinner of his will be getting cold.

Jean Indeed it will. I wonder where he is! (*Men pass.*) All the men seem to have passed. (*Stands just outside the door and looks down the street to the* R, *sheltering her eyes from the sun.* **Hutton**, *a workman, passes, and stops to speak to her.*)

Hutton Good morning, Mrs Creyke: a fine day again!

Jean It is indeed, Mr Hutton. What's got my husband this morning, do you know? Why is he so long after the rest?

Hutton He's stayed behind to see about something that's gone wrong with the machinery. It's the new saw, I believe – that's what happens when folks try to improve on the old ways. I don't believe in improvements myself, and in trying these new-fangled things no one can understand.

Jean No one? I'll be bound Alan understands them well enough.

Hutton Well, happen he does, more than most, and that's why the manager called him back to fettle it up – but I doubt he won't be much longer now.

Jean Ah, well, that's all right, as long as I know what keeps him. Good morning. (**Hutton** *moves on.*) You see, Mother, how they turn to Alan before all the rest!

Mrs Holroyd Ah, well, when a lass is in love she must needs know better than her mother, I suppose.

Jean Ah, Mother dear, wasn't there a time when you were a girl – when you knew better too?

Mrs Holroyd (*shaking her head*) Eh, but that's a long time ago.

Jean But you remember it, I'll be bound! I think I'd best be setting that dish in the oven again; it will be getting cold. (*Exit with dish.*)

Mrs Holroyd (*alone*) Well – (*shakes her head with a little smile as she goes on knitting*) – there's nowt so queer as folk! (*Shakes her head again.*)

Jean (*coming back*) I wonder what makes him bide so long?

Mrs Holroyd You had far better give over tewing, and sit quietly down with a bit of work in your hands till he comes.

Jean No, Mother, I can't! (*Smiling.*) I'm too busy – watching for him! (*Leans over railing and looks along road to the* R.)

Mrs Holroyd That'll be Jamie coming along. (*Looking off to the* L.)

Jean (*looking round*) So it is. (*Indifferently.*) Well, Jamie, good morning. (**Warren**, *a small delicate man, wearing a wide-awake hat and carrying a stick in his hand, comes along the road from the* L.)

Warren Good morning, Jean. Well, Mrs Holroyd, how are you?

(**Jean** *stands and leans against the railing to the* R, *looking down the road and listening to what the others are saying.*)

Mrs Holroyd Good morning, my lad: sit down a bit. And what have you been doing the day? You look tired.

Warren (*takes off his hat wearily, passing his hand over his brow*) I've been doing my work – giving the Word to those who can hear it.

Mrs Holroyd And yon will have been edifying, that it will! And ye'll have done them good with it, for ye always were a beautiful speaker, Jamie!

Jean (*from the back*) Mother, I doubt you should call him Mr Warren now he's a minister.

Mrs Holroyd Eh, not I! I mind him since he was a bit of a lad running barefoot about the village at home.

Jean And do you mind, Jamie, that when you had a book in your hand I'd snatch it from you and throw it over the hedge? (*Laughs.*)

Warren Yes, you always pretended you didn't like books, Jean – but you used to learn quicker than anybody else when you chose.

Mrs Holroyd And so she does still, I'm sure. She likes her book as well as any one, though she will have it that she doesn't. She'll sit and read to Alan, when he's smoking his pipe, for half an hour at a time.

Warren And what does he think of it?

Mrs Holroyd (*smiling*) Between you and me, Jamie, I don't think he minds much for what she reads.

Jean (*hotly*) Indeed, but he does! Alan can understand what I read just as well as me.

Mrs Holroyd Eh, lass, it isn't the strongest in the arm that's the best at the books!

Warren Yes, it's rather hard upon the rest of us poor fellows if a fellow like Creyke is to have everything – if we mayn't have a little more book-learning to make up for not being a Hercules, like him.

Jean Why, Jamie, you wouldn't care to be a Hercules, as you call it – you never did.

Warren That's what you say.

Jean (*lightly, still watching road to the* R) Well, I say what I think, as honest folk do! (*Sheltering her eyes with her hand.*) Where can he be? His dinner will be burnt to a cinder directly.

Mrs Holroyd I wish he'd come and be done with it. She can't mind for anything else but yon dinner while she's waiting for him.

Warren Well, well, that's how it should be, I daresay.

Mrs Holroyd And have you got settled in your new house against the chapel?

Warren Pretty well, yes.

Mrs Holroyd Ah, I doubt you find it hard. A man's a poor creature at siding up, and getting things straight.

Warren He is indeed!

Mrs Holroyd (*sympathetically*) You'll be lonesome at times, my lad, isn't it so?

Warren (*shakes his head*) Indeed I am!

Mrs Holroyd Come, you must get yourself a little wife, and she'll make it nice and homely for you.

Warren (*shakes his head*) No, I don't think I shall be taking a wife yet a bit, somehow. (*Gets up.*) Well, I must be going. (*Looks at his watch.*) I said I would look in at the school for a bit after dinner, and the children go in again at half-past one.

Jean Yes, I always see them bustling past – some of them so little that if they didn't take hold of each other's hands they'd be tumbling down! (*She laughs.*)

Warren Yes, there are some very weeny ones in the infant school. Canny little bairns! Good-bye, Jean – good-bye, Mrs Creyke.

Jean Good-bye, Jamie! (*Exit* **Warren** *to the* R.)

Mrs Holroyd Eh, but he has a tender heart. I like a man that can speak about the little ones that way.

Jean So do I. Oh, Mother, I like to watch Alan with a child – the way he looks at it and the way he speaks to it! Do you know, with those strong arms of his he can hold a baby as well as you, Mother? He picked up a little mite that was sobbing on the road the other day, and carried it home, and before a minute was over the bairn had left off crying, and nestled itself to sleep on his shoulder.

Mrs Holroyd Ah, yes, he'll make a good father some day!

Jean A good father and a happy one, too! Yes, we shall be happier then than we are now even. Oh, Mother, is that possible? – shall I be happier when I have my baby in my arms?

Mrs Holroyd Ah, my child, yes, you will

that, in truth. People talk of happiness and the things that bring it, and the young people talk about it and dream of it – but there's one happiness in the world that's better and bigger when it comes than one ever thinks for beforehand – and that is the moment when a woman's first child lies in her arms.

Jean Is it, is it really? Oh, Mother, to think that this is coming to me! I shall have that too, besides all the rest! Isn't it wonderful?

Mrs Holroyd (*moved*) God keep you, honey!

Jean Yes, when I think of the moment when my child will lie in my arms, how he will look at me –

Mrs Holroyd (*smiling*) He! It's going to be a boy then, is it?

Jean Of course it is! Like his father. He shall be called Alan, too, and he will be just like him. He will have the same honest blue eyes, that make you believe in them, and the same yellow hair and a straight nose, and a firm, sweet mouth. But that's what he'll be like when he grows up a little; at first he'll be nothing but a pink, soft, round, little baby, and we will sit before the fire – it will be the winter, you know, when he comes – and he'll lie across my knee, and stretch out his little pink feet to the blaze, and all the neighbours will come in and see his sturdy little limbs, and say, 'My word, what a fine boy!' He'll be just such another as his father. Oh, Mother, it's too good to be true!

Mrs Holroyd No, no, honey, it isn't! It will all come true some day.

Jean Oh, Mother, Mother, what a good world it is! (*Kisses her.*) Ah, I see some more people coming – he'll soon be here now! (*Goes in to* R.)

Mrs Holroyd (*looking along road*) Yes, there

they come. (*Gets up, puts her knitting down, begins straightening table, then goes in as though to fetch something.*)

Gradual signs of commotion, two boys rush along stage from R to L, then return with two more, and go off, R. Two children rush past; then two women enter at back, L, and stand a little to the R of cottage, shading their eyes. **Mrs Holroyd** *comes out of door with a brown jug in her hand.*

Mrs Holroyd What is it? Anything happened?

1st Woman Ay, it's an accident, they say, at the works.

Mrs Holroyd (*alarmed*) An accident?

2nd Woman Yes, yes, look there! (*She points off to the R.*)

Jean (*leaning out of room to the L, with her arms crossed on window sill*) And, Mother, I've been thinking we shall have to call him wee Alan, to tell him from his father, you know. Mother! (*Looks.*) Mother, what has happened?

Mrs Holroyd (*hurriedly*) Nothing, honey, nothing. (**Jean** *comes hurriedly out of room and down passage.*)

Jean No, Mother, I am sure there is something! What is it? (*To woman.*) Do you know?

1st Woman It will be an accident, they say, at the works.

Jean At the works! Any one hurt?

2nd Woman Eh, with yon machines, ye never know but there'll be something.

Jean With the machines? (*Sees* **Warren** *coming hurriedly past, R.*) Jamie, Jamie, what is it? What has happened?

Warren Jean, dear Jean, you must be prepared.

Jean Prepared? For what?

Warren There has been an accident.

Jean Not to Alan? Ah, do you mean he has been hurt? (**Warren** *is silent.*) But he's so strong it will be nothing! I'll make him well again. Where is he? We must bring him back!

Warren No, no! (*He looks back at something approaching.*)

Jean What is that? (*Pause.*)

Warren God's will be done, Jean; His hand is heavy on ye. (*A moment of silence.* **Jean** *is seen to look aghast at something coming.* **Hutton** *and two more, carrying a covered litter, come to the gate, followed by a little crowd of men, women and children.*)

Jean Oh, they're coming here! (*Rushes to them.*) Hutton, tell me what has happened?

Hutton Best not look, missis – it's a sore sight! (**Mrs Holroyd** *holds* **Jean** *back.*)

Jean Let me be, Mother – I *must* go to him!

1st Woman Na, na, my lass – best keep back!

Mrs Holroyd Keep back, honey! you're not the one to bear the sight!

Jean I *must* – let me go! (*Struggles, breaks away, and rushes forward – lifts up cover.*) Alan! (*She falls back with a cry into* **Mrs Holroyd**'*s arms.*)

Curtain.

Scene Two

A room in **Jean**'*s cottage. Fireplace to the R, with chimneypiece on which are candlesticks, tapers, etc.; door at back, L C. Window to L with curtains; kitchen dresser to L with plates, jugs, and a bowl with green spray in it. A mahogany* *bookcase on back wall, a table back* C, *chairs, etc.; a cradle half way down the stage to the* L *of* C.

Jean *discovered sitting listlessly by the fire. She is in a white gown with a black shawl over it.* **Mrs Holroyd** *and* **Mrs Ridley** *are standing one on each side of the cradle,* **Mrs Holroyd** *bending over it, smoothing the clothes, etc.,* **Mrs Ridley** *standing by admiringly.*

Mrs Holroyd (L *of cradle, finishing tucking it up*) There now, he looks the picture of comfort, the dear! and so sound asleep, it's a pleasure to see him.

Mrs Ridley (R *of cradle, looking at him*) It is indeed; but I doubt you've got him too hot, Mrs Holroyd.

Mrs Holroyd (*doubtfully*) Too hot, do you think so? Well, perhaps we might put off this quilt. (*Takes it off and stands with it in her hand.*) And yet, I don't know, I am all for weeny babies being kept warm enough. (*Puts the quilt on again.*)

Mrs Ridley Warm enough! Yes, but not stifled – ye'll fair smother the bairn with all yon clothes! (*Takes off quilt.*)

Mrs Holroyd Ay, now, it's difficult to know what one should do for the best! (*Stands looking doubtfully at cradle.*)

Mrs Ridley Well, I always say with a baby, you can't do better than take a neighbour's advice, and one that's had eleven too. My bairns used just to lie in the cot with a patchwork counterpane over them – it's a grand thing for a baby is the patchwork – and they grew up fine, sturdy lads as you'd wish to see.

Mrs Holroyd Ah, fine and sturdy – that's just it! But it's very different with this poor little mite.

Mrs Ridley (*her arms folded as she holds the quilt, shaking her head and looking*

compassionately at the baby) Ay, poor wee thing, indeed! well, the Lord's will be done! He must have His own way with the bairns, as with everything else.

Mrs Holroyd Do you know, I think I'll leave the quilt on. (*Takes it.*) I am fearful of the draughts down the chimney coming to him.

Mrs Ridley Eh, yes – every chimney'll blow both hot and cold, as the saying is. I'm all for keeping the fresh air from a baby till he's turned the twelvemonth. Eh, but his mother should see him now, looking so fine and comfortable! (*Looking round at* **Jean.** **Jean** *pays no attention.*) Jean, he's looking as happy as a prince, the dear! (**Jean** *is absorbed in thought.*)

Mrs Holroyd (*shakes her head. Half aside to* **Mrs Ridley**) Ah, it's not much his mother wants to see him, I'm afraid. Jean!

Jean (*as though waking out of a reverie*) Yes, Mother, what is it? (*Sits up.*)

Mrs Holroyd The baby has gone to sleep – he's quite comfortable now.

Jean Asleep, is he? Yes. (*Leans forward, her head on her right hand, her elbow on her knee.* **Mrs Holroyd** *puts her hand down to the ground near the cradle.*)

Mrs Holroyd I thought I felt a bit of a draught here, near the cradle head.

Mrs Ridley (*putting her hand to the ground with an anxious look*) No, no! There's no draught; it's just yourself that's made it, whisking round with your petticoats.

Mrs Holroyd Well, happen you're right. (*Holds her skirts carefully together, then feels for the draught again.*) Na, na, there's no draught here. He'll sleep now, right enough.

Mrs Ridley If he does it'll be more by

good luck than good management, with all yon clothes on the top of him!

Mrs Holroyd He should – he's not had much sleep this day, nor last night either.

Mrs Ridley And you look tired with it, Mrs Holroyd.

Mrs Holroyd We've had a restless day with him, haven't we, Jean?

Jean (*indifferently*) Yes, he's cried.

Mrs Ridley It's too much for you, Mrs Holroyd, to have been after that bairn ever since daylight.

Mrs Holroyd Eh well! It's my Jean's bairn, you know.

Mrs Ridley Yes, that's just it! It's Jean's bairn, and it's Jean ought to be tewing with it – it would do her good, Mrs Holroyd.

Mrs Holroyd Eh, I doubt she's not strong enough yet! But you are right: she should take an interest in it, all the same. I can't get her to seem as though she minded for it, do what I will.

Mrs Ridley You should rouse her a bit, and not let her sit mounging that way. (*Cheerily.*) Come, Jean, do you think the cradle is out of the draught there, or shall we get it moved a bit?

Jean (*half looking round, then subsides again*) Oh, I think it will do very well where it is.

Mrs Holroyd Ah, honey, I don't like to see you sitting there as though you had nothing to do with the bairn.

Jean Nay, Mother, I know it's well cared for with you looking after it – and Mrs Ridley.

Mrs Holroyd Ah, but that's not enough. Ah, Jean, how little I thought when you used to talk of your baby, and long to have it in your arms, that you would be so hard

to the little fatherless child when it came, and not bear to look at it, just because it isn't the fine lusty lad you wanted! (**Jean** *shudders as she sits and looks into the fire.* **Mrs Holroyd** *is bustling about, arranging the room as she talks.*)

Mrs Ridley Yes, poor wee thing! He can't help being a cripple; you should care for him all the more because he won't walk and run like other boys. What's a mother for, if it's not to care for the bairn that needs it most?

Jean (*looks into the fire*) Yes, yes, I suppose so! that is what's left – there'll be nothing else in my life.

Mrs Holroyd Nothing else! You ought to be thankful for having the child!

Jean (*bitterly*) Thankful!

Mrs Ridley Ah, Jean, I doubt you have a hard heart! You don't know the blessings you have.

Jean (*covers her face, then goes on after a minute*) No, maybe I don't. Do you remember, Mother, that last afternoon that we talked about the child that was to come? You told me how beautiful everything would be, and that I should be happier than ever I'd been before. Happier – ah!

Mrs Holroyd It's not ours to tell the future, and it's very wicked to repine when things are not as we hoped.

Jean (*half to herself – looking into the fire*) I used to hope, all those happy weeks before that day, and then afterwards, when my only hope was in the bairn – and now I have no hope left . . . only horrible certainty!

Mrs Holroyd (*arranging room*) Eh, Jean, yours is sinful talk – you must just be a good mother to the bairn now that it is here.

Mrs Ridley (*kneeling in front of fire, takes up fire-irons in her hand, and sweeps hearth*) Ay, there's many a mother with a family of fine boys and girls has thought more of her one deformed child than all the rest!

Jean (*covering her face*) Deformed! Yes, that's what they'll call him. (*Pause.*)

Mrs Ridley Why, there's Meg Dowden who used to live beside the Green at home – how she used to go about with that little Tommy of hers, who could only sling along the road instead of walking! and she was as proud of him as you please. Then there's Kate Lockerby, when one of her bairns wasn't right in her head –

Jean Don't! Don't! I can't bear it!

Mrs Ridley Ah well, child, you must try to bear it, and to put up with things that can't be mended.

Mrs Holroyd Yes, honey, you must put off that hard, rebellious spirit, and put on a meek and submissive one, else you will be punished for your pride some day. (*Goes on dusting and arranging room, etc.*)

Mrs Ridley Ah, but a young thing like that will feel it! I mind when my Johnnie was born, that only lived a week –

Jean Don't tell me about it, I say, don't tell me about any other woman's child!

Mrs Ridley My word, Jean, but you've got your saucy tongue in your head still! I'll tell you what, Mrs Holroyd, you ought to have the minister to her when she speaks that way; he would bring her to a better way of thinking.

Mrs Holroyd (*aside to* **Mrs Ridley**) I've told him today just to step in and see her. Ye see, Mrs Ridley, when the lass has been about a bit longer, she'll be better; she hasn't got her strength yet.

Mrs Ridley Ay, that's true – any one can

see that to look at her. She's as white as a sheet tonight.

Mrs Holroyd Indeed, she is that! Come, dearie, get to bed with you, and you'll feel better in the morning.

Jean (*wearily*) To bed – very well!

Mrs Holroyd Everything is ready for you in the next room – and Mrs Ridley will sit here and be a bit of company for you while I go back home to see how things are going on.

Mrs Ridley Eh, that I will. I'll sit here as long as you please. (*Sits by table to the* L. *Gets out her knitting.*)

Jean No, no! I don't want anyone to stay with me.

Mrs Ridley Eh, I can knit just as well here as at home. My boys are on the night shift this week, and won't be in for supper.

Mrs Holroyd (*to* **Mrs Ridley**) And if the baby cries you can just put it over again.

Mrs Ridley No need to tell me what to do with a baby, that's had eleven to look after; and I can do for Jean too, if she wants anything.

Jean No, no; I can quite well fend for myself. I shan't want anything.

Mrs Holroyd (*anxiously*) But what about the baby? I doubt you won't be able to manage him, Jean?

Jean Yes, yes, I shall! Didn't you say that's what a mother's for? (**Mrs Ridley** *gets up.*)

Mrs Ridley (*to* **Mrs Holroyd**) Well, neighbour, I believe the lass is right; and if you take my advice, you'll do as she says, and leave her to tew with the baby; she'll soonest get to care for him that way.

Mrs Holroyd Maybe you are right after all.

Mrs Ridley Well, if I'm not wanted then, I'd best be getting home. Good night to you! (*Shakes her head to herself as she goes out.*) Eh, but some folks are bad to do with when they're in trouble! (*Exit.*)

Jean You go too, Mother; I shall be all right.

Mrs Holroyd Suppose you wanted anything, or the baby wasn't well?

Jean Well, if the worst came to the worst, I could step up so far and fetch you: it's only a few doors off.

Mrs Holroyd Yes; you could do that after all. Good night, then, honey! Go to bed, say your prayers, and wake up stronger and better in the morning. All that comes to us is for the best, you know, if we can but see it.

Jean Good night! (*Her mother kisses her.* **Mrs Holroyd** *goes out, after giving a last look at the baby, and a general straightening touch to things as she passes.*) At last! Oh, if they would only give over telling me it's for the best! (*Looks at cradle.*) For the best! *That* for the best! (*Bends over cradle.*) But he has got a darling little face all the same! Poor little bairn – my poor little bairn! They say I don't love you – I don't care for you at all! Yes, yes, I do, dear, yes, I do! (*Buries her face and sobs. Knock heard at the door. Gets up, drying her eyes, and stands at foot of cradle, looking at child.* **Jean** *looks round, crosses to fire – another knock.*) Yes? who is it? (**Warren** *on the threshold.*)

Warren Good evening, Jean! (*Pause –* **Jean** *still looking into fire –* **Warren** *stands hesitating, and a little embarrassed at her inhospitality.*) Your mother asked me to look in, and –

Jean And tell me of my sinful ways – yes, I know! Come in, Jamie!

Warren (*comes forward*) Jean, how ill you look! You're fretting; you mustn't rebel so against the visitation o' God! His laws are –

Jean Good and merciful. Yes, I've heard that!

Warren Eh! I hope you're not doubting His loving-kindness, Jean!

Jean I'm not thinking about God, nor about loving-kindness.

Warren But you must, child. It'll steady and strengthen ye. Ye'll find His mercy everywhere.

Jean Do you think I'll find it in the cradle, yon?

Warren Eh? (*Shaking his head.*) Yes, I know what you mean. I've heard –

Jean (*with smothered anguish, breaking in*) Then you *forgot*, Jamie Warren, or you wouldn't talk of loving-kindness. You forgot God couldn't even take Alan away without – without – (*Covers her face and shudders.*)

Warren Jean! You're tempting the Almighty!

Jean Ye hadn't heard, maybe, that a little child was sent, hideous and maimed, to stumble through this terrible world – eh?

Warren Hush, hush, my girl! You're ill, or you wouldn't talk that wild and wicked way! (*As* **Jean** *is about to break in.*) When you're stronger you'll see how the child'll comfort you.

Jean (*slowly*) But how shall I comfort the child?

Warren He'll grow up to be a scholar and a God-fearing man yet, Jean. It's no ill fate.

Jean He'll grow up, you think?

Warren (*cheerily*) Aye, why not? He may quite well live to be old.

Jean You don't think that? (*Seizes* **Warren** *by the arm.*)

Warren Of course. Why not? He's not rightly formed, poor bairn, else he's sturdy enough, they say. He may outlive us all, yet!

Jean (*hoarsely*) You think he'll live longer than any of us?

Warren Well, in the course of nature and if God wills it; (**Jean** *turns away.*) but if it's the will of God that the child should be taken, Jean, you must bow to His will.

Jean You're sure the bairn would go to heaven, Jamie?

Warren How can you doubt it? Ye'll be having him baptised?

Jean Baptised! (*Listlessly.*) Yes, I suppose so.

Warren Ah, Jean, take care lest it be too late! The innocent bairn mustn't suffer for the sinful neglect of others. Unless he be baptised, who can be sure? Jean, see to it that the child is saved.

Jean Saved! Why was he not saved from *that*?

Warren We are not here to ask that. It is enough for us to know that it is the will of God.

Jean (*passionately*) The will of God! I won't believe it!

Warren Jean!

Jean Or if you're right, so much the worse, then! If God were full of mercy and loving-kindness as you say, how could He be so cruel to a little harmless child? (*Crosses to cradle, and drops on her knees beside it.*)

Warren Jean, Jean, ye tempt the Almighty by your wicked words. But I doubt you're sore at heart. His mercy endureth for ever; He will forgive you, and He'll have pity on you.

Jean (*with a burst of agony*) Pity on *me*, man! It's the child! It's the *child*! Don't you think I'd be glad to give up my health and strength to my baby? If God was angry at *me*, why didn't He strike *me* down? If I'd been doing wrong, He should have cursed *me*, and not hurt Alan's little bairn! *I* could have borne it. This minute I could stand up and let them hack me all to pieces if they'd make my baby straight and strong. (**Jean** *walks unsteadily back towards fireplace.*)

Warren Hush! hush! You'll come to better reason as the time goes on (**Jean** *absorbed in her grief.*) if you'll but strive in prayer to be given a meek spirit, and strength to bear your burden bravely, Jean. There's many a one has had to go through the world before bearing a cross as heavy as yours.

Jean And does it make it any better for me to think of those other wretched women?

Warren Ah, Jean, seek for strength where alone it can be found – pray for it, only pray, and it shall be given you! (**Jean** *stands looking at the fire trying to control herself.*) (*Moved.*) Jean, my poor Jean, good-bye! I'll pray for you and for the bairn – I'll pray that God may bring you peace. (*Exit.*)

Jean (*alone – wildly*) Pray for the bairn – pray, pray! (*She falls on her knees.*) Oh God! If I've been wicked, don't make it worse for the child – punish me some other way – don't hurt him any more – he's so little, dear God – so helpless, and he never did any wrong! *He* hasn't been drunk with life and strength and love – he hasn't walked through the world exulting and fearless and forgetting You. That was I, oh, Father in heaven! Punish *me* – and take the baby away. This is a hard place – this world down here. Take him away! Take him away! (*She staggers to her feet – listens.*) He is stirring. (*Goes and looks in cradle – leans over it.*) Ah, how little you must know to be smiling in your sleep! (*Drops on her knees by* *the cradle.*) Dear little face! Ah! It's brave of you to smile when God has laid such heavy burdens on you! Do you think you will be able to smile later on when you see other boys running and leaping and being glad – when you're a man, dear, and see how good it is to be strong and fair? Can you bear it, little one? (*She rocks the cradle as if to hush him, though the child sleeps on – she croons drearily.*) Never mind, never mind! Mother'll be always at your side – always – always. (*She stops, horror-stricken.*) Always? Who can say so? I might die! It's natural I should go first and leave him to the mercy of – Oh, I cannot, I cannot! I *dare* not! (*Bows her head over the cradle's edge – then half recovering, and yet with suppressed wildness, whispers.*) Baby, I'm frightened! Listen, I don't know what to do. Do you *want* to live? Tell me, shall you ever hate me for this horrible gift of life? (*With wide vacant eyes.*) Oh, I seem to see you in some far-off time, your face distorted like your body, but with bitterness and loathing, saying, 'Mother, how *could* you be so cruel as to let me live and suffer? You could have eased my pain; you could have saved me this long martyrdom; when I was little and lay in your arms. Why didn't you save me. You were a coward – a coward!' (*She bows her head over the cradle again, overcome – then she lifts a drawn white face.*) It would be quite easy – only to cover the dear face for a little while – only to shut out the air and light for a little while, and remember I'm fighting for his release. Yes, it would be quite easy – if only one's heart didn't sink and one's brain grow numb! (*Leans against the cradle, faint – her eyes fall on the child.*) Are your lips moving, dear? (*Pause.*) Are you asking for life? No, you don't want to live, do you? No, no, you cannot! Darling, it will be so easy – you'll never know – it will only be that you'll go on sleeping – sleeping, until you wake up in heaven! (*Clutches quilt together quickly, then stops.*) In heaven! No –

what did Jamie say? 'Unless he be baptised' – (*Stands a minute – repeats to herself.*) He said, 'See to it that the child is saved'. Yes, darling, that's what I'm trying to do save you! (*Lets quilt fall – stands staring into space – moves like a woman in a dream; brings two candles; returns, brings a bowl of water, and a big book with silver clasps; puts all on table by cradle – lights candles – lifts the great book, and goes to the cradle and looks at the child – turns away with a sob, and, standing by the candle-light, opens the book and tries to find the place – passes her hand across her eyes.*) Where is the place? I can't find it! I can't find it! (*Tries again – then falls on her knees between the table and the cradle – she closes the great book and whispers.*) Have pity on us, Lord – show us the way! (*Still on her knees, she lets the book fall to the floor, dips her hand in the water and sprinkles the child.*) I baptise thee, Alan! (*Prays a moment – then stands looking yearningly at him.*) Alan, my little Alan! (*Rises – looks anxiously over her shoulder to door and window, blows out the candles one by one, and goes stealthily towards cradle with a long wailing cry, the eider quilt hugged to her breast as the curtain falls.*)

Scene Three

Room in the prison.

(**Colonel Stuart** *sitting at writing-table with papers to the* R. *Chief warder standing by him. Door* C. *Door to the* L.)

Col Stuart You have nothing more to report, Roberts?

Roberts No, sir; nothing.

Col Stuart And Jean Creyke?

Roberts Just the same, sir. Can get nothing out of her.

Col Stuart (*shaking his head*) Ah! Well, you can take these. (*Gives him papers.* **Roberts**

gathers up papers and is turning away. Enter a **Warder** *at* C.)

Warder Please, sir, there is some one to see the woman Creyke.

Col Stuart Who is it?

Warder An old woman, sir, of the name of Holroyd. She is Creyke's mother, I believe.

Col Stuart Her mother? Bring her in here. (*Exit* **Warder**.) I can't help feeling that there must be some extenuating circumstance if only we could get at it.

Roberts Well, sir, maybe there is. It's a bad business, anyway! (*Salutes, and goes out with papers at door* L. *Enter* **Mrs Holroyd** *with* **Warder**. *Exit* **Warder**.)

Col Stuart Mrs Holroyd?

Mrs Holroyd (*with her handkerchief to her eyes*) Ay, yes, your worship, my name is Holroyd.

Col Stuart (*kindly*) I am very sorry for you; it must be a hard trial.

Mrs Holroyd Ah, it's hard indeed to think that a girl of mine should have taken her own child's life.

Col Stuart Yes, it's a very terrible story. (*Pause.*)

Mrs Holroyd (*anxiously*) What will they do to her, your worship? (**Col Stuart** *is silent.*) They won't take her life, will they? There must be a chance for her yet.

Col Stuart I fear not much; a reprieve has been asked for, but –

Mrs Holroyd Yes, I know – Jamie Warren said he would bring the news this morning, the moment it was known.

Col Stuart Jamie Warren?

Mrs Holroyd Yes; he's the minister down at our place; he's always been a good friend to our Jean, and if she would have listened to him, and not taken up with Creyke, things would have been very different.

Col Stuart Well, there seems to be very little here to found an appeal for mercy on. We know so little of the whole thing. What could have made her kill the child? Do you think her mind was at all affected at the time?

Mrs Holroyd Her mind! My Jean's? No, indeed! Why did she kill the little baby? Well, it was a poor wreckling, the lamb, and it well-nigh broke her heart that it wasn't fine and sturdy like the father – she wanted a boy like the husband she lost – she never seemed to take to the baby, never from the first, and she never would tew with it as mothers do.

Col Stuart Do you mean that that's why she killed the poor little helpless child – that she could find it in her heart to kill it because it wasn't strong and sturdy?

Mrs Holroyd Ah, yes, your worship, it's hard my Jean should have done it. I well-nigh can't believe it of my own bairn.

Col Stuart It's hard to believe of any mother.

Mrs Holroyd And if they spare her life what will become of her? Can I have her back with me to her home again?

Col Stuart No, my poor woman, she can't go back to you again. The best will be that her sentence will be commuted to penal servitude for life.

Mrs Holroyd (*crying out*) For life! My Jean? Oh Lord, oh Lord, Your hand is heavy on us!

Col Stuart You shall see her. (*Rings bell.*) (*A* **Warder** *comes in.*) Jean Creyke is to come here. (*Exit* **Warder**.) (*To* **Mrs Holroyd**.) Perhaps you can bring her to a better frame of mind. She seems strangely hardened.

Mrs Holroyd Ah, your worship, I am afraid she won't mind for me; she always knew I hadn't the wits to be up to her, or find the words to say to her. Oh, my poor girl, she always was too proud, I always told her she was. The Lord has punished her. (*Enter* **Jean** *with two* **Warders**.)

Mrs Holroyd Oh, Jean, Jean! (**Jean**'s *sentences are given as a stage direction of what she is silently to convey, but she does not speak until nearly the end of the Act.*)

Jean (*silent*) Mother!

Mrs Holroyd Honey, tell his worship how you came to do it. Tell him you hadn't your wits right; that you didn't know what you were doing to the little bairn!

Jean (*silent*) I knew well enough.

Mrs Holroyd Oh, my dear, if you could tell him something that would make them let you off – now think, Jean, think, honey! it may be you could tell him something that would save you.

Jean (*silent – stares vacantly into space*) I can tell him nothing.

Col Stuart Nothing you can say, of course, will clear you now; but, for the sake of the memory you will leave behind you, can you give no sort of reason, no explanation of the impulse that led to your terrible crime? (**Jean** *shakes her head.*)

Mrs Holroyd Oh, your worship, your worship!

Col Stuart (*to* **Mrs Holroyd**) No, it is no use, I'm afraid; she hasn't opened her lips from the beginning. (*Looks at watch.*) You have twenty minutes together. (*Exit.*) (*The two* **Warders** *stand at the back, apparently not listening.*)

Mrs Holroyd (*in tears*) Oh, my Jean, my bonny Jean! That it should have come to this! (**Jean** *stands motionless.* **Mrs Holroyd** *turns away, distractedly wringing her hands.*)

Mrs Holroyd (*coming back to the girl*) Jean, Jean, do you know they will have the life of ye?

Jean (*silent – makes motion of assent*) Yes, I know.

Mrs Holroyd How could you do it, my lass? Can't you remember? If you could have told them all about it and asked for mercy you could have got it.

Jean (*silent – smiles strangely*) I don't want mercy.

Mrs Holroyd You're not afraid to die with your sins about ye?

Jean (*silent – shakes her head*) No, I am not afraid.

Mrs Holroyd Ah, Jean, but I am afraid for ye. No, I cannot bear it. Jean! (*With a fresh outburst.*) Are ye not thinking of your mother at all?

Jean (*silent – puts out her hand to her mother*) Poor mother!

Mrs Holroyd Oh, Jean, you're very hard. You don't think of those who are left when you won't ask for mercy. And Jamie Warren, poor lad – his heart is broken as well as mine. (*Pause –* **Jean** *stands erect seeming not to hear.*) But there is still a chance, Jean – honey – there is indeed. Maybe Jamie'll come back here this morning with the blessed news. He should be here soon, very soon. (*In an agony.*) Jean, Jean, if only I could get you to speak! His worship's been asking me about you. What can I tell him? Try to recollect, lassie – try to think on that night when I left ye with the baby – try to think just how it all was. I left ye sitting by the fire, just after Mrs

Ridley had gone out; ye'll mind she was a bit vexed, poor body, at the way ye'd spoken – and the baby was asleep in the cradle, I'd just covered him up warm with the quilt. (**Jean** *gives a sharp cry, and makes a motion to stop her mother.*)

Jean (*silent*) Ah! (*The door opens, and* **Jamie Warren** *comes in hastily with a* **Warder**, *who points to* **Jean** *and goes out again.*)

Mrs Holroyd Jamie! Well, Jamie – what news do you bring? Speak, lad, tell us!

Warren (*looks at* **Mrs Holroyd** *and shakes his head, and then looks at* **Jean**.) The news I bring is – bad.

Jean (*silent – unmoved*)

Warren No, Jean, they won't grant it; they say the sentence must be carried out. (**Jean** *clasps her hands with a look of relief, almost of gladness.*)

Mrs Holroyd Oh, Jean, honey, it will kill me too! (**Jean** *seems not to hear.*) Jamie, Jamie, she doesn't seem to mind for me one little bit! Speak to her, my lad, try to soften her hard heart! (*Re-enter* **Col Stuart**.)

Col Stuart (*to* **Jean**) You have heard the result of the appeal?

Jean (*silent – bows*) Yes.

Mrs Holroyd Oh, your worship, is there no hope?

Col Stuart None – absolutely none.

Warren Jean, your only hope is in Him who alone can pardon your sin: turn to Him before it is too late. Do not die unforgiven.

Jean (*silent*) I shall not die unforgiven.

Col Stuart Take care, Jean Creyke; remember your time is running short – the end is very near.

Jean (*aloud*) When?

Col Stuart Tomorrow morning at eight.

Jean Tomorrow! (*Her lips form the word.*)

Mrs Holroyd (*crying out*) Tomorrow morning!

Warren Yes, the time is short, indeed! Jean, confess! Confess, and turn you to the Lord your God.

Mrs Holroyd Tomorrow! Tomorrow! Ah, but it's too soon for her to die! Jean, Jean, my honey, my little lass! Oh, my Jean! (**Jean**, *as if in a dream, turns to go.*)

Col Stuart My poor woman, all you can do for her now is to pray for her, and say good-bye. You won't see her again.

Mrs Holroyd (*horror-stricken and bewildered*) Not see her again! What do you mean? You'll let me come tonight, and tomorrow? (*Looks round – reads answer in faces of bystanders.*)

Col Stuart No, this is the last time.

Mrs Holroyd The last time! No, no! You can't take her from me like that! Your worship, she's the only child I've ever had – the only thing I have in the world! Eh, but ye'll let me bide with her the day, till tonight, only till tonight! Just these few hours longer! Think, your worship – I must do without her all the rest of my life!

Col Stuart (*compassionately*) My poor woman! (*He makes a sign to the* **Warders**.)

Mrs Holroyd (*rushing forward as* **Warders** *are going to take* **Jean** *out*) Oh, wait, only wait! Jamie, don't let her go! Tell them they mustn't take her to die yet. She isn't ready to die, ye know she isn't ready. (*To* **Jean**.) Oh, my honey! Speak, speak, before it is too late. Tell them why you did it. Put away your rebellious heart! (*To* **Stuart**.) You think she's bad and wicked, but she's not wicked – she's not indeed! Jean, Jean, why did ye kill the poor little bairn?

Warren Jean, listen to me – tomorrow you are to appear before your Maker. Confess your crime, and lay down your burden before the throne of God.

Jean (*aloud*) Crime!

Col Stuart Not a crime, that you in cold blood took the life of a poor, helpless, little baby, because you hadn't the courage to bear the sight of its misfortunes?

Jean I hadn't courage? I've had courage just once in my life – just once in my life I've been strong and kind – and it was the night I killed my child! (*She turns away to door.*)

Warren Jean! (**Mrs Holroyd** *cries something inarticulate as she tries in despair to hold* **Jean** *back.*)

Jean Don't, mother, don't! You don't think I could live after this, do you? I had to do what I did, and they have to take my life for it. I showed him the only true mercy, and that is what the law shows me! Maybe I shall find him up yonder made straight and fair and happy – find him in Alan's arms. Good-bye – Mother – goodbye!

She goes out as the curtain falls.

Diana of Dobson's

Cicely Hamilton

Cicely Hamilton (1872–1952)

Cicely Hamilton was an active feminist campaigner. She was a member of the Womens' Freedom League, and a founder-member of the Actresses' Franchise League and the Women Writers' Suffrage League, and was on the advisory committee of the Pioneer Players, Edith Craig's feminist theatre company. She wrote suffrage plays for the Actresses' Franchise League and the Pioneer Players, amongst them *A Pageant of Great Women* and *How the Vote Was Won*. In several of her many plays she attacks women's economic dependency on men through marriage, and the lack of reasonable alternatives to marriage for women – arguments which she developed at length in her book, *Marriage as a Trade* (1909), and which were the subject of her play, *Just to Get Married*, performed in 1911 at the Little Theatre, under the management of feminist and suffragist Gertrude Kingston. In the play, Georgiana Vicary, the 'redundant woman', speaks of her position in being forced to find a husband as her only means of economic survival:

> I'm a perfectly useless woman. And what is a perfectly useless woman to do but marry? . . . Even when she does not care for the man who asks her. . . . Every woman is expected to get herself a husband, somehow or another, and is looked on as a miserable failure if she doesn't. . . . I've got nothing to look forward to if I don't marry. And then, if you haven't married, you've failed. There's nothing else – and people look down on you. And as you get older there's no one to care about you – and you just don't matter. It's so dull and miserable – no sort of a future. I dread it so. (Act 2)

After the war, Hamilton continued writing plays, novels, travel books and journalism, acted as a director of *Time and Tide* and worked on the editorial committee of the *Englishwoman*. She was a member of the 'Six Point Group', campaigning for equal opportunities for women, and of the Open Door Council, which opposed protective legislation for women which was seen as hampering them economically. She also campaigned for birth control and abortion rights for women: 'If I have a bee in my bonnet, the name of that insect is birth-control; the right of men and women (but especially of women) to save themselves suffering, to spare themselves poverty, by limiting the number of their children'. (*Life Errant*, p. 55)

Diana of Dobson's, submitted to the licenser under the title *The Adventuress*, was so great a success when it was first performed by Lena Ashwell at the Kingsway Theatre in February 1908 – it ran for 143 performances – that she revived it to open her season in January of the following year, when it played for a further month. It was toured by Ashwell in 1908 and successfully performed in the provinces by three other companies in that year, and Hamilton rewrote and published the play as a novel in the same year. It was her first playwriting success, although she had worked as an actress in the provinces, and as a writer for some years, supporting herself by writing 'sensation' stories for weekly magazines. When her first play, a curtain-raiser, had been produced, she was advised by its producer 'to conceal the sex of its author until after the notices were out, as plays which were known to be written by women were apt to get a bad press. . . . Certain it is that the one or two critics who had discovered that C. Hamilton stood for a woman were the one or two critics who dealt out hard measure to her playlet' (*Life Errant*, p. 60). *Diana of Dobson's*, however, came out under her full name.

When Ashwell revived the play in 1909, she published a note in the programme: 'I think the revival may have some special points of interest for you, as the theme of the play is so intimately connected with a subject which is at present attracting a large amount of attention. I refer, of course, to the discussion which has been going on in the Press on the "Living In" System.' But while the *New Age* (29 February 1908) wanted the first act to be longer in order to strengthen the revelation of 'the servility of living-in' – 'we get an impressionist vision of "living-in" life when a more detailed and extended realism would have served as a heightened contrast to the society life shown in the next act' – most contemporary reviews praised the play as 'a bright little comedy', and *The Times* (12 January 1909) believed that the first act was 'as "romantic" as the rest of the comedy'.

It is the play's romanticism that might be the puzzling part today, given Hamilton's political activism in opposing the expectation that women would be economically dependent on men. In her autobiography, *Life Errant* (1935), she wrote of her involvement in the suffrage campaign:

If I worked for women's enfranchisement (and I did work quite hard) it wasn't because I hoped great things from counting female noses at general elections, but because the agitation for women's enfranchisement must inevitably shake and weaken the tradition of the 'normal woman'. The 'normal woman' with her 'destiny' of marriage and motherhood and housekeeping – and especially no interest in the man's preserve of politics! My personal revolt was feminist rather than suffragist. (p. 65)

In *Marriage as a Trade* she analyses the ways in which young women are taught to sell themselves into the business of marriage, for want of any other possibilities being open to them to support themselves. Diana shows herself, in Act One of *Diana of Dobson's*, to be quite aware that marriage is an economic proposition: for the young women working in the drapery shop, it is the only alternative to the 'grind and squalor and tyranny and overwork' of the shop, where they are paid 'five bob a week for fourteen hours work a day', obliged to live in the shop dormitory, and are chaperoned and punished for misdemeanours such as leaving the lights on after hours. In Diana's discussion with her suitor, Bretherton, in the third act, she again highlights the economic base of marriage. In the proposed match, it is money that matters most: when he finds that she hasn't enough to support him, he decides that he hasn't enough to support her. Economics, not romance, is the basis of the bargaining. But in the final act, romance takes over: they meet on the Embankment, both without work and seemingly penniless. Bretherton has undergone his fairy-tale trial for the princess, and now has his reward – she marries him. But Diana makes it clear that not only does she get the man she wants, she also gets and needs a share of his £600 a year. Her lack of training for work, because she is middle-class, gives her no other way of controlling her economic circumstances. The play mixes fantasy with realism: the fantasy of the legacy, of Bretherton's trial, of their meeting on the Embankment at dawn and marrying; the realism of the dormitory at Dobson's, of the limitation of women's opportunities for decent work, of the economic base of marriage, and of the recognition that under capitalism the way to make money is 'to get other people to work for you for as little as they can be got to take, and put the proceeds of their work into your pocket'. The play was dubbed a 'romantic comedy', and in the second act Diana defines romance as 'the prospect of a new sensation . . . something that their everyday life fails to give them'. Undoubtedly the romantic ending contributed to the play's success with critics and audiences. But the formulaic ending can also suggest to the audience that this sort of solution is possible in romances, but not in life where women cannot afford, economically, to be romantic. As Georgiana says in *Just to Get Married*:

> Surely you're not romantic enough to imagine that all the married women of your acquaintance have selected their more or less unsuitable husbands out of pure affection! . . . When you're a pauper you've got to take what comes along. (Act 1)

Linda Fitzsimmons

Select Bibliography

Diana of Dobson's: a novel (London, Collier, 1908)

Marriage as a Trade (London, Chapman and Hall, 1909; repr. London, The Women's Press, 1981, intro. Jane Lewis)

A Pageant of Great Women (London, The Suffrage Shop, 1910; repr. in *Sketches from the Actresses' Franchise League*, ed. Viv Gardner (Nottingham, Nottingham Drama Texts, 1985))

Just to Get Married: a novel (London, Chapman and Hall, 1911)

How the Vote Was Won, with Christopher St John [Christabel Marshall] (London, Edith Craig, 1913; repr. in *How the Vote Was Won and Other Suffragette Plays*, ed. Dale Spender and Carole Hayman (London, Methuen, 1985))

Just to Get Married: a comedy in 3 acts (London, Samuel French, 1914)

The Child in Flanders (London, French, 1922)

Diana of Dobson's: a romantic comedy in 4 acts (London, Samuel French Ltd., 1925)

The Old Adam (Oxford, Blackwell, 1926)

The Old Vic, with Lilian Baylis (London, Jonathan Cape, 1926)

Life Errant (London, J. M. Dent and Sons, 1935)

Diana of Dobson's was first performed at the Kingsway Theatre, London, on 12 February 1908, with the following cast:

Miss Smithers	Miss Nannie Bennet
Kitty Brant	Miss Christine Silver
Miss Jay	Miss Muriel Vox
Diana Massingberd	Miss Lena Ashwell
Miss Morton	Miss Doris Lytton
Miss Pringle	Miss Ada Palmer
Mrs Cantelupe	Miss Frances Ivor
Waiter	Mr W. Lemmon Warde
Mrs Whyte-Fraser	Miss Gertrude Scott
Sir Jabez Grinley	Mr Dennis Eadie
Captain the Honourable Victor Bretherton	Mr C. M. Hallard
Old Woman	Miss Beryl Mercer
Police Constable Fellowes	Mr Norman McKinnel

Produced by Lena Ashwell

Act One
One of the Assistants' Dormitories at Dobson's Drapery Emporium

Act Two
The Hotel Engadine, Pontresina

Act Three
The Hotel Engadine, Pontresina

Act Four
The Thames Embankment

Between Acts One *and* Two *14 days elapse.*
Between Acts Two *and* Three *12 days elapse.*
Between Acts Three *and* Four *14 weeks elapse.*

Act One

Scene: one of the Assistants' Dormitories in the large suburban drapery establishment at Messrs Dobson's.

As the curtain rises the stage is almost in darkness except for the glimmer of a single gas jet turned very low. A door opens – showing light in passage beyond – and **Miss Smithers** enters and gropes her way to the gas jet, which she turns full on. The light reveals a bare room of the dormitory type. Very little furniture except five small beds ranged against the walls – everything plain and comfortless to the last degree. On the doors are some pegs.

As **Miss Smithers** turns away from the gas, **Kitty Brant** enters, sighs wearily, and flings herself down on her bed. **Miss Smithers** is well over 30, faded and practical looking. **Kitty Brant** is about 20, pretty, but pale and tired.

Smithers (at bureau, looking towards **Kitty**) Very tired tonight, Miss Brant? (Removes ribbon, tie and collar, takes out brush and comb from drawer.)

Kitty (on bed) Oh no, thank you, not more than usual. I'm always glad when bedtime comes round.

Smithers (commencing to undress) So's most of us. You look white, though – (still at bureau) – you are not strong enough – (unhooks dress) – to stand the long hours, and that's the truth.

Kitty (smiling shyly) Well, I shan't have to stand them for so very much longer now, shall I? (Begins to undo her tie.)

Smithers (with a half sigh) That's true. Ah, you're a lucky girl, you are, to be able to look forward to having a little home of your own. (Looks round the bare walls, then shrugs her shoulders.) Wish I could. (Puts waist over foot of bed – returns to bureau and takes out hairpins from puff and switch.)

Kitty (unbuttoning dress) Perhaps you'll be having a home of your own some day, Miss Smithers.

Smithers (back turned to **Kitty** – standing in front of looking glass) Me, bless you – no such luck. I'm one of the left ones; I am left high and dry. I made up my mind to that long ago. But what's the use of grumbling? It'll be all the same in a hundred years' time.

Kitty (removes waist) You don't often grumble.

Smithers (turning towards **Kitty** with puff in her mouth) No, what's the good? It only makes things more uncomfortable for yourself and for everybody else. No use quarrelling with your bread and butter, even if the butter is spread thin and margarine at that. (Removes other puffs.) Not that I wouldn't grumble fast enough if there was anything to be got by it – except the sack. (Deposits puffs on bed.) When is it coming off – the wedding?

Kitty He – Fred – wants it to be at the beginning of October.

Smithers (taking off switch, lets down her own hair) The beginning of October – that's less than three months! It won't have been a long engagement.

Kitty No. You see, Fred has always been very careful and steady, and he has got a good bit put by.

Smithers (unbraids switch and combs it) Well – (sits in chair) – I won't say that I'm sorry you're leaving Dobson's, because it's about the best thing that could happen to you. But I do say this, we shall all of us miss you.

Kitty It's very kind of you to say so, Miss Smithers.

Smithers (*turns chair round, sits combing her switch*) And as for Miss Massingberd, I really don't know however she'll manage to get on without you – if she stays on herself, that's to say.

Kitty (*sitting up anxiously at lower end of bed*) Why do you say that? Do you think Mr Dobson is going to turn her off?

Smithers (*continues to comb switch*) Oh, I haven't heard anything about it – if that's what you mean. But it's as plain as the nose on your face that Dobson don't like her.

Kitty *removes shoes and stockings.*

And she has managed to put up Miss Pringle's back as well, so she'll have to mind her p's and q's if she wants to stay on. (*Lays switch across her knees and again combs her own hair.*)

Kitty I wish she didn't hate Miss Pringle so. (*Drops shoes side of bed.*)

Smithers Oh, well, of course we all hate – (*combing hair vigorously*) – Miss Pringle, with her mean, nagging ways, and her fines and spying, but the rest of us aren't quite such fools as to let her see it, like Miss Massingberd does.

Kitty Poor Di! I really don't think she can help it, Miss Smithers. She can't keep her feelings in. Even when she doesn't say anything, you can tell what she's thinking by her face.

Smithers That you can.

Kitty (*a little timidly*) I wish – now I'm leaving – that you'd try and be a little better friends with her, Miss Smithers.

Smithers Oh, you mustn't think I dislike her. It's only that she's a bit – well – queer – (*rises*) – what the French call *difficile*. (*Puts switch on bureau, takes up collar, tie, etc., and puts them on bed.*)

Kitty She's had such a hard time. (*Undoing clothes and shaking out nightdress.*)

Smithers (*takes waist and rolls up things*) Well, so have most of us, as far as that goes. And we're having a hard time now, just the same as she is. You get used to anything if you only stick at it long enough. (*Puts roll she has just made on box at foot of bed.*)

Kitty (*puts feet in slippers*) You know Di wasn't brought up to earn her own living.

Smithers (*removes shoes and puts on slippers*) Wasn't she? Of course it always falls hardest on that sort.

Kitty (*gets nightgown from under her pillow, stands on bed, and puts on nightgown – speaking quickly*) She told me the other day that her father was a doctor. She kept house for him until he died, six years ago, and never had the least idea, till then, that – (*the nightgown is over her head, and her movements under it show that she is undoing skirts, etc.*) – she would have to turn and work. When he died – quite suddenly – there was nothing for her – nothing at all. She hasn't got a penny in the world except what she earns, or anyone to turn to.

Smithers No relations? (*Sees tear in skirt.*)

Kitty (*same business*) None near enough to be of any good to her. She's had an awful struggle these last six years. Oh, I do hope Mr Dobson isn't going to sack her. After she left Grinley's shop at Clapham she was out of work for weeks – (*slips her arms into sleeves of nightgown and finishes wriggling into them*) – before she came here, and I don't suppose she has been able to save anything since.

Smithers (*crosses to washstand*) Not likely. She's always being fined for one thing – (*opens drawer of washstand and looks inside*) – she's careless, and then Miss Pringle's so down on her – (*closes drawer, turns to box foot of bed, addressing* **Kitty**) – hates her like poison. (*Opens box and kneels – takes out workbox, closes lid, and sits on box and sews.*) There must have been precious little left out of her screw last week.

Kitty (*takes skirt from under nightgown*) Poor Di – I wish –

Enter noisily **Miss Jay**, *a fair girl with very frizzy hair. She speaks with a strong Cockney accent, and giggles frequently.*

Miss Jay Hallo, girls – aren't you in bed yet? (*Crosses to bureau, removing tie and collar.*) Thought I'd better come up or I shouldn't have taime to put my hair in pins before the gas is turned off. It's just on the quarter to eleven naow. (*Viewing herself in looking-glass.*) Heard from him today, Miss Brant? (*Removes waist, showing pink corset. Turning to* **Kitty**.)

Kitty (*seated on bed, combing hair*) No, not today.

Miss Jay Thought you were looking a bit paile. Cheer up – he's thinking of you so hard he forgot to write. Where's Miss Morton? Oh, I forgot, she's got an evening aeout. (*With skirt loosened about hips looks in mirror, then takes off skirt and tosses it on box.*) My, what a fright I do look tonight – this damp weather takes every bit of curl out of my hair. (*Curls hair vigorously.*) Miss Massingberd not come up yet?

Smithers No.

Miss Jay I wish she was in somebody else's dormitory and not mine.

Kitty (*hotly*) Why?

Miss Jay (*at glass with back to* **Kitty**) Oh, she gives me a fair hump, she does – going about with a face as long as a fiddle. I don't laike her.

Kitty That's only because you don't understand her.

Miss Jay (*turning to* **Kitty**) Of course it is. I haite things I can't understand – and people I can't understand too.

She breaks off as **Diana Massingberd** *walks in.* **Diana** *is about 27 or 28 – she is pale with dark lines under her eyes, her movements are nervous and overwrought. She walks to her box at the foot of bed, sits on it, and begins pulling off her tie and collar with a quick impatient gesture.*

Kitty (*after* **Diana** *is seated*) How are you feeling tonight, Di – any better?

Diana (*undoing tie with a jerk*) Better – no, I'm feeling murderous.

Smithers Murderous?

Diana That's the word.

Kitty *goes to door and hangs up her skirt and returns to bed.*

Miss Jay (*putting curlers in her hair*) And who do you want to murder, Miss Massingberd?

Diana Anyone – but first and foremost Dobson and the Pringle woman.

Kitty Has she been fining you again?

Diana Fining and nagging.

Kitty (*anxiously*) Oh, Di, you didn't answer her back?

Diana (*removing shoes – bitterly*) No – I didn't dare.

Miss Jay What did she fine you for this time?

Diana Need you ask? (*Begins to unbutton waist.*) Usual thing – unbusinesslike conduct. According to her, every single thing I do comes under the heading of unbusinesslike conduct. Oh, how I loathe the words – and how I loathe the Pringle. I

wish we were living in the Middle Ages.
(*Puts belt over foot of bed.*)

Smithers In the Middle Ages – what for?

Diana So that I could indulge in my
craving for the blood of Miss Emily
Pringle.

Miss Jay (*giggling*) You do saiy funny
things, Miss Massingberd.

Diana They strike you as funny, do they?
It must be delightful to have your keen
sense of humour. (*Waist loosened.*) I wish I
could see anything at all humorous about
Messrs Dobson's high-class drapery
emporium. Grind and squalor and tyranny
and overwork! I can see plenty of those –
but I fail to detect where the humour
comes in. (*Waist off.*) Wonder how long it
will be before I get the sack, Kit?

Kitty Di, you mustn't –

Diana What's the good of saying that to
me? You must talk to Dobson. I can't help
getting the sack if he gives it me, can I?
And I'd bet a shilling, if I had a shilling,
that I get kicked out within a fortnight.

Kitty Oh – Di –

Smithers (*has finished mending skirt – rises
with work-basket and opens box*) Well, I don't
want to be unkind, Miss Massingberd –

Diana That means you are going to say
something particulary nasty. Fire away.
(*Begins to undo boots, then puts on pair of
slippers, placing boots R of box.*)

Smithers (*on her knees – talks over her shoulders
– nettled*) Well, you've been going on lately
as if you rather wanted to be turned off.
Time after time you've given Miss Pringle
the chance to drop on you – and this
morning you all but contradicted Mr
Dobson himself about those suède
gauntlets.

Diana Miss Smithers, I wish I had had the
pluck to contradict Mr Dobson right down
– flat – direct – about those suède
gauntlets.

Smithers That's where you're a fool, if
you'll excuse me saying so.

Diana (*goes to bed*) Oh, I'll excuse you –
you can call me whatever you like. I don't
mind. I dare say I am a fool – and anyway
I know for certain that I'm something
that's very much worse than a fool.

Miss Jay Something that's very much
worse than a fool?

Diana (*takes off skirt*) Yes – a pauper.

Miss Jay *sniggers.*

There's another of my funny remarks for
you, and it's not only funny, it happens to
be true as well.

Smithers (*rises*) I don't quite understand
what you're driving at, Miss Massingberd,
but what I mean to say is that the way
you've been carrying on the last week or
two isn't the way to go to work if you want
to stay on with Dobson.

Diana (*shakes out skirt*) The question is – do
I want to stay with Dobson?

Kitty Oh, you do – for the present you do.

Diana For the present –

Smithers (*shrugging her shoulders*) Of course,
you know your own business best.

Diana You wouldn't say that if you
thought it. (*Puts skirt at foot of bed.*)

Smithers Well, as you said the other day
you were all alone in the world with no one
to look to, and as I don't imagine that
you've been able to save very much since
you were taken on here –

Diana Save – good Lord – me save! On

thirteen pounds a year, five bob a week, with all my clothes to find and my fines to pay.

Smithers (*crosses – stiffly*) I suppose, you know, Miss Massingberd, that the firm prefer that the assistants should not discuss the amount of their salaries.

Diana (*at lower corner of bed*) I don't wonder – I'm glad the firm have the grace to be ashamed of themselves sometimes. Well, I'm not bound to consider their feelings, and I shall discuss the amount of my totally inadequate salary as often as I like. I get five bob a week – with deductions – and I don't care who knows it. I only wish I could proclaim the fact from the housetops. Five bob a week for fourteen hours' work a day – five bob a week for the use of my health and strength – five bob a week for my life. And I haven't a doubt that a good many others here are in the same box. (*Sits quickly.*)

Miss Smithers *shaking skirt outside door. An awkward silence –* **Miss Jay** *frizzles her hair hurriedly –* then **Kitty** *lays a hand on* **Diana***'s shoulder.*

Kitty Di, what's come over you lately? You usen't to be like this – not so bad. It's only the last fortnight that you've been so dreadfully discontented.

Diana Oh, it has been coming on a great deal longer than that – coming on for years.

Kitty For years?

Diana I have fits of this sort of thing, every now and then. I can't help myself. They come and take hold of you – and you realise what your life might be – and what it is – I'm about at the end of my tether, Kit.

Kitty But why? What is the matter just now, in particular?

Diana There isn't anything particular the matter. That's just it.

Kitty What do you mean, dear?

Diana Everything's going on the same as usual – the same old grind. As it was in the beginning, is now, and ever shall be: world without end. Amen.

Miss Jay (*with a shock*) Oh, Miss Massingberd – that's in the prayer book.

Diana (*imitating her*) Ow, Miss Jay, you do surprise me –

Kitty *sits on edge of bed.*

Is it really? –

Miss Jay *turns back to bureau annoyed.*

You're going to have done with it, Kitty. In three months' time you'll be married. However your marriage turns out, it will be a change for you – a change from the hosiery department of Dobson's.

Kitty (*hurt*) Di –

Diana (*still seated, her arm round* **Kitty***'s waist*) Oh, I didn't mean to be unkind, Kit. You're a dear, and if I'm nasty to you it's only because I envy you. You're going to get out of all this: in three months' time you'll have turned your back on it for good – you'll have done with the nagging and the standing and this horrible bare room – and the dining-room with the sloppy tea on the table and Pringle's sour face at the end of it. Lucky girl! But I haven't any prospect of turning my back on it, and it doesn't seem to me I ever shall.

Smithers (*significantly*) You will, and before very long too, if you don't look out. (*Crosses to bed, sits up on middle of bed with her back to audience, combing hair.*)

Diana Oh, I shan't be here much longer – I can quite see that. But when I am fired out I shall only start the same old grind somewhere else – all over again. The delectable atmosphere of Dobson's will follow me about wherever I go. I shall crawl round to similar establishments, cringing to be taken on at the same starvation salary – and then settle down in the same stuffy dormitory, with the same mean little rules to obey – I shall serve the same stream of intelligent customers – and bolt my dinner off the same tough meat in the same gloomy dining-room with the same mustard-coloured paper on the walls. And that's life. Kit! (*Clapping* **Kitty** *on the shoulder.*) That's what I was born for. (*Rises.*) Hurrah for life! (*Tosses* **Miss Smithers***'s puffs and switch in the air.*)

Miss Jay (*with grease pot, greasing her face*) Well, I never, you do – (*Checks herself.*)

Miss Smithers *retrieves her hair with indignation.*

Diana Say funny things – yes, I know.

Smithers Look here, girls, it's only five minutes now till we have to turn the light out. Instead of listening to Miss Massingberd's nonsense, we'd better –

Enter hurriedly **Miss Morton** – *she wears dark – not black – skirt, jacket and hat and white shirt waist. She is unbuttoning jacket as she runs in – the others are beginning to undress, plaiting hair, etc., with the exception of* **Diana.**

Miss Morton Hallo, girls! Gas not out yet. (*Closes door, hangs hat on peg.*) That's a blessing.

Smithers Had a nice evening out, Miss Morton?

Miss Morton Tip-top, thanks. (*Removes jacket.*) Been at my cousin's at Balham. I hurried back though.

Miss Jay *crosses with skirt, etc., and stands.*

I was afraid I shouldn't get in till after

eleven – and I do so hate having to go to bed in the dark. (*Hangs jacket on a peg.*)

When **Miss Morton** *goes up –* **Miss Jay** *crosses to bed with things. As she does so she sees a letter sticking out of pocket.*

Oh, Miss Massingberd, I brought this up for you. (*Gives letter to* **Diana**.) It was in the hall. I suppose it came by the last post. (*Goes to box foot of bed, sits and unlaces shoes.*)

Diana (*rises and goes to gas, surprised*) A letter for me? (*Moves a few steps, looking at envelope.*)

Miss Morton (*unlacing boots*) My cousin Albert sent his kind regards to you, Miss Jay. Said I was to be sure not to forget 'em.

Miss Jay (*has hung skirt on peg and is now rolling up waist, etc.; giggling*) Ah! Did he?

Miss Morton He asked most particular which department you was in.

Miss Jay Whatever did you say? You never went and told him it was corsets?

Miss Morton Didn't I just? (*Getting into slippers.*)

Miss Jay Well, I never – you are a caution. What did he say when you taold him?

Miss Morton Said he was downright disappointed, and he wished you'd been in the tie department – then he could have dropped in now and again to buy a new tie and have a chat.

Miss Jay Oh, go on!

Miss Morton He was afraid he'd be too shy to ask to look at a pair of corsets even for the pleasure of seeing you.

Miss Jay (*giggling more than ever*) Well, I must saiy, he has got a nerve. Did you ever –

Diana (*who has been standing under the gas*

reading her letter – then staring at it incredulously) Girls – girls –

Smithers *comes down to below bed.*

Kitty (*on bed – foot of it*) Di, what is it?

Smithers What's the matter, Miss Massingberd?

Diana (*hysterically*) The letter – it says – (*Holding it out.*) Read it – oh no, let me read it again first.

Kitty It's not bad news, is it?

Diana Bad news – bad news. (*She laughs.*)

Miss Jay She's got hysterics.

Miss Morton (*moves to and picks up glass of water from washstand*) Have a glass of water, Miss Massingberd, dear.

Diana No, no – I'm all right.

Miss Morton *returns glass of water to washstand.* **Diana** *pulls herself together.*

Kitty Tell us what it is?

Diana It's this letter – the letter Miss Morton brought up.

Miss Morton Yes.

Diana It comes from a lawyer – a solicitor in Manchester –

Kitty Yes?

Diana It seems that a cousin of my father's used to live in Manchester – a distant cousin whom I never knew, and who was in some sort of business there. He died suddenly a while ago, without leaving a will. His money is all to be divided up among the next of kin – and I'm one of them – one of the next of kin – and I get three hundred pounds!

Chorus of 'Oh! Three hundred pounds! Oh, you lucky girl!'

Kitty Di, I'm so glad – so glad, dear.

Diana I can't believe it yet – I can't get myself to believe it. Read the letter, some one. (*Gives letter to* **Smithers**.) Read it aloud to me – and tell me if it is really true.

Business of dropping letter and picking it up, etc. They hoist **Smithers** *on the chair under the gas.*

Smithers (*reading*) 'Madam, *re* R. C. Cooper, deceased. I beg to inform you that, by the recent death of my client, Mr Edward Chamberlain Cooper, you, as one of his next of kin, are entitled to a share in his estates – '

Diana (*snatching letter from her*) It's true then – it is really true.

The girls crowd round her.

Kitty Of course it is.

Diana Girls, I'm not a pauper any more. I've got three hundred pounds of my own. Think of it – three hundred golden sovereigns.

Miss Jay What are you going to do with it?

Diana I don't know – I haven't had time to think yet. I'll stand you all a treat on Sunday, for one thing. (*The girls cheer.*) And Kitty shall have a wedding present – what shall it be, Kit?

Kitty (*shaking her head*) You mustn't be extravagant and waste your money. You ought to put it straight in the bank.

Diana Put it in the bank – not me. What's the good of that?

Smithers You should invest it in something really safe. (*Sits.*)

Diana And get nine or ten pounds a year for it at the outside. No, thank you – not good enough. Now I've got three hundred pounds –

Diana *sits on box,* **Kitty** *sits on bed,* **Miss Morton** *sits on floor at* **Diana**'s *feet and* **Miss Jay** *on box.*

– three hundred pounds to do as I like with – I intend to have some fun out of it.

Miss Morton You'll chuck Dobson's, I suppose?

Diana (*scornfully*) What do you think?

Miss Morton (*sitting on floor in front of* **Diana**) Tomorrow?

Diana (*nods*) I can get an advance tomorrow – the solicitor – Mr Crampton – says so. So this is my last night here, girls. You don't suppose I'll stay in this beastly den a moment longer than I can help! Dobson's hosiery department has seen the last of me. I'd clear out of the place tonight if it wasn't so late. No, I wouldn't, though – if I went tonight I shouldn't be able to have an interview with Mr Septimus Dobson – to tell him what I think of him.

Chorus of – 'OH!'

Miss Jay You're not really going to?

Diana Not going to – you wait and see. Why, it'll be glorious – glorious. Girls, have you ever grasped what money really is? It's power! Power to do what you like, to go where you like, to say what you like. Because I have three hundred pounds in my pocket, I shall be able tomorrow morning to enjoy the priceless luxury of telling Dobson to his fat white face, what we all whisper behind his mean old back –

Miss Morton Shall you dare?

Diana Dare? With three hundred pounds in my pocket I'd dare any mortal thing on earth.

Smithers I think you're forgetting, Miss Massingberd, that three hundred pounds won't last for ever.

Diana Oh, no, I'm not. But while it does last, I mean to have everything I want – everything.

Kitty Oh Di, don't do anything silly –

Smithers It won't last you very long at that rate.

Diana I know – but I don't care. Who was it said something about a crowded hour of glorious life? Well, that's just what I'm going to have – a crowded hour, and it *shall* be crowded. For once in my life I'll know what it is to have a royal time – I'll deny myself nothing. I have had six years of scrape and starve – now I'll have a month of everything that money can buy me – and there are very few things that money can't buy me – precious few.

Smithers (*sarcastically*) And when it's all spent? (*Combing her hair.*)

Diana (*defiantly*) When it is all spent –

Smithers Yes?

Diana I shall go back, I suppose – back to the treadmill grind. But I shall have something to remember – I shall be able to look back at my crossing hour – my one little bit of life. For one month I shall have done what I chose – not what I was forced to. For one month I shall have had my freedom – and that will be something to remember. But I'm not going to think of the afterwards yet – I'm going to think of the *now*. What shall I do, Kit? For one thing, I shall travel – I've always longed and craved to see something of the world besides one narrow little piece of it.

Miss Morton Where shall you go?

Diana Haven't thought yet, but of course I shall begin with Paris.

Miss Morton Paris?

Diana To buy my clothes. I'll know what it is to wear a decently cut frock before I die.

Miss Jay I saiy, you are going it.

Diana Also boots that cost more than seven and elevenpence a pair. I'm going to have the best of everything, I tell you, and I'll start with Paris for clothes. (*Rises.*) Then I shall go on – move about – Switzerland, Italy, where I feel inclined –

Kitty It will be lovely – but – Diana –

Diana (*goes to* **Kitty**) No buts – Kitty – for the next month I am not going to have any buts. For part of the time I think I shall go somewhere in the mountains – I've always longed to see real mountains – I shall stay at the best hotels – I shall call myself Mrs Massingberd, I think. You're ever so much freer when you're married. I shall be a widow. (*Sits on box.*)

Kitty A widow!

All laugh.

Smithers Mrs Massingberd! Hush, the Pringle!

The door is suddenly flung open, and **Miss Pringle** *enters, middle-aged, sour-faced, and wearing a palpable transformation. All except* **Diana** *rush to their beds.* **Diana** *whistles.*

Miss Pringle What is all this noise about? It's past eleven, and the gas ought to have been out long ago. Miss Massingberd – (*one step down, on line with* **Diana**) – was it your voice I heard?

Diana Miss Pringle, it was.

Miss Pringle Then –

Diana (*interrupting*) The usual thing, I suppose? We're all of us fined. Gas burning after eleven o'clock at night – unbusinesslike conduct – sixpence all round. Never mind, girls, don't you worry. I'm standing treat for this lot.

Miss Pringle Miss Massingberd!

Diana Miss Pringle!

Miss Pringle Do you wish me to report you?

Diana For more unbusinesslike conduct? Certainly, if you like. Please yourself about it – I don't really care a row of brass pins.

Miss Pringle Are you out of your senses?

Diana Now you mention it, I do feel rather like it.

Miss Pringle You'll be sorry for your impertinence tomorrow.

Diana I assure you, you are entirely mistaken. (**Miss Jay** *rises in bed.*) The combination of fury and astonishment in your face will always remain with me as a pleasing memory – grateful and comforting. I may add that the effect is singularly unbecoming.

Miss Jay *giggles audibly – then chokes as* **Miss Pringle** *turns round.*

Miss Pringle (*viciously*) Miss Massingberd –

Diana Allow me to remind you that you have made that remark before. If you have nothing to add to it, we need not detain you any longer. I'll turn out the gas when I've done with it – which won't be for a few minutes yet. (*Rises.*)

Miss Pringle (*beside herself with fury*) Miss Massingberd – (*makes a step towards* **Diana**) – I believe you're drunk.

Girls Oh!

Diana (*coming back towards box*) You are quite at liberty to believe any mortal thing you like – you are quite at liberty to say any mortal thing you like. What you choose to think and what you choose to say are matters of perfect indifference to me now. It has ceased to matter to me in the very least whether you are satisfied with me or whether you are not – whether you fine me or whether you don't. This morning the stony glare in your eye would have made me shiver – tonight, it merely makes me smile. In short – (*Takes belt from foot of bed.*) – Miss Pringle, you are no longer in a position to bully me, so take my advice and don't try it on.

She sits on box and faces **Miss Pringle**.

Miss Pringle Miss Massingberd, the first thing in the morning – the *very* first thing in the morning – I shall make it my business to inform Mr Dobson –

Diana (*composedly*) *Damn* Mr Dobson.

Quick Curtain.

Act Two

A few bars of waltz music behind scene with rise of curtain.

Evening: about 9.30 p.m.
Scene: sitting-room Hotel Engadine – three large windows at back looking on to Swiss Mountains.

Mrs Cantelupe *discovered in window* L. *When curtain is well up, enter* **Waiter**.

Waiter Mrs Whyte-Fraser.

Enter **Mrs Whyte-Fraser**. *Exit* **Waiter**.

Mrs Cantelupe (*comes down, shakes hands*) My dear Eleanour – delighted! I was just wondering if you had arrived. And where's the Major? You haven't brought him with you?

Mrs Whyte-Fraser No. He said he was too dead beat to talk to anyone – even to you. So he sent his love and retired to the smoking-room. (*Sits.*) And how long have you been here, Mrs Cantelupe?

Mrs Cantelupe Just over a week. (*Sits on Chesterfield.*)

Mrs Whyte-Fraser Captain Bretherton is with you, isn't he?

Mrs Cantelupe Yes, I insisted on his coming to look after me on the journey and keep me company for a little.

Mrs Whyte-Fraser And like a dutiful nephew, he complied.

Mrs Cantelupe He couldn't very well refuse, after all I've done for him lately.

Mrs Whyte-Fraser Indeed?

Mrs Cantelupe My dear, you know how fond I am of Victor – he has always been my favourite of all the Bretherton boys –

but – well – he has cost me a pretty penny lately. His bills, my dear Eleanour, his bills – monstrous. Raynesworth went on strike four years ago – declared he would never pay his brother's debts again. I told him pleasantly that it was impossible for a man with Victor's tastes to keep up the position in the Guards on a miserable six hundred pounds a year.

Mrs Whyte-Fraser Six hundred pounds a year? Of course he couldn't remain in the Guards on that.

Mrs Cantelupe He quite saw that, too. And, as I was only willing to pay his debts, he had to send in his papers.

Mrs Whyte-Fraser I suppose Lord Raynesworth will get him into some sort of Government appointment.

Mrs Cantelupe Oh, of course – it's the only thing he's fit for, poor boy. Meanwhile, I have brought him out here with me – even *he* can't manage to spend anything very outrageous half-way up a Swiss mountain.

Mrs Whyte-Fraser It's almost a pity you can't establish him half-way up a Swiss mountain for the term of his natural life.

Mrs Cantelupe I declare, I wish I could – though even then I believe he could get into mischief.

Mrs Whyte-Fraser (*going to Chesterfield and sitting beside* **Mrs Cantelupe**) Does that mean that he's got into mischief already?

Mrs Cantelupe Well, to tell you the truth, my dear Eleanour – I am not quite sure.

Mrs Whyte-Fraser What is the nature of the mischief?

Mrs Cantelupe Feminine.

Mrs Whyte-Fraser Oh – who is she?

Mrs Cantelupe A Mrs Massingberd, who is staying at this hotel.

Mrs Whyte-Fraser *Mrs* Massingberd?

Mrs Cantelupe A widow.

Mrs Whyte-Fraser Genuine or Grass?

Mrs Cantelupe Oh, genuine – at least I have no reason to suppose otherwise.

Mrs Whyte-Fraser Young?

Mrs Cantelupe About eight and twenty, I should say.

Mrs Whyte-Fraser Any connection of Mrs Jimmy Sinclair's – she was a Massingberd.

Mrs Cantelupe I don't know. I have never heard her mention any of her people – except her husband.

Mrs Whyte-Fraser And who was he?

Mrs Cantelupe That I don't know either; but I understand from Victor that the late Mr Massingberd was considerably older than his wife.

Mrs Whyte-Fraser What is she like? Pretty – smart?

Mrs Cantelupe Both.

Mrs Whyte-Fraser Then what is the objection – no money?

Mrs Cantelupe That, my dear Eleanour, is exactly what I want to find out before I let things go too far.

Mrs Whyte-Fraser I see. When did he first meet her?

Mrs Cantelupe When she arrived here – five days ago.

Mrs Whyte-Fraser Only five days ago! He isn't usually so susceptible, is he?

Mrs Cantelupe No – that is what makes me think it is serious. *Apparently* she is very well off.

Mrs Whyte-Fraser But you are inclined to mistrust appearances?

Mrs Cantelupe My dear, one has to be so *careful* in these foreign hotels. Of course, an elderly husband *sounds* like money – and if she is as well off as she seems, it would be the best thing that could happen to Victor. A sensible marriage of the kind is what I've always hoped for him. But with only six hundred a year and his extravagant habits, it would be simply madness for him to marry a woman without money.

Mrs Whyte-Fraser Surely a skilful cross-examination ought to reveal something.

Mrs Cantelupe I assure you, Eleanour, I have only been waiting for the opportunity, and I am rather relying on your good nature to help me to it.

Mrs Whyte-Fraser On my good nature?

Mrs Cantelupe Yes. I have asked Mrs Massingberd to have coffee with us tonight.

Mrs Whyte-Fraser Here?

Mrs Cantelupe Yes – I generally sit here after dinner. No one seems to come to this little room. Now –

Sir Jabez *crosses at back on balcony.*

– what I want you to do is to carry Victor off with you, as soon as you have swallowed your coffee, and leave me alone for a quiet chat with Mrs Massingberd. Will you?

Mrs Whyte-Fraser I will – (*leans back in chair*) – even at the risk of earning Captain Bretherton's undying hatred.

Enter **Sir Jabez** *at window, comes slowly down. He has a cigar in his mouth, as he passes the window he stops, throws away cigar and comes in.*

Mrs Cantelupe You can set my undying gratitude against it.

Sir Jabez Surely that's Mrs Whyte-Fraser?

Mrs Whyte-Fraser It is. (*Rises.*) I congratulate you, *Sir Jabez.* (*Shakes hands.*) My husband and I were delighted to see your name in the Honours list – *really* delighted.

Sir Jabez Many thanks – so was I! It is an excellent form of advertisement, and taking all things into consideration, remarkably cheap at the price.

Mrs Whyte-Fraser *sits again.*

Mrs Cantelupe (*seated*) An excellent form of advertisement?

Sir Jabez That's how I look upon it, Mrs Cantelupe. My new dignity has a direct commercial value.

Mrs Whyte-Fraser Then will the fact of your having been created a baronet increase the volume of trade at your innumerable shops?

Sir Jabez Very considerably, I hope. Whom His Majesty delights to honour, His Majesty's loyal subjects delight to patronise.

Pause. **Sir Jabez** *goes up to window, giving impression that he feels he is not wanted.*

Mrs Cantelupe Do you know if my nephew is still in the garden, Sir Jabez?

Sir Jabez He was smoking a cigar there a minute or two ago.

Mrs Cantelupe We are waiting coffee for him and Mrs Massingberd.

Sir Jabez (*in window*) Mrs Massingberd? (*Comes down.*) You're expecting her?

Mrs Cantelupe I suppose you have never met her before?

Sir Jabez No. At first I fancied I had – her face seemed familiar to me somehow – but

she assured me she had never seen mine, so I must have been mistaken. I see so many faces. She's quite an acquisition here. Talks well and dresses well and has a style of her own. I like her.

Enter **Captain Bretherton**.

Mrs Cantelupe Oh, here you are, Victor.

Bretherton Ah! how do, Mrs Whyte-Fraser? When did you turn up?

Crosses to her and shakes hands. **Sir Jabez** *drifts up stage again.*

Mrs Whyte-Fraser Only a couple of hours ago.

Bretherton You don't look any the worse for the journey.

Mrs Whyte-Fraser That's nice of you.

Bretherton How's the Major?

Mrs Whyte-Fraser Oh, he says he's worn out, but I believe, if the truth were known, he's only saving himself for his first climb. I forget – you a climber?

Bretherton No, I'm not keen – I prefer golf. There's some quite decent links at Samaden – eighteen holes – and you can get over there on a 'bus.

Sir Jabez Been golfing this morning?

Bretherton No. Walked to the Morteratsch Glacier with Mrs Massingberd. She's coming in, isn't she?

Sir Jabez *goes up to chair.*

Mrs Cantelupe Yes. We're only waiting for coffee till she arrives. Ah! Here she is.

Enter **Diana** *from window, comes down. All rise.*

Diana Did I hear you say you were waiting coffee for me, Mrs Cantelupe? I'm afraid that means I've been a hopelessly long time over dinner. But I was so hungry.

Mrs Cantelupe Not at all. Just ring the bell, will you, Victor?

Bretherton *rings bell by fire-place, then returns to* C.

Mrs Whyte-Fraser Mrs Massingberd. Where will you sit? I am sure you must be tired.

Diana Tired? Oh no – why should I be? (*Sits top end of Chesterfield.*)

Sir Jabez *moves over.*

Mrs Cantelupe (*sits*) My nephew was just telling me that you had walked to the Morteratsch Glacier. That's a long way, isn't it?

Mrs Whyte-Fraser *sits.*

Diana Only six miles there and back. I don't think anything of that.

Sir Jabez (*comes down*) You're a great walker, I suppose, Mrs Massingberd?

Diana I don't know that I should describe myself as a great walker, but – (*Looks at* **Sir Jabez**.) – I'm used to being on my feet all day.

Enter waiter with salver with letters for **Mrs Cantelupe**, *who takes them, and tray with coffee – crosses to table up* C *by window, puts tray on table, moves table down stage a little and exits.*

Mrs Whyte-Fraser Really? How delightfully strong you must be.

Mrs Cantelupe Will you all excuse me if I just glance(*goes up* C) – at my letters – I see they've been sent on from London. You pour out for me, Eleanour. There's one thing about this place, they do give you excellent coffee – otherwise the cooking isn't up to the mark. (*Sits – opens and reads letters.*)

Bretherton (*crossing to* **Diana** *on Chesterfield – hands cup to her, then takes cup for himself and*

Mrs Cantelupe – *goes up to* **Mrs Cantelupe** *with cup – then comes down*) No, it isn't. The soup tonight was a disgrace – mysterious brown lumps cruising about in a plateful of warm grease. A revoltin' concoction, I call it. Didn't you think so, Mrs Massingberd? (*Comes and sits on* **Diana**'s L *on Chesterfield.*)

Diana The soup? Do you know, I really didn't notice?

Bretherton You don't mean to say you actually swallowed the stuff?

Sir Jabez *goes to window, crosses veranda to window* L *and re-enters.*

Diana I suppose I must have done so. Yes, I remember I did, and that I not only swallowed it, but enjoyed it.

Bretherton Enjoyed it – no!

Diana Yes – in the first place, because I was exceedingly hungry, and in the second place, because I came here to enjoy everything – even that revolting soup.

Bretherton What an extraordinary idea!

Diana To want to enjoy yourself?

Bretherton No, but the soup –

Diana Captain Bretherton, I am not going to allow indifferent soups or anything else to be the fly in my ointment. If the fly gets in without asking my permission, I simply pretend he isn't there.

Bretherton Then I suppose you're a what d'you call it – Christian Scientist?

Diana Oh no, I'm afraid I'm much too material to be a Christian Scientist. I like the good things of life – when I can get them – and plenty of them.

Sir Jabez While at the same time you don't seem to mind the bad ones. That's a very comfortable frame of mind.

Diana Oh, I assure you, I'm not so philosophical as all that. I hate the bad things of life when they are really bad. But, just at present, I'm having a good time, a really good time – and I refuse to allow any little disagreeables to interfere with it.

Bretherton Bravo! Have some more coffee? (*Rises, and takes cup to tray.*)

Diana Thanks! I will.

Sir Jabez (*coming down to head of Chesterfield*) You take a holiday in the right spirit, Mrs Massingberd; you're determined to get your money's worth.

Diana That's exactly what I came here for, Sir Jabez – to get my money's worth, and I'm getting it.

Mrs Cantelupe *gives an exclamation.*

Mrs Whyte-Fraser What's the matter?

Mrs Cantelupe (*rising*) My dear Eleanour, what do you think? Milly Cantelupe, the pretty one, insists on marrying that dreadful Mr Wilks – you remember him – the man with no eyebrows and projecting teeth. And Adelaide says he literally hasn't a penny.

Mrs Whyte-Fraser Poor Adelaide!

Mrs Cantelupe She's in despair about it. She's written me pages, and the letter has been following me about. She'll think it so unkind of me not to have answered. Will you all forgive me if I scribble a line –

Sir Jabez *crosses to open door.*

– otherwise I shan't catch the early post. You won't run away till I come back, Mrs Massingberd. Poor Adelaide, such a blow – and Milly is the only good-looking one of all. (*At door.*) Those girls.

She exits.

Sir Jabez *closes door after* **Mrs Cantelupe** *and moves up* L.

Bretherton Take 'em all round, Aunt Emma's nephews and nieces are an awful lot of rotters. (*Handing coffee to* **Diana**.) You do take sugar?

Diana Yes – thanks.

Mrs Whyte-Fraser So you like Pontresina, Mrs Massingberd?

Diana Like it? That's a very mild way of expressing it. I delight in it –

Captain Bretherton *hands sugar bowl to her – she takes one lump and returns with bowl. Then he lights a cigarette.*

– it's a new sensation.

Mrs Whyte-Fraser A new sensation?

Diana Yes – the mountains, the air, everything. You see, I have never been in Switzerland before.

Mrs Whyte-Fraser Really?

Diana No, and until the other day, except in a picture, I had never seen a mountain with snow on it. I haven't got over the thrill yet.

Sir Jabez *drops down* C, *watching* **Diana.**

Bretherton (*comes to below Chesterfield and sits on bottom end*) Ah, now I understand why it is that you're so keen on seeing all these glaciers and waterfalls and things round here.

Diana Which means, I suppose, that you have reached the blasé stage and are no longer keen on seeing them.

Bretherton Well, you know, you find that when once you've got used to 'em, one mountain's awfully like another, especially when it's got snow on the top. There's a strong family likeness about Alps – I can hardly tell which of 'em I'm looking at myself.

Diana I wish you'd told me that before.

Bretherton Why?

Diana Because for the last two or three days, I have been dragging you out in different directions to look at what you probably imagined was the same monotonous mountain with the same identical snow on the top. I really ought to apologise.

Bretherton Oh, come now, Mrs Massingberd, you know I didn't mean that. I've enjoyed the walks awfully, even though I'm not so great as you are on mountain scenery, and all that sort of thing. It's tremendously good of you to let me go with you.

Diana Very kind of you to say so, but after the confession you have just made, I shan't dare to ask you again.

Bretherton Oh, come now –

Diana I shall have to look out for some unsophisticated Cook's tourist to keep me company and share my enthusiasms.

Bretherton The sort of cheerful bounder that takes his five guineas' worth of lovely Lucerne, eh? Suit you down to the ground.

Mrs Whyte-Fraser Do you know, I always wonder who those extraordinary people can be, and what they do at other times when they're not having five guineas' worth of lovely Lucerne? (*With a side glance at* **Sir Jabez**.) Tom says he believes they spend the remaining fifty-one weeks of the year in handing stockings or sausages over a counter.

Sir Jabez (*coolly*) Very likely.

Diana Quite likely. You see, that sort of person is usually in the unfortunate position of having its living to earn.

Mrs Whyte-Fraser I have no doubt of it, but need that make the poor things so aggressively – unornamental?

Diana I am rather inclined to think that there are great difficulties in the way of being useful and ornamental at the same time. Strictly speaking, we of the ornamental class are not useful; and the useful class – the class that earns its own living and other people's dividends – is seldom decorative.

Mrs Whyte-Fraser Well, it is to be hoped, then, that the five-guinea tourist is only half as useful as he looks. If your theory is correct, his value to the community must be enormous. There were dozens of him – and her – in the train yesterday, and I must say, greatly as I dislike the species, I really pitied them. Nearly all of them staggered ashore, palpably and unbecomingly the worse for the crossing – it was simply atrocious – and were forthwith packed away like sardines into second-class carriages, with the prospect of a night of unmitigated misery before them. I wondered what on earth induced them to spend their money in undergoing all that torture?

Sir Jabez Some form of mild insanity, I should say. They'd much better keep their savings in their pockets, and stop at home.

Diana I don't agree with you –

Sir Jabez Oh!

Diana And I know what the inducement was. It was the prospect of a new sensation – of romance –

Sir Jabez Romance?

Diana Yes, romance. Something that their everyday life fails to give them.

Bretherton And a jolly good thing, too, I should say. You wouldn't like to spend your daily life sitting five a side in a railway carriage, would you?

Diana Of course I shouldn't – and no more would they. But I can quite imagine that there are times when even a night in a stuffy railway carriage would come as a relief to some people – people whose lives have gone on, day after day, in the same dull, mean, little round, without any hope of change or betterment or advancement.

She has been speaking more and more earnestly, but as she sees the others looking at her, she breaks off with a laugh.

I'm afraid you don't quite share my sympathy for the globe-trotting counter-jumper and his fellows. You may consider me very extraordinary, but I really like to think that when he gets away from his daily round and common task he really enjoys himself in his own vulgar fashion.

Bretherton Of course – why shouldn't he enjoy himself, poor beggar? As long as he don't spoil the place for other people and get in the way.

Diana Of the ornamental classes! I quite agree with you – the two don't mix. Their views of life are so hopelessly dissimilar. . . . Would you mind putting down my cup?

Both **Sir Jabez** *and* **Captain Bretherton** *start to take the cup –* **Captain Bretherton** *gives him a look.*

Bretherton I beg your pardon. (*Rises and takes cup.*)

Sir Jabez *coughs and goes up to window.*

Mrs Whyte-Fraser Is that the right time? (*Glancing at clock and rising.*) I really must be off, or Tom will wonder what has become of me. Captain Bretherton, whether you like it or not, I am going to drag you to the Victoria with me.

Bretherton Me – oh – er – delighted. (*Backs – with his eye on* **Diana**.)

Mrs Whyte-Fraser To see Tom. He told me I was to be sure and capture you if I ran across you. So I must absolutely insist on your coming in with me . . . I hope *you* will look us up, Mrs Massingberd.

Diana *rises – shakes hands.*

My husband and I are at the Victoria.

Diana Thank you – it is very kind of you.

Mrs Whyte-Fraser I shall expect you then . . . any afternoon. (*Goes up to window.*) Come along, Captain Bretherton!

She exits through window, followed by **Captain Bretherton**.

Diana *goes to table and turns over papers.* **Sir Jabez** *comes to table.*

Sir Jabez Would you care to take a turn in the garden, Mrs Massingberd? It's a lovely night.

Diana No, thank you. I should like it very much, but I think I ought to wait till Mrs Canteloupe comes back.

Sir Jabez Then perhaps you won't have any objection to my waiting and keeping you company?

Diana None at all. (*Sits on* R *of table, still looking at papers.*) On the contrary, you interest me very much, Sir Jabez.

Sir Jabez (*stands* L *of table*) Delighted to hear it. May I ask why?

Diana Oh, certainly. But perhaps you won't be flattered when you hear the reason. When I am with you – when I am talking to you – I can't help thinking of the hundreds of men and women whose lives you control. I mean the people who work for you.

Sir Jabez Oh, my employees.

Diana Yes . . . that's how you think of them, of course, just as your employees.

What a different sort of creature you must seem to them from what you do to me.

Sir Jabez (*good-naturedly*) I suppose I do.

Diana Of course you do. You strike me as being quite an amiable and good-natured person – but I don't imagine that there is a man or woman in your employment who has a good word to say for you behind your back.

Sir Jabez (*astonished*) Upon my soul!

Diana Well, is there? You are far too clever not to know that you aren't popular with the people who work for you.

Sir Jabez (*recovering his equanimity*) Oh yes, *I* know – but I was wondering how *you* did!

Diana (*lightly*) Feminine intuition, I suppose – I can feel it in my bones. You're quite charming as an equal, but you would be just the reverse as a – tyrant. And you are a tyrant, aren't you? You like to be feared?

Sir Jabez By people who have to work for me – yes. It keeps 'em up to the mark. And the business of an employer is to keep his hands up to the mark.

Diana Fancy spending one's life in keeping other people's noses to the grindstone! How I should hate it! (*Rises and moves to window.*)

Sir Jabez (*good-naturedly*) Apparently you've got an idea that I'm a regular ogre to my employees. But I assure you I treat 'em just as well as most other firms. They're no worse off than they would be anywhere else.

She turns from window.

If you're interested in that sort of thing, you must have a look around one of our establishments some day – let me know when you can go and I'll show you over myself – I'm not afraid of inspection,

Government or otherwise – in the long run it doesn't pay to play tricks with the Factory Acts.

Diana *comes down* C.

And – (*laughing*) – it would be a new experience for you to see one of my shops. Don't suppose you've ever set foot in any of 'em – they're not quite your style.

Diana Oh, you're wrong. I used to know one of them very well indeed – the one at Clapham –

Sits on Chesterfield facing **Sir Jabez**.

Sir Jabez Did you?

Diana That was in my hard-up days – you may be surprised to hear it, but I was hard up once. At that time I used to – well, I may say I used to frequent your Clapham establishment – especially the mantle department.

Sir Jabez You've given up dealing with us now – eh?

Diana I must confess I have.

Sir Jabez Well, I shan't ask you to continue your esteemed patronage. I frankly admit that Jabez Grinley & Co. couldn't turn you out as you're turned out tonight. (*Pointing to her dress.*)

Diana No, I don't think you could. You won't mind my saying so, but your latest Paris models at thirty-five shillings and sixpence always struck me as being painfully uncertain with regard to fit.

Sir Jabez They are. They are! I've often remarked it myself. But you can't do better at the price. If you're well enough off to avoid our thirty-five-shilling-and-sixpenny reach-me-down made in Shoreditch and labelled Paris – why, avoid 'em! Avoid 'em! But we cater for the woman with the short purse.

Diana See advertisement – 'Grinley's is the place where a short purse is as good as a long one anywhere else'.

Sir Jabez That's it. The lower-middle-class woman – she's our best customer – and she's quite satisfied with Paris models that don't fit. So she gets 'em. That's business, Mrs Massingberd. Give people what they want – good or bad, silk or shoddy – and give it 'em a halfpenny cheaper than they can get it anywhere else, and you're a made man. (*Moves to and sits on arm of Chesterfield, above her.*)

Diana The question is – how do you manage to give it them a halfpenny cheaper than anyone else?

Sir Jabez That's the secret – organisation – keep down working expenses.

Diana Working expenses – that means wages, doesn't it?

Sir Jabez Wages is one item.

Diana And generally the first to be kept down. Oh, that's the way to make money – to get other people to work for you for as little as they can be got to take, and put the proceeds of their work into your pockets. I sometimes wonder if success is worth buying on those terms.

Sir Jabez You're a bit of a sentimentalist, Mrs Massingberd. Not that I object to that – in a woman. On the contrary – But sentiment is one thing and business is another. Business, my dear lady, is war, commercial war, in which brains and purses take the place of machine guns and shells.

Diana And in which no quarter is given to the weaker side.

Sir Jabez Why should it be? In every healthy state of society the weakest goes to the wall, because the wall is his proper place. If a man isn't fit to be on top, he must go under – if he hasn't the power to rule, he must serve whether he likes it or not. If he hasn't brains enough to lift himself out of the ruck, in the ruck he must stay. That's what makes success all the more worth winning. It's something to have fought your way, under those conditions, step by step, inch by inch, from the foot of the ladder to the top.

Diana As you have done.

Sir Jabez Yes, as I have done, Mrs Massingberd. I like to remember that I began my career as a brat of a boy running errands.

Diana And I like you for remembering it.

Sir Jabez I should be a fool to try and forget it; nobody else would. (*Sits at end of settee.*) Besides, I'm proud of the fact – proud to think that a little chap who started on two bob a week had grit and push and pluck enough to raise himself out of the ruck and finish at the top. It shows what a man can do when he sets his mind on a thing and sticks to his business.

Diana (*with her arm on Chesterfield top, not looking at* **Sir Jabez**) And doesn't indulge in sentiment – or spend his money in cheap trips to the continent.

He feels the quality of goods in her sleeve, she withdraws her arm slowly, still not looking at him.

Sir Jabez (*coughs when caught*) Quite so. But I can see that it's the shiftless chap who has your sympathy.

Diana Of course he has my sympathy – he wants it.

Enter **Mrs Cantelupe**.

Sir Jabez *rises and crosses.*

Mrs Cantelupe Oh, they have gone! So

sorry to have left you all this time, Mrs Massingberd. I must apologise.

Diana (*rising*) Oh, please don't! Sir Jabez has been entertaining me. We've been talking economics.

Mrs Cantelupe (*relieved*) Economics? How very dull!

Sir Jabez Then we'd better adjourn the discussion to a more favourable opportunity, Mrs Massingberd. I'll leave you and Mrs Cantelupe to talk chiffons for a change while I have a cigar in the garden. Good night.

He moves up towards window.

Diana Good night, Sir Jabez.

Sir Jabez *continues to window; when near it, stops, says to* **Diana** 'Good night again' *and exits through window.*

Pause – **Mrs Cantelupe** *sits.*

Mrs Cantelupe Dreadful person, isn't he? But one has to know him – everybody does. I'm afraid he must have bored you horribly.

Diana Not at all.

Enter **Waiter** *– he replaces small table in original position – and crosses with tray and exits after arranging papers on table and taking up cup, etc.*

On the contrary, he rather interests me. (*Sits on Chesterfield.*)

Mrs Cantelupe You don't mean to say so. Will you have another cup of coffee?

Diana No, thank you.

Mrs Cantelupe Is this your first visit to Pontresina, Mrs Massingberd?

Diana My first visit to Switzerland. It is the fulfilment of a dream.

Mrs Cantelupe You are fond of travelling, I can see.

Diana I am – all the more, perhaps, because I have been very little abroad.

Mrs Cantelupe Circumstances have prevented you, I suppose?

Diana Yes, circumstances have always prevented me.

Mrs Cantelupe I dare say your husband did not share your pronounced taste for globe trotting?

Diana He strongly objected to it.

Mrs Cantelupe I wonder – Massingberd is not a very common name –

Diana (*on the alert, watching her*) It *is* rather unusual.

Mrs Cantelupe There was a Mr Massingberd I met seven or eight years ago at the Wetherbys' place in Lincolnshire – Cyril Massingberd. Could it have been – ?

Diana (*composedly places a pillow at her back, as she realises that she is being pumped*) My husband's name was Josiah.

Mrs Cantelupe Josiah?

Diana Josiah Massingberd.

Mrs Cantelupe Then it could not have been the same.

Diana Of course not.

Mrs Cantelupe Still, they may very possibly have been related.

Diana Very possibly.

Mrs Cantelupe The man I was speaking of – Cyril Massingberd – was one of the Wiltshire Massingberds, I think.

Diana One of the Wiltshire Massingberds? You will probably think me very extraordinary, Mrs Cantelupe, but I haven't the faintest idea whether or not my husband was a Wiltshire Massingberd. I really know hardly anything about his relations.

Mrs Cantelupe Indeed?

Diana (*with a deep sigh*) You see, our married life was so brief, so very brief.

Mrs Cantelupe (*sympathetically*) Indeed?

Diana So very brief. I sometimes feel as if it had never been – as if my life with Josiah had been nothing but a dream.

Mrs Cantelupe May I ask – ?

Diana (*putting her handkerchief to her eyes*) Forgive me, but I had rather you didn't – I had so much rather you didn't . . .

Mrs Cantelupe I beg your pardon –

Diana There are some things which it is painful to recall.

Mrs Cantelupe My dear Mrs Massingberd, I shall never forgive myself. I had no idea your bereavement was so recent – I ought not to have –

Diana (*apparently mastering her emotion*) Oh please, please, Mrs Cantelupe. It is I who ought to apologise for giving way to my feelings like this. (*Dabbing her eyes.*) It is very foolish of me.

Mrs Cantelupe Foolish of you – no.

Diana Oh yes, it is. I ought to have more self-control. But you see, my attachment to my husband's – to Josiah's – memory is – peculiar.

Mrs Cantelupe Peculiar?

Diana You do not know how much I owe to Josiah, Mrs Cantelupe. (*Moves to end of settee.*) Every day, I realise more and more that everything that makes my life worth living – comfort, amusements, friends –

even, if I may use the word in connection with myself, social success – that they are all due solely to my position as Josiah Massingberd's widow. No wonder that I am grateful to him for all that he has done for me.

Mrs Cantelupe My dear Mrs Massingberd, surely you are a great deal too modest. As regards social success, your own very charming personality – if you will permit an old woman to say so – has had something to do with that.

Diana (*shaking her head*) Personality does not go very far in society as we understand it, unless it is backed by money.

Mrs Cantelupe That is true, unfortunately.

Diana And I have very good reason to know it. I was not always as well off as I am now – in fact, I don't mind confessing to you that, after my father's death and before I – became the wife of Josiah Massingberd – I was in very straitened circumstances – very straitened indeed.

Mrs Cantelupe Dear, dear, how trying.

Diana It was – very.

Mrs Cantelupe But your marriage changed all that, of course?

Diana I should not be here otherwise.

Mrs Cantelupe It must have been a relief to you. Straitened circumstances are always so very unpleasant.

Diana Oh, they are – I assure you they are.

Mrs Cantelupe You must be thankful to feel you have done with them. I can quite understand your very right and natural feeling of gratitude towards a husband who has placed you beyond the need for petty economies.

Diana (*mischievously – enjoying the joke*) Yes, petty economies are rather out of my line, just now. Of course, I don't mean to say that I am a millionaire or anything near it. On the contrary, I dare say my income would seem comparatively small to you. But, coming after the period of petty economies, I find that three hundred pounds a month is quite adequate for all my little wants.

Mrs Cantelupe Three hundred pounds a month – that is three thousand six hundred a year.

Diana Yes, I suppose my income is at the rate of three thousand six hundred pounds a year – for the present.

Mrs Cantelupe Does that mean – ? (*She stops – moves chair towards* **Diana**.)

Diana Yes – you were going to say?

Mrs Cantelupe I really don't know – perhaps you would consider it an impertinence on my part.

Diana Not at all, pray go on.

Mrs Cantelupe Well, – I was going to ask, as you have been so very frank about your affairs and we seem to have become quite old friends during our little chat – but please do not answer the question if you think it impertinent or inquisitive.

Diana I am quite sure I shall not.

Mrs Cantelupe Well, then, by your saying that your income was three thousand six hundred a year for the present, did you mean that your husband imposed any restriction in his will?

Diana Restrictions?

Mrs Cantelupe I mean, with regard to your marrying again?

Diana With regard to my marrying again?

Oh, dear no – no restrictions whatever. (**Mrs Cantelupe** *sighs*.) I beg your pardon.

Mrs Cantelupe It has always seemed to me that such restrictions – and I have known of several cases where they have been imposed by men who left their property to their wives – are so exceedingly unfair. Don't you think so?

Diana Oh, certainly. Most unfair.

Mrs Cantelupe Especially where a young woman is concerned.

Diana I quite agree with you. But from what I know of Josiah, I am certain that such an idea would never have entered his head.

Mrs Cantelupe You forgive my curiosity in asking?

Diana (*with an undercurrent of sarcasm*) I understand that it was entirely prompted by your very kindly interest in myself.

Mrs Cantelupe Exactly.

Diana (*with arm on sofa, next* **Mrs Cantelupe**) But at the same time I think it most unlikely that I shall ever marry again.

Mrs Cantelupe Oh, you will change your mind when the right man comes along. (*Pats her hand.*)

Diana (*rising*) I don't think so.

Mrs Cantelupe You are not going? (*Rises and pushes chair back.*)

Diana Indeed I am. I have two or three letters I must write – and besides, I have stayed an unconscionable time already. (*Turns.*)

Mrs Cantelupe On the contrary, it has been very good of you to waste your time chatting with me. You are staying on here for the present, I think you said?

Diana Oh yes. These mountains fascinate me; I don't think I can tear myself away from them just yet.

Mrs Cantelupe (*pressing her hand affectionately*) Then I hope we shall see more of you – a great deal more of you.

Diana It is very sweet of you to say so. (*Going towards door.*)

Mrs Cantelupe By the way, have you made any arrangements for tomorrow?

Diana Tomorrow? No. (*Turns at door.*)

Mrs Cantelupe Because I was thinking of asking Eleanour Whyte-Fraser to join me in a little excursion to the Bernina Hospice – carriages to the Hospice and then those who like a scramble can go farther. Victor will come to look after us, and I shall be so pleased if you will make one of the party.

Diana It is really very kind of you. I should enjoy it immensely. I haven't been as far as the Bernina Hospice yet.

Mrs Cantelupe Then that is settled. I shall arrange it with Eleanour and let you know the time we start.

Diana Goodbye till then.

Mrs Cantelupe Au revoir.

Exit **Diana**, *closing door after herself.* **Mrs Cantelupe** *with a satisfied smile takes up her work from table – sits on Chesterfield humming strain of* Merry Widow *waltz.*

Enter **Bretherton** *at window.*

Ah, Victor.

Bretherton Oh! Mrs Massingberd gone? Can't think what Mrs Whyte-Fraser wanted – dragging me off like that. Said her husband wanted to see me. He didn't at all, though. (*Lights a cigarette.*)

Mrs Cantelupe No?

Bretherton Looked quite surprised when I turned up, and said he hadn't heard I was here. (*Picks up* The Sketch *from table.*)

Mrs Cantelupe (*doing her work*) Oh – curious – Eleanour must have made a mistake. (*Looks at* **Captain Bretherton**.) I have been chatting with Mrs Massingberd since you went.

Bretherton Have you?

Mrs Cantelupe She has only just gone. I must say I like her – very charming and very frank about herself. She was telling me that she had quite hard times before her marriage, but it seems that her husband has left her very comfortably off.

Bretherton Oh!

Mrs Cantelupe (*pointedly*) She has three thousand six hundred a year, I understand.

Bretherton (*unimpressed*) Lucky woman!

Mrs Cantelupe I am quite taken with her. (*Looks at him.*) I have asked her to drive with Eleanour and ourselves to the Bernina Hospice tomorrow. You are not doing anything else, I suppose?

Bretherton (*still looking at* The Sketch) Oh no – I'll come!

Mrs Cantelupe *hums waltz with a self-satisfied air. Ring curtain bell as* **Mrs Cantelupe** *swells melody.*

Curtain.

Act Three

Scene: same as Act Two. Daylight outside.

As the curtain rises **Diana** *is discovered seated at table with a* Continental Bradshaw *before her, jotting down figures on a piece of paper. Enter* **Waiter**.

Waiter Did you ring, madame?

Diana Yes, how long does it take to drive to Samaden Station?

Waiter A little over half an hour – madame – thirty-five to forty minutes.

Diana Forty minutes – and the train starts at 2.17. I haven't much time, then. Will you order a carriage to take me to the station at five and twenty past one.

Waiter At five-and-twenty past one – all right, madame.

Diana And will you ask Herr Ritter to send me up my bill as soon as possible. (*Looks down at memoranda on table before her.*)

Waiter All right, madame. (*Does not move.*)

Diana (*after pause – looks up*) That's all, thank you.

Waiter Thank you, madame.

He exits.

Diana (*running her finger down time-table, murmuring*) Arrive Zürich eight-twenty – leave Zürich nine-twelve – arrive Basle eleven-five – leave Basle . . .

Enter **Mrs Cantelupe**, *crosses to table.*

Mrs Cantelupe My dear Mrs Massingberd, I have been hunting for you all over the place.

Diana Have you? I'm so sorry.

Mrs Cantelupe I have just met Eleanour Whyte-Fraser, and she horrified me by telling me that you were leaving Pontresina today. Surely it isn't true?

Diana I'm afraid it is, Mrs Cantelupe.

Mrs Cantelupe But why?

Diana I have stayed a good deal longer than I intended already, and now I find that I must go back to London at once.

Mrs Cantelupe Dear, dear, that is most unfortunate.

Diana I shall never forget the good time I've had at Pontresina – never as long as I live. It will be something to remember at any rate even if I never see mountains like that again – (*looks through window, still seated*) – and sky and clean air and white snow. Yes, at least it will be something to remember.

Mrs Cantelupe But there's no reason why you shouldn't see them again, you know. If you like the place so much why not come back again next year?

Diana Why not? (*She laughs quietly.*) Why not indeed?

Mrs Cantelupe Only if you come back, I should most strongly advise you to try the Hotel Victoria.

Diana Thank you. I shall certainly try the Victoria – on my next visit.

Mrs Cantelupe (*going towards her*) I can't tell you how distressed I am that you are going. I shall miss you dreadfully.

Diana It's very nice of you to say so.

Mrs Cantelupe (*meaningly*) And I am sure that Victor will miss you – more than I shall. I know how thoroughly he has enjoyed all your walks and little excursions together.

Diana (*constrainedly*) It has been most kind of him to show me my way about.

Mrs Cantelupe Most kind of him – my dear Mrs Massingberd! Now I hope, I really do hope – that this unexpected departure of yours isn't going to put an end to our very pleasant friendship.

Diana (*with an embarrassed little laugh*) Oh – why should it?

Mrs Cantelupe Exactly – why should it! I shall be at home by the middle of October at latest. But what are your plans?

Diana I really hardly know yet. I am very unsettled at present, and I can't tell in the least what I shall do till I get back to England.

Mrs Cantelupe Well, as soon as you have fixed your plans you must write and let me know. Now will you?

Diana Oh, of course I will.

Mrs Cantelupe That's a promise. Victor will be most anxious to know that you haven't forgotten your Pontresina friends.

Clock strikes off.

Diana You can be quite certain I shall not do that. Is that twelve? I must hurry upstairs and see to my packing. (*Rises, and stands near table.*)

Mrs Cantelupe So soon?

Diana The train starts from Samaden at 2.17, and the carriage is to be round for me at five-and-twenty past one.

Mrs Cantelupe And it is twelve o'clock now. Has Victor any idea that you are leaving so soon?

Diana (*coldly*) I really don't know. (*Moves to* R *a bit.*) It was only this morning that I found it would be necessary for me to start today.

Mrs Cantelupe And you have not seen him this morning – since you made up your mind?

Diana No, I have not seen him.

Mrs Cantelupe Then of course he doesn't know – I wonder where he is? (*Going towards* L.)

Diana If he hasn't come back by the time I start you must say goodbye to him for me. (*Moves to table and picks up her memoranda.*)

Mrs Cantelupe But, my dear – I really don't know what he will say – he will never forgive me if I let you go –

Diana I'm afraid I can't expect the Zürich train to wait till Captain Bretherton comes back from his walk, can I? If I don't see him mind you give him a pretty message from me. (*Moves* C.)

Enter **Sir Jabez** *from window with paper which he places on small table.*

Mrs Cantelupe But I – (*Breaking off as she sees* **Sir Jabez**.) Oh, Sir Jabez, have you seen my nephew anywhere about?

Sir Jabez Not a sign of him. Want him particularly?

Mrs Cantelupe I do. Mrs Massingberd is leaving here suddenly, and I know Victor will be so distressed if – perhaps some of the waiters know where he has gone. (*Rings bell violently.*)

Sir Jabez You're leaving today, Mrs Massingberd?

Diana Yes, today. Going back to England.

Mrs Cantelupe Why doesn't the man answer the bell?

She exits hurriedly, calling 'Waiter, waiter!'

Sir Jabez You've been called back suddenly?

Diana Rather suddenly – but holidays can't last for ever.

Sir Jabez (*nervously*) No, of course not, of course not – business is business – must be attended to.

Diana (*holding out her hand*) Goodbye, Sir Jabez – I must run upstairs and pack.

Sir Jabez One moment, Mrs Massingberd . . . one moment. I've a question to put to you before you go – a straightforward question – (*Hesitates.*)

Diana Yes, what is it?

Sir Jabez How should you like me for a husband?

Diana (*astonished*) Sir Jabez!

Sir Jabez A plain answer, please – yes or no – I'm a business man.

Diana Then I'm afraid it must be – no! (*Pause – gently.*) I'm so sorry!

Sir Jabez Not sorry enough to change your mind?

Diana I'm afraid not.

Sir Jabez Yet most women would consider it a good offer – an offer worth considering.

Diana I have no doubt of that.

Sir Jabez Forty thousand a year, to say nothing of the title. It's brand new, of course – but –

Diana (*coming down*) You wouldn't like me to accept you for what you've got.

Sir Jabez (*doggedly*) I'm not so sure that I shouldn't. If you'd have me now for what I've got I believe I'd chance your caring – later on –

Diana (*gently*) Some day you'll be glad that I didn't let you chance it. (*Crossing to door.*)

Sir Jabez It *is* no, then?

Diana It *is* no. (*Over her shoulder going, near door.*)

Sir Jabez That's straightforward, anyhow. (*Pauses.*) Perhaps it's the drapery sticks in your teeth, eh? You look down on it.

Diana I – look down on it – oh no. I've no right to look down on the drapery trade.

Sir Jabez (*crossing*) I believe you're the first woman I ever met who cared nothing for money.

Diana (*trying to speak lightly*) That shows how little you understand me. I'm not at all disinterested. I've known the time when I felt as if I could sell my soul for a five-pound note.

Sir Jabez Have you? Have you? Then your soul's gone up in price. What's sent the price up so high? Another bidder in the market, eh?

Diana (*starts angrily, then quietly*) Goodbye, Sir Jabez. (*Moves rapidly.*)

Sir Jabez (*going up to her*) There is – you can't deceive me.

Diana (*coldly – facing him*) I haven't the least wish to deceive you, but having refused you as a husband, I am scarcely likely to accept you as a father-confessor.

Sir Jabez You're not going to throw yourself away on that fool of a guardsman – a – clever woman like you?

Diana Sir Jabez! –

Sir Jabez You are! That brainless puppy who's spent his life playing at soldiers – who hasn't the sense to stick to the little money he's got.

Diana (*with a flash of indignation*) Or the heartlessness to grind a fortune out of underpaid work-girls?

Sir Jabez One for me. So you mean to marry him?

Diana That is a grossly impertinent question.

Bretherton *strolls in* – **Sir Jabez**, *seeing her face, turns and sees him, and walks away from her to the Chesterfield.*

Bretherton Ah, Mrs Massingberd, there you are.

Sir Jabez *moves and stands with his back to audience.*

I've been looking round for you. Feel inclined for a stroll?

Diana (*nervously and without looking at him, conscious that* **Sir Jabez** *is watching her*) A stroll? No, thank you, Captain Bretherton. I'm afraid I haven't time this morning. I have other things to do.

Exit **Diana** *quickly, closing door after her.*

Bretherton (*after pause, begins to whistle 'British Grenadiers', takes cigarette from case which he carries in coat pocket*) Got a match about you? (*Comes down to and sits on Chesterfield.*)

Sir Jabez Eh?

Bretherton Match?

Sir Jabez *feels in pockets – tosses him box silently and takes* Bradshaw *from table.* **Bretherton** *apparently burns his fingers with the lighted match, then transfers match to* L *hand and box to* R *hand –* **Sir Jabez** *looks at him for a moment, then snatches box and crosses to table where he sits, consulting* Bradshaw.

(*As* **Sir Jabez** *snatches box*) Thanks.

Sir Jabez Ugh!

Bretherton Thinking of moving on?

Sir Jabez Yes.

Bretherton Where to?

Sir Jabez London.

Bretherton What's taking you to London in August?

Sir Jabez Business. (*Coughs.*)

Bretherton What a beastly nuisance.

Sir Jabez No doubt you'd find it so.

Bretherton Don't you?

Sir Jabez No.

Bretherton There's no accounting for tastes. (*Stretching himself on Chesterfield, his head towards the end of it.*)

Sir Jabez There isn't. (*Closes book with a slam.*) Your lounging life would knock me out in three months.

Bretherton Thanks.

Sir Jabez And my sort of life – hard work and stick at it from morning till night – would kill you in three days.

Bretherton (*irritated*) Thanks, awfully.

Sir Jabez (*laughs roughly, rises, and goes up to table*) Fact! But you needn't mind. It's your sort that gets the best out of life after all – at any rate, as far as the women are concerned. (*Throws Bradshaw on table.*)

Bretherton That's a comfort.

Sir Jabez (*comes down* C) It's just the shiftlessness and helplessness of you that appeals to 'em, I suppose – they know you aren't capable of looking after yourselves, so they take the job on to their own shoulders. And perhaps they're right. You couldn't get along without 'em and the rest of us can, if we must. We've always got our work to turn to, whatever else fails us, and that's something to be thankful for.

He goes towards window and meets **Mrs Cantelupe**.

Mrs Cantelupe (*in window*) You haven't found my nephew, Sir Jabez?

Sir Jabez (*impatiently*) No, madam, I have not, but he's there if you want him.

Exit **Sir Jabez** *who crosses on veranda. Pause.*

Bretherton (*sitting up*) What's the matter with Sir Jabez? –

Mrs Cantelupe *puts parasol on table, then comes down* C.

– sun or liver, or whisky or what?

Mrs Cantelupe (*impatiently*) I really don't know. (*Sits.*) Has he told you?

Bretherton (*settles himself back this time with his head on pillow*) Told me?

Mrs Cantelupe Then he hasn't.

Bretherton What is it? Anything wrong?

Mrs Cantelupe Yes.

Bretherton What?

Mrs Cantelupe Mrs Massingberd is leaving for England by the next train.

Bretherton God bless my soul, no! (*Sits up.*)

Mrs Cantelupe Yes.

Bretherton Are you sure?

Mrs Cantelupe She is packing her trunks at this moment.

Bretherton But what – what's taking her away so suddenly?

Mrs Cantelupe (*significantly*) I can guess easily enough.

Bretherton What do you mean?

Mrs Cantelupe You have said nothing to her?

Bretherton Said nothing? Oh, you mean . . . why no – nothing definite.

Mrs Cantelupe Then you ought to have

done it; it is disgraceful of you, Victor – simply disgraceful.

Bretherton Disgraceful?

Mrs Cantelupe To let your opportunities slip in this idiotic manner; I have no patience with you. And it has been most unfair to her as well – most unfair.

Bretherton My dear Aunt Emma, as far as that goes, though I haven't said anything definite to Dia – to Mrs Massingberd, I'm sure I have shown her quite plainly what – er – what my feelings are towards her.

Mrs Cantelupe My dear Victor, that is not enough. You ought to have spoken before now.

Bretherton Come now, we haven't known each other so very long – less than three weeks.

Mrs Cantelupe That doesn't matter. What does matter is that I am perfectly certain she is offended by your silence – as she has every right to be. Her manner was very constrained when I mentioned you just now – I could see that she did not wish to meet you again before she went. (*She goes up towards window.*)

Bretherton But why – ?

Mrs Cantelupe You really are hopelessly dense. (*Comes down.*)

Mrs Cantelupe She feels of course that she has given you plenty of chances and is naturally piqued that you have never attempted to take advantage of them.

Bretherton Never attempted – why?

Mrs Cantelupe (*crosses to Chesterfield – slams first cushion – then the one* R *corner*) Don't argue. Victor . . . listen to me. (*Business shaking cushions – then sits.*) You have behaved most foolishly, Victor – most foolishly. You ought to have realised that a woman in her position, a woman who, to put it vulgarly, can pick and choose, does not expect to be kept dangling on in uncertainty while a man is making up his mind whether or not he means to propose to her.

Bretherton 'Pon my soul. I'm awfully sorry if I've offended her.

Mrs Cantelupe So you ought to be.

Bretherton I wouldn't have hurt her feelings for the world.

Mrs Cantelupe (*sarcastically*) You have not only hurt her feelings, my dear boy, but you have gone within an ace of losing her altogether. I conclude you do intend to ask her to be your wife?

Bretherton Of course I do. (*Rises.*) I – well – I don't mind saying it to you, Aunt Emma – I've got to like her awfully. She's – she's a downright good sort. (*Sits on arm of Chesterfield.*)

Mrs Cantelupe Then why on earth haven't you told her so before now? You've had plenty of opportunity – I've seen to that.

Bretherton It's such a deuced awkward thing to do.

Mrs Cantelupe Nonsense.

Bretherton I've been just on the point of getting it out half a dozen times, and then either I've funked it or else something has happened to put me off my stroke. Once – (*he smiles*) – just when I'd got the words on the very tip of my tongue that ass Grinley came floundering in and it was all up with me.

Mrs Cantelupe (*scornfully*) Really, Victor.

Bretherton Oh, it's all very well for you to be so down on me, but after all, I'm not at all sure in my own mind that she cares a snap of the fingers about me.

Mrs Cantelupe Of course she does.

Bretherton H'm! I've thought so sometimes, but other times she's different.

Mrs Cantelupe Different!

Bretherton Yes, seems to shut up and draw into herself – says such queer things –

Mrs Cantelupe What sort of things?

Bretherton Oh, contemptuous and sarcastic – and I can't exactly explain – but once or twice it has struck me that she was trying to put me off before I had gone too far.

Mrs Cantelupe Rubbish – all your imagination.

Bretherton Oh, you can call it rubbish if you like, but that doesn't make me any more certain that she'll have me when I do summon up courage to ask her. (*Rises, crosses, then turns to her.*) And, when you come to think of it, why on earth should she? I'm not much of a catch as far as money goes – and even if I were it strikes me that I'm not half clever enough for her.

Mrs Cantelupe Nonsense, Victor. (*Rises, crosses, rings bell and returns.*)

Bretherton And I can tell you –

Mrs Cantelupe *stops to listen to him.*

– that when a man feels that as soon as he opens his mouth he may be told he's not wanted and sent about his business, it – well, it gives him a sinking sensation in the inside.

Mrs Cantelupe (*comes towards* c) Does it – that must be very uncomfortable, but as far as you are concerned, you will have to get over that sinking sensation in the inside now.

Bretherton What do you mean?

Enter **Waiter.**

Waiter Your ring, madame?

Mrs Cantelupe Yes. Will you send up to Mrs Massingberd – she is packing in her bedroom – and tell her I shall be exceedingly obliged – Mrs Cantelupe will be exceedingly obliged – (*glare of fury at* **Bretherton** *who is making efforts to speak*) – if she will spare me a few minutes down here. Say I am sorry to disturb her, as I know she is busy, but it is on a matter of importance.

Waiter All right, madame.

He exits.

Bretherton I say, Aunt Emma, you surely don't mean –

Mrs Cantelupe Now, Victor, no shuffling.

Bretherton Oh, hang it all, you needn't have rushed me into it like this.

Mrs Cantelupe If I hadn't rushed you into it, my dear boy, it is my firm belief that you would have let her go without a word.

Bretherton But I shouldn't have let her go altogether – I could have written to her.

Mrs Cantelupe Idiot! My dear Victor, if you are labouring under the delusion that letter-writing is one of your strong points, all I can say is that you are most woefully mistaken; besides, no self-respecting woman likes a man who hasn't the pluck to tell her that he loves her. So take your courage in both hands – you'll find that you'll muddle through somehow.

Bretherton I'm not so sure of that.

Mrs Cantelupe I shall allow you half an hour. (*Goes up to table for parasol.*) And at the end of that time I shall appear on the scene armed with suitable congratulations.

She opens parasol – with a bang – and exits through window.

Bretherton Good Lord! (*He goes up after her.*)

Diana *enters – crosses to* C. **Bretherton** *comes down* C.

Diana Oh, isn't Mrs Cantelupe here? I heard she wanted to see me.

Bretherton (*confused*) Yes, I know she did, that is to say, she sent a message – I mean she has just gone out for a stroll –

Diana Gone out for a stroll?

Bretherton She'll be back soon – in twenty minutes.

Diana In twenty minutes – oh, very well –

She turns quickly towards the door – **Bretherton** *gets in front of her.*

Bretherton Don't go for a moment, Mrs Massingberd. I – I want to speak to you.

Diana I am rather in a hurry. (*Tries to get to door –* **Bretherton** *backs towards it.*) Captain Bretherton.

Bretherton Yes, I know, but – I – I – (*with a rush*) – I hear you're leaving us.

Diana Yes. I find I must get back to London at once.

Bretherton I'm awfully sorry – awfully.

Diana It is very nice of you to say so.

Bretherton We – we've had a ripping time together, haven't we?

Diana I've enjoyed it immensely.

Bretherton The walks round here are splendid – aren't they?

Diana Yes.

A short pause, during which he attempts to speak

and fails. **Diana** *waits nervously for him to move away from the door.*

I'm afraid I really must go now, Captain Bretherton. I have to catch the 2.17 at Samaden, and the carriage will be round for me directly. (*Holding out hand.*) Goodbye.

Bretherton (*taking her hand*) Goodbye – I hope you'll have a comfortable journey and – no, I don't mean that – Mrs Massingberd – Diana – I – oh, hang it all, what does a fellow say when he wants to ask the nicest woman in the world to marry him? Diana, do you think you could possibly manage to put up with me as a husband? I know I'm an awful fool at putting things into words, but what I mean is that I've never met a woman like you and – I love you – 'pon my soul, I love you, Diana.

Diana (*turning to him with a sort of wistful, restrained eagerness*) Do you?

Bretherton (*joyfully going towards her*) Diana – does that mean?

Diana (*turning away quickly*) No, it doesn't – it doesn't – wait.

Bretherton Diana, for heaven's sake, don't keep me in suspense. Just let me know my fate in one word – tell me one way or the other.

Diana (*in a low voice*) That is just what I can't do.

Bretherton You can't? Why not?

Diana (*troubled*) Because . . . – (*more firmly*) – Captain Bretherton, you have just made me a proposal of marriage for which I – thank you. But, until you have heard what I have to say to you, I shall consider that proposal of marriage unspoken.

Bretherton Unspoken – but it isn't unspoken. What on earth – I don't – understand.

Diana Of course you don't understand – yet – but I wish to make the position clear to you.

Bretherton The position? What position?

Diana (*pointing to chair*) Will you be good enough to sit down and listen to me quietly – for a few minutes?

Bretherton (*taken aback*) Of course – er – certainly – delighted. (*Crosses her and sits on chair.*)

Diana *sits at end of Chesterfield – she is outwardly quite calm.*

Diana Do you realise, Captain Bretherton, that we have only been acquaintances for a little over a fortnight – to be exact, for seventeen days?

Bretherton Is that all? I feel as if we had been *friends* for seventeen years.

Diana And you know practically nothing about me – nothing, I mean, of my life and history before I met you here less than three weeks ago.

Bretherton (*surprised, and beginning to be uneasy*) Er – no – of course not. Except what you have told me yourself.

Diana (*leaning back and leisurely placing her finger-tips together*) Let me see – and what have I told you exactly?

Bretherton (*still more astonished*) Well, for one thing, you've told me that you are the widow of Mr Josiah Massingberd.

Diana (*calmly*) That, of course, was a lie to begin with.

Bretherton Diana, what do you mean?

Diana I mean, Captain Bretherton, that that estimable old gentleman, Mr Josiah Massingberd, is in exactly the same position as the celebrated Mrs Harris –

Bretherton Mrs Harris?

Diana There never was no such person!

Bretherton What?

Diana And that being the case, he couldn't very well have left a widow, could he?

Bretherton What on earth are you saying?

Diana (*leaning forward and looking him straight in the face*) Nor, which is more to the point, perhaps, could he have bequeathed the very comfortable income of three thousand six hundred pounds a year to his imaginary relict.

Bretherton (*stupefied*) His imaginary relict.

Diana Those were my words.

Bretherton I say, you're joking!

Diana I assure you, I'm not. On the contrary, I'm in black and deadly earnest.

Bretherton (*starting up, but remaining by chair*) Then if you aren't Diana Massingberd, who the deuce are you?

Diana Oh, I'm Diana Massingberd right enough. That's my name – my legal and lawful name – and the only thing about me that isn't a snare and delusion.

Bretherton Am I going mad or are you?

Diana Neither of us, I hope. I'm perfectly sane. All I'm trying to do is to make you understand that instead of being a rich widow, I'm a poor spinster – a desperately poor spinster.

Bretherton (*stammering*) But – then – how?

Diana I've been taking you in, of course.

Bretherton Taking me in?

Diana You and all your friends – sailing under false colours.

Bretherton *turns face aside.*

No doubt it was a disgraceful thing to do –

He makes movement of anger.

But before you get angry with me, I have a right to ask you to hear my story –

He sits again.

Diana (*she goes on more rapidly and with less self-control as her feelings get the better of her*) My father was a country doctor – an underpaid, country doctor. When he died there was nothing – nothing at all – and I was thrown upon my own resources for a living. I earned it how and when I could – and a little more than a month ago I was a shop assistant in London.

Bretherton A shop assistant – you?

Diana My last situation was at Dobson's – a big draper's. I was in the hosiery department.

Bretherton The hosiery department –

Diana Earning five shillings a week and having a hell of a time. I shan't apologise for the unparliamentary expression – it is justified. I'd had six years of that sort of slavery – been at it since my father died. Then one night, I got a solicitor's letter, telling me that a distant cousin of mine was dead, and that I had come in for three hundred pounds.

Bretherton Three hundred pounds?

Diana Of course, if I'd been a sensible woman I should have hoarded up my windfall – invested it in something safe and got three per cent for it. But I didn't. I was sick of the starve and the stint and the grind of it all – sick to death of the whole grey life – and so I settled to have a royal time while the money lasted. All the things that I'd wanted – wanted horribly, and couldn't have – just because I was poor – pretty dresses, travel, amusement, politeness, consideration, and yes, I don't mind confessing it – admiration – they should be mine while the cash held out. I knew that I could buy them – every one – and I wasn't wrong – I have bought them, I've had my royal time. I've been petted and admired and made much of, and – only for the sake of my imaginary fortune I know, but still I have enjoyed the experience – enjoyed it down to the very ground. . . . And now, it's over and the money's spent, and . . . I'm going back. (*She leans back against cushion.*)

Bretherton Going back? (*He rises.*)

Diana Yes. To work – to the old life and the old grind. I've just enough left out of my three hundred pounds to settle my hotel bill, tip the servants, and pay for my ticket home. I expect I shall land in England practically broke to the wide!

Bretherton Good Lord!

Diana Oh, my dresses will fetch something, of course. In that state of life to which it will please Providence to call me, I shall have no further use for smart frocks. They ought to bring me in enough to live upon until I get work.

She pauses – her face, which is turned away from him, showing him that she is painfully anxious for him to speak. He is silent, tugging irritably at his moustache – she faces round on him defiantly.

Well – now you know the whole story – and having heard it, you are no doubt feeling very much obliged to me because I refused to allow you to commit yourself a few minutes ago.

Bretherton (*faces front – sullenly*) You've put me in a deuced awkward position – deuced awkward –

Diana (*sarcastically*) I assure you, it is just as awkward for me.

Bretherton (*turns to her quickly*) You had no right to – to –

Diana (*still seated*) No right to enjoy myself as I pleased for once in my life, and to play the fool with my own money? Are you so very scrupulous as to the wisdom with which you spend yours?

Bretherton That's not the point. You must see that it was most – unfair – to me – to all of us – to deceive us as to your real position.

Diana (*mockingly*) In other words, as to the extent of my monetary resources. . . . Then I am to understand that it was entirely due to my imaginary three thousand six hundred a year that I owe all the attention and courtesy I have received from you during my stay here. I guessed as much from the moment Mrs Cantelupe tried to pump me about my income.

Bretherton Oh, it's all very well to talk like that, but surely you must realise that you have treated me shamefully.

Diana Indeed?

Bretherton Abominably. By deceiving me in this way – by allowing me to suppose –

Diana That – I was in a position to support a husband?

Bretherton (*going up to table, throws his hat down and comes down – losing his temper*) Oh, hang it all, I know I'm no match for you in an argument. But however much you may sneer and jeer at me, you must know perfectly well that your conduct has been that of an adventuress.

Diana (*lightly*) An adventuress! So I'm an adventuress, am I? Doesn't this rather remind you of the celebrated interchange of compliments between the pot and kettle?

He turns away.

For if I'm an adventuress, Captain Bretherton, what are you but an adventurer?

Bretherton I?

Diana You were ready and willing and anxious to run after me, so long as you believed that I had money and in the hope that I should allow you to live upon that money –

Bretherton Diana – Mrs – Miss Massingberd!

Diana It's true – and you know it – (*rises*) and what is that, may I ask, but the conduct of an adventurer? You are far too extravagant to live on your own income – you are far too idle to work to increase it – so you look round for a wife who is rich enough to support you in idleness and extravagance. You cannot dig, but to sponge on a wife you would not be ashamed.

He turns away.

And what, pray, have you to offer to the fortunate woman in exchange for the use of her superfluous income? Proprietary rights in a poor backboneless creature who never did a useful thing in his life!

Bretherton Miss Massingberd, this is insulting – intolerable.

Diana Captain Bretherton, it may be insulting and intolerable, but it is also the truth. Common, vulgar people like me – people who work for their living instead of living on other people's work – have an awkward knack of calling a spade a spade . . .

He turns from her.

at times. And remember . . . (*dryly*) it wasn't I who started calling names . . .

A short silence – **Diana** *pulls herself together and speaks coolly.*

Well, goodbye, Captain Bretherton –

She starts up – he stops her by his movement – goes up towards her.

as I told you just now, my money is spent, and my time here is up. I must hurry off to my room and finish packing all my earthly possessions in a couple of trunks and a handbag. (*Goes towards door.*) Make my final adieux to Mrs Cantelupe and – (*shrugging her shoulders*) tell her – whatever you think fit.

Bretherton Diana – Miss Massingberd . . .

Diana Yes?

Bretherton Before you go, I want you to see – I want to tell you that you have been very unjust to me.

Diana Unjust . . . how?

Bretherton You can't believe all that you have said about me. . . . It is not only money. . . . Surely you see that – and surely you must know that I would give a great deal – a very great deal – if circumstances did not keep us apart –

Diana (*contemptuously*) Circumstances!

Bretherton If it were not a moral impossibility for a man – a man in my position – (*He stops.*)

Diana If it were not a moral impossibility for a man in your position to marry a shop girl. That's what you mean, isn't it?

He is silent.

A shop girl – that is to say, a woman who has so far degraded herself as to work for her own living. Believe me, I quite realise the impossibility of the thing from your point of view – only, for the life of me, I cannot understand how you and your like have the impertinence to look down on me and mine? When you thought I had married an old man for his money, you considered that I had acted in a seemly and womanly manner – when you learnt that, instead of selling myself in the marriage market – I have earned my living honestly, you consider me impossible. And yet, I have done for half a dozen years what you couldn't do for half a dozen months.

Bretherton And what's that?

Diana Earned my bread, of course – without being beholden to any man and without a penny at my back. I wonder if it has ever entered into your head to ask yourself what use the world would have for you if you hadn't got money enough to pay your own way with?

Bretherton (*nettled*) No, it hasn't!

Diana (*coolly*) Well, it's a question that you might turn over in your mind with considerable advantage to your moral character. Personally I imagine that you would find the answer to be that under those circumstances the world hadn't any use for you at all. (*Turns.*)

Bretherton Upon my word.

Diana If you don't believe me, you have only to try the experiment for yourself. Stand with your back against the wall as I've stood for the last six years, and fight the world for your daily bread on your own hand. . . . You simply couldn't do it – you'd throw up the sponge in a week.

Bretherton Do you take me for an absolute fool, then?

Diana No. But I take you for a man brought up in sloth and self-indulgence and therefore incapable of seeing life as it really is. Your whole view of life is – must be – false and artificial. What is the meaning to you of the words, 'If a man will not work neither shall he eat?' Just nothing – they have no meaning to you. You don't understand them – and how should you?

Bretherton (*a step towards her*) If I'm the

idiot you make out, I wonder you've ever had anything to do with me at all.

Diana (*bitterly*) It would have been very much better for me if I hadn't.

She walks rapidly to door and exits, closing door after her.

The curtain falls.

Act Four

Scene: the Thames Embankment in the small hours of a November morning. Nearly in the centre of the stage, is a seat on which, as the curtain rises, are seen three huddled figures of two sleeping men, and the **Old Woman***, of the hopelessly unemployed class.* **Police Constable Fellowes** *enters when curtain is well up. He looks at the seat and stalks to it.*

Fellowes (*shaking the first loafer by the arm*) Now then – wake up – wake up, d'you hear? This here seat ain't a doss-house – you've got to move on.

He repeats the shaking operation – one of them – the extra man – gets up and shuffles away off the stage – the other, **Bretherton***, takes a good deal of rousing.*

(*Returns to* **Bretherton***.*) Now then (*shaking him violently*), are you deaf? Move on, when I tell you.

Bretherton (*rising reluctantly*) Why on earth can't you let me alone? I wasn't doing any harm. This moving on of poor harmless devils is a perfectly inhuman practice.

Fellowes Can't help it – it's our orders. Now then, quick march. (*Pushes him and starts.*) Why – it's never you, sir – Captain Bretherton.

The lights are raised a trifle here.

I beg your pardon, sir.

Bretherton Why, who the –

Fellowes Don't you remember me, sir? I served in the Welsh Guards afore I got my discharge and joined the force – and in your company, sir – Private Fellowes.

Bretherton Why, of course, I remember you, Fellowes. Glad to see you – that's to say I hope you're doing well.

Fellowes Yes, sir, thanks. I – I'm afraid you're not, sir.

Bretherton Well, it doesn't look very much like it, does it?

Fellowes (*looking him up and down with respectful sympathy*) I'm sorry to see you come to this, sir – so rejooced in circumstances.

Bretherton Thank you – er – that's very kind of you.

Fellowes We all liked you in the regiment, sir. There wasn't an officer that the men thought more of – and if there was anything I could do –

Bretherton Well, if it wouldn't get you into any serious trouble with your superiors, perhaps you'd allow me to resume my seat? Thank you. (*Sitting.*) And, Fellowes –

Fellowes Yes, sir.

Bretherton I suppose you haven't got a morsel – just a morsel of tobacco about you?

Fellowes I have, sir. (*Produces first pocket-book, which he puts in his mouth, then tobacco pouch from his coat-tail pocket.*)

Bretherton Ah! (*With a sigh of satisfaction he takes a battered pipe from his pocket, fills and lights it.*) That's good – three days since I had a whiff of the blessed stuff.

Fellowes You don't say so, sir.

Bretherton I do. Cash hasn't run to it. Total takings for the last four-and-twenty hours, threepence-halfpenny. And the half-penny was a French one.

Fellowes (*shaking his head*) It's a bad job! 'Eavy financial losses, I suppose, sir?

Bretherton Why, not exactly – light financial gains would be nearer the mark.

Fellowes (*puzzled*) Beg pardon, sir?

Bretherton The truth is, Fellowes, that as regards money I am not quite so badly off as I look.

Fellowes I'm very glad to 'ear it, sir – but –

Bretherton But why am I masquerading on this Embankment in these delectable garments, eh? Well, it's on account of what you might call a challenge.

Fellowes A challenge, sir?

Bretherton Yes, a – a sort of a bet.

Fellowes You're walking about all night with your feet coming through your boots for a bet, sir?

Bretherton For a sort of bet.

Fellowes If I was you, sir, I'd stick to the 'orses.

Bretherton I think I will – after next February!

Fellowes After next February?

Bretherton Yes. I've got to go on with this sort of thing till then.

Fellowes You've got to go on sleeping out till next February, sir. Why, you'll never stand it – it'll be your death.

Bretherton I don't always sleep out, Fellowes. When I possess the necessary twopence, I patronise the doss-house.

Fellowes But what's the hobject of it all, sir? What's the hobject of sleeping in a twopenny doss when you've got a comfortable 'ome of your own?

Bretherton The object, Fellowes, is to discover whether or not I am capable of earning my living by the work of my own unaided hands for the space of six calendar months.

Fellowes Well, I'm damned – beg pardon, sir.

Bretherton I suppose now, you can't give me any tips on how to manage it? How on earth does a man set about earning his livelihood? I don't mean a man who has been through a Board School and has had a trade at his fingers' end, but a man who has muddled through Eton and Oxford and had practically no education at all?

Fellowes (*thoughtfully*) Why 'is friends usually gets him some sort of berth, don't they, sir?

Bretherton But if he hasn't got any friends – if he has to worry along on his own?

Fellowes It's a bit difficult to say. I suppose he looks out for a job.

Bretherton But how the deuce does he get that job? From my experience of the last few weeks, I should say that all trades were closed to the man whose education has cost his father more than five hundred a year. For the last three months I've been trying to earn my living by the sweat of my brow – net result, a few odd jobs at the docks and a shilling for sweeping out an old gentleman's back garden. My present profession is that of a cab chaser.

Fellowes That's not much of a trade, sir?

Bretherton I agree with you – it's not. Occasionally, at the end of a two-mile trot, I receive sixpence in return for the privilege of carrying several trunks up four flights of stairs – but more often my services are declined – without thanks.

Fellowes I should give it up, sir, if I was you.

Bretherton I'll be hanged if I do, Fellowes.

Fellowes Just pride, sir.

Bretherton That's it, I suppose, just pride.

Hang it all, it makes a man feel so small when he realises that he hasn't any market value at all.

Fellowes I expect it does, sir.

Bretherton I don't mind confessing, that if I had known what I was letting myself in for three months ago, I should have thought twice – several times – before I joined the ranks of the unemployed. But now I've started I've got to see the thing through – somehow.

Fellowes *coughs doubtfully.*

Meanwhile, the devil only knows where my next meal –

Fellowes *looks at him.*

comes in. I suppose you couldn't suggest any means of acquiring it – honest, if possible?

Fellowes I'm afraid I can't at this moment, sir. But I'm sure you won't think it a liberty, sir – if the loan of a shilling – I'd be proud – (*Hand in pocket.*)

Bretherton (*hesitates*) No – you're a good chap, and thank you – but I won't.

Fellowes You'd better, sir – there's a coffee-stall just along there. (*Pointing off.*)

Bretherton (*rises*) I know there's a coffee-stall, Fellowes – there's no need to remind me of that fact. For the last half-hour I've been trying not to see it – and smell it. Don't think I'm too proud to accept a loan from you, but I'm playing this game on my own.

Fellowes Well, if you won't, sir, I must be moving along my beat. (*Crosses in front to side of seat.*) But if you change your mind by the time I'm round this way again –

Bretherton (*sits*) Don't tempt me, Fellowes, don't tempt me.

Fellowes (*shaking* **Old Woman**) Come on, Mother. Come on!

Bretherton There's plenty of room for me and that wretched old scarecrow. You'll let her have her sleep out, eh?

Fellowes That's all right, sir.

Exit **Fellowes**, *slowly.*

Business of **Bretherton** *trying to put his feet up on seat and lie down. His foot touches* **Old Woman** – *she starts and wakes.*

Bretherton Beg pardon.

Woman Is the copper coming back?

Bretherton No, he's gone by.

Woman That's a blessin'. I didn't want to be moved on from this 'ere seat – I chose it perticler so as to be near the cawfee-stall. I'm 'avin' my brekfus there later on.

Bretherton You're lucky – wish I was.

Woman (*suspiciously – moves to end of seat*) It's no use 'inting for me to stand yer treat if that's what you're after.

Bretherton Oh, I assure you – I hadn't the least idea.

Woman (*mollified*) Not that I wouldn't be willin' if I'd more than enough to pay for myself. What's brought a nice-spoken young man like you down to this?

Bretherton Oh, various things – can't get work.

Woman (*who gradually gets more drowsy as she speaks*) Take my advice, dearie – an old woman's advice – and leave it alone.

Bretherton What – work?

Woman No, dearie – not the work – the drink.

Bretherton I haven't touched a drop for weeks.

Woman (*getting sleepier*) I dessay you haven't – but that's because you haven't had the money. If you'd been flush it 'ud ha' bin another story – I know yer. (*Returning to* C *of seat.*) You take my tip – when the luck turns, leave it alone – leave it alone. (*Very sleepy.*) And now you an' me 'ull 'ave our forty winks till the copper comes round again. . . . Pleasant dreams, dearie.

Bretherton (*settles himself down – groans*) Oh, Lord!

Woman What's the matter, dearie?

Bretherton I was only thinking what a silly fool I am.

Woman We're all of us that – dearie – or we – shouldn't be here. (*Last words almost inaudible as she falls asleep.*)

Bretherton Lord, what a fool I am – what a silly fool.

Enter **Diana Massingberd**. *She wears a shabby hat and coat, a short skirt, muddy boots and woollen gloves with holes in several of the finger-tips. She carries a small brown-paper parcel – sits at end of seat.* **Bretherton**'s *pipe has gone out – he strikes a match – lights pipe – turns, shades the light from match on to her face with his hand, recognises her and throws down match.*

God bless my soul – Miss Massingberd!

Diana (*turning quickly*) Who are you?

Bretherton (*apologetically*) My name's Bretherton.

Diana Bretherton – not Vic – Captain Bretherton?

Bretherton The same.

Diana What on earth are you doing here?

Bretherton What are you?

Diana (*defiantly*) If you want to know, I'm here because I have no where else to go. I'm resting on this seat until a policeman moves me on.

Bretherton That's exactly my case – only I've got one advantage over you. The policeman on this beat happens to be an old friend of mine and he says I may stay here as long as I like.

Diana As you have so much influence with the powers that be, perhaps you'll intercede with them for me.

Bretherton With pleasure.

Diana (*harshly*) What are you masquerading like this for? Are you trying to eke out your totally inadequate income by sensational journalism?

Bretherton (*puzzled*) Sensational journalism?

Diana I thought perhaps you were writing up the Horrors of Midnight London for the *Daily Mail*. If you are, I dare say I can be of some assistance to you.

Bretherton (*humbly*) You know I'm not nearly clever enough for that.

Diana Then what are you doing?

Bretherton Looking for work.

Diana What? . . . you don't mean to tell me that this is — genuine — that you — are penniless — like me?

Bretherton Are you penniless?

Diana Quite.

Bretherton (*under his breath*) My God! . . . Tell me about it.

Diana What's the use?

Bretherton Tell me.

Diana I've had hard times . . . since I saw you.

Bretherton No work?

Diana Very little. I got a job soon after I came back to London, but I only kept it for a fortnight.

Bretherton How was that?

Diana Knocked up – got some sort of a chill – and was ill for weeks. That took the rest of my money. Since then – (*She looks before her – her face working.*) Oh, I've no right to grumble, of course. If I hadn't played the fool with my little fortune – my three hundred pounds – I shouldn't have been turned out of my lodgings. . . . But after all, I don't regret it – no, I don't. I had my good time – my one glorious month, when I made fools of you all and – no, (*impulsively*) I didn't mean that – I oughtn't to have said that to you, now. Forgive me.

Bretherton Of course I forgive you.

Diana (*more gently*) And now, it's your turn. Tell me, how long is it since you lost your money?

Bretherton I've been at this sort of game for three months now.

Diana Three months – why, it's not much more than that since I was at Pontresina.

Bretherton Not much more.

Diana *suddenly laughs.*

What's the joke?

Diana I can't help it. If anyone who knew us then – at the Engadine – could see us now.

Bretherton They'd notice a difference.

Diana We were both rather smart in those days, weren't we?

Bretherton We certainly aren't now.

Diana (*holding up her hand*) Look at my glove.

Bretherton (*lifting foot*) Not worse than my boots.

Diana (*chokily*) You poor fellow. You poor fellow. You must find it horribly hard?

Bretherton I do.

Diana But won't your people do anything for you? Surely your brother –

Bretherton I haven't asked him.

Diana Have you quarrelled with him, then?

Bretherton No. The fact is, he doesn't know. None of them know.

Diana They don't know that you have lost your money. But they must know. You must tell them. They'll give you a start –

Bretherton Miss Massingberd, I'm trying to do what you said I couldn't.

Diana What's that?

Bretherton Fight the world on my own.

Diana You surely don't mean that because of all the ridiculous things I said when I was angry –

Bretherton They were not ridiculous. My own experience has proved that they were perfectly correct – except in one particular. You said that I should throw up the sponge in a week – I haven't done that.

Diana Then it is through me – that you have come down to this?

Bretherton Through you.

Diana (*shakily*) I am – very sorry.

Bretherton Sorry – you ought to be glad.

Diana Glad to see you suffer like this – when you might have applied to your friends for help. You must apply to them at once, do you hear?

Bretherton Miss Massingberd, it is only fair to tell you that you have made a mistake.

Diana A mistake?

Bretherton A very natural one, of course. Finding me apparently homeless on the Embankment, you have jumped to the conclusion that I am a ruined man. I am not – I have still got six hundred a year when I choose to make use of it.

Diana (*drawing away from him*) Oh!

Bretherton And six hundred a year seems a great deal more to me now than it did three months ago.

Diana But if you have still got all that money, what on earth are you doing on the Embankment at three o'clock in the morning – and in those boots?

Bretherton Don't you remember what you said to me that last day at Pontresina?

Diana I remember – some of the things I said.

Bretherton You told me that I wasn't man enough to find myself a place in the world without money to bolster me up – that I was a poor backboneless creature and that I should go to the wall if I were turned out to earn my bread for six months. I didn't believe you then, but I've found out since that you were right, though I set out to prove you wrong.

Diana Then do you really mean –

Bretherton I do. Even the ornamental classes have a certain amount of pride, you know – it isn't only labour that stands on its dignity. For the last twelve weeks I have been existing on the work of my two hands

and such brains as I possess. I haven't touched a penny that I haven't earned.

Diana (*with a little sob*) You –

Bretherton And you were quite correct – nobody wants my services. I'm no use to anyone. You were entirely justified in looking down on me –

Diana No, no, I had no right –

Bretherton But you had – (*Strikes seat first time.*) All that you said was perfectly true. The world only tolerated me because I could pay my way – more or less – with money I never earned. For every useful purpose I'm a failure. (*Bangs back of seat with his hand, which wakes* **Old Woman**.)

Woman (*half aroused, drowsily, without opening her eyes*) We're – all of us – that, dearie – or we shouldn't be here. (*Snores faintly.*)

Diana and **Bretherton** *look at her.*

Diana I've no right to look down on you because you're not successful. If you're a failure, what else am I? If nobody wants you, nobody wants me either.

Bretherton I do.

Woman (*gives a sort of snort and opens her eyes, looks knowingly from one to the other, unties a knot in her shawl and takes out a penny*) I think it's abaht time I 'ad my brekfus. (*Sniffing.*) The cawfee-stall smells invitin', don't it, miss? (*Coin business.*) And you two 'ull be able to chat more comfortable without me sittin' in the middle of yer. (*To* **Bretherton**.) Move along, and tike my plice, dearie.

She exits.

Bretherton (*moves to* C, *but not from his section of seat*) Diana, I remember telling you once that my income was a miserable pittance, hardly enough for me to live upon. I've found out my mistake since then. It's not only enough for *one* to live upon – it's ample for *two*.

Diana (*harshly*) Do you realise what you're saying?

Bretherton I'm offering you 'proprietary rights in a poor backboneless creature who never did a useful thing in his life'.

Diana Don't.

Bretherton You refuse to – to entertain the idea? I'm sorry.

Diana (*turning on him almost fiercely*) Captain Bretherton – I'm homeless and penniless – I haven't – tasted food for nearly twelve hours – I've been half starved for days. And now, if I understand you aright – you offer to make me your wife.

Bretherton You do understand me aright.

Diana That is to say, you offer me a home and what is to me a fortune.

Bretherton And myself.

Diana (*laughing harshly*) And yourself – please don't imagine I forget that important item. But, under the circumstances, don't you think that you are putting too great a strain upon my disinterestedness?

Bretherton I understand what you mean. Perhaps I ought not to have spoken tonight – perhaps I ought to have waited. It might have been fairer to you – to us both. But –

Diana But what?

Bretherton I am going to tell you what is in my mind, even if you are angry with me.

Diana Go on.

Bretherton Perhaps, in my blundering

conceit, I made a mistake; but it seemed to me that last day at Pontresina, that if I had said to you, 'I care for you, not for your money but for your own sake' – it seemed to me that you would have come to me then. . . . Tell me – was I wrong?

Diana (*in a low voice*) No – then I would have . . .

Bretherton And now?

Diana (*hesitates – then with an effort*) No.

Bretherton Because you are too proud. Is that it?

Diana I suppose so – yes. I *am* too proud.

Bretherton Are you trying to make me still more ashamed of myself?

Diana Why?

Bretherton I was willing enough to marry you when you were the plutocrat and I the pauper. Haven't I put my pride in my pocket and for you, Diana? Haven't I trailed about the streets of London for the last three months to justify my existence in your eyes? (*Taking her hand, he moves over* C *partition and sits beside her.*) Diana, a much humiliated failure asks you to lead him in the way he should go.

Diana (*half laughing, but with tears in her voice*) It will be the blind leading the blind, then – and the end of that is the ditch.

Bretherton Never mind. Even the ditch can't be much worse than the Embankment in November.

Diana (*hurriedly, drawing away her hand*) Someone's coming – a policeman.

Enter **Fellowes.**

Bretherton That you, Fellowes?

Fellowes Yes, sir. (*Stops.*)

Bretherton (*rises*) Glad you've come back. Look here, I've changed my mind about that shilling. If you could oblige me with the loan of it for a few hours –

Fellowes (*giving it*) You're very welcome, sir.

Bretherton Thanks. I've changed my mind on the other point too. I'm going back to civilisation in the morning. (*Crosses in front of* **Fellowes**.)

Fellowes Glad to hear it, sir.

Bretherton And meanwhile this lady and I are going to breakfast off the coffee-stall at your expense.

Exits, running.

Fellowes (*looks after him, then surveys* **Diana** *curiously, then under his breath*) Well, I'm blowed!

Exit **Fellowes** *behind the seat.*

Re-enter **Bretherton**, *carrying two cups of coffee and some thick slices of bread and butter. The sandwiches are carried each on top of a coffee-cup. He puts his cup down on seat and hands the other to* **Diana.**

Bretherton (*speaking as he enters*) Had rather a difficulty in getting the chap to trust me with the crockery, but I told him we were close by and he could keep an eye on us. (*Putting down cups on seat and sitting.*) Two cups of coffee – and four doorsteps – that's what they call 'em.

Diana I know.

Bretherton Do you – poor little woman!

Diana Oh! they're not half bad when you're hungry.

Bretherton Not half bad – they're delicious. (*Takes a bite and speaks with his mouth full.*) Good chap, Fellowes, eh? We'll ask him to the wedding.

Diana (*also with her mouth full*) M'm.

She nods and smiles over her cup as the curtain falls.

Chains

Elizabeth Baker

Elizabeth Baker (1876–1962)

Chains was Elizabeth Baker's first performed play. It was given one performance on Sunday 18 April 1909 by the Play Actors subscription society, at the Court Theatre. The Play Actors were one of a number of groups promoting the performance of new plays which were unlikely to attract commercial production. It was performed again the following year during Charles Frohman's seventeen-week repertory season at the Duke of York's Theatre where, in May and June, with Sybil Thorndike and Lewis Casson newly in the cast, it was given fourteen performances, and was the fourth-most performed play of the season. It went on to be performed by the provincial repertory companies and to gain some minor recognition in histories of the theatre as a realist piece.

Baker wrote and had published and produced at least fifteen plays, several of them one-acters, the last apparently in 1931. A number of her plays were performed by the early repertory theatres in Manchester and Birmingham. In February 1912 her one-acter, *Edith*, was given a matinée performance at the Princes Theatre in London, produced by the Women Writers' Suffrage League. The play argues that women are capable of managing money and being successful in business. Between 1918 and 1920 she was a member of the Pioneer Players. The focus in her plays is usually on her women characters, who are mainly lower-middle-class, and the moral dilemmas they find themselves in are often related to the conflicts for women in the areas of work and marriage. She frequently presents the workplace, and women working, on stage. Her characters work in shops (*Miss Tassey*, 1910), are secretaries (*Miss Robinson*, 1918), are milliners (*The Price of Thomas Scott*, 1913), are dress-makers (*Partnership*, 1921), are domestic servants (*Bert's Girl*, 1925). She presents the notion that marriage is a woman's only possible course of action in a highly critical manner.

Contemporary reviews of *Chains*, while being mostly favourable, were also patronising, insisting that Baker, as a typist herself – 'a typist employed by a City firm' (*Era*, 24 May 1909) – was merely recording her observations of a milieu and class she knew first-hand. This not only took away from her any credit in creating the piece – it was mere journalism – it also served as a put-down in class terms. The play was about boring, vulgar people so she must be one of them too:

> Miss Baker aims at no effects of the theatre; she paints with faithfulness and sincerity the things she knows (*Sketch*, 25 May 1910)

and:

> No one, it is safe to say, could have painted a picture so faithful in detail, so true in essentials, who had not lived the life depicted therein. . . . Miss Baker apparently has known and felt these things, and out of a full experience has written her play. . . . [She] reveals that particular phase of existence of which, clearly, she has an intimate and personal knowledge. (Unidentified cutting, British Theatre Association library)

The reviewers were also much taken by the fact that she was a new playwright, the *Athenaeum* (28 May 1910) describing the play as 'the work of a young girl who, according

to report, has had no training in stage technique' (she was in her early thirties) and the
Era suggesting that maybe someone with more experience should have helped her in her
apparent lack of familiarity with theatre:

> The piece itself might be made suitable for production in a West End theatre if it
> received certain strengthening touches at the hands of an experienced dramatist. (24
> April 1909)

There was an insistence that the carefully constructed, detailed theatrical realism of the
play was mere ignorance of a more flamboyant style:

> We were told in advance that Miss Baker had little knowledge of the theatre and had
> scarcely troubled about stage technique. . . . [*Chains*] shows promise enough to justify
> Miss Baker in studying in earnest the rudiments of the art and in trying again. (The
> *Stage*, 22 April 1909)

What impresses me, however, is the play's astute use of theatrical devices, for example in
the creation of a sense of the constriction of Lily's and Charley's home by the use of stage
space and of off-stage action, the building to the climax of the row in Act Three, the use of
everyday objects unobtrusively to carry symbolic value, and the double movement at the
end of the play so that Maggie asserts herself as Charley is defeated.

Just as Archer claimed credit for initiating *Alan's Wife* so Edward Knoblock (dramaturg,
playwright and novelist) claimed credit for *Chains* in his autobiography, *Round the Room*
(1939):

> Miss Baker had sent in [to Lena Ashwell's company] a one-act play. I wrote her urging
> her to write a three-act play on her own experience – her own world. The result was
> *Chains*. I begged Miss Ashwell to reconsider her decision [not to produce the play]. But
> when a leading actress is not attracted to a play it is as well not to persist. . . . So that I
> finally sent *Chains* to Miss Edith Craig, who produced it in her 'Pioneer Society' on a
> Sunday night. . . . I met Miss Baker later on at some reception – but she did not
> remember me. When I recalled myself to her, she seemed equally vague. I couldn't help
> being a little surprised. It has taken me a long time in life to realise that people resent
> being put under obligations to others. (p. 90)

Perhaps Baker, unlike Knoblock, remembered that the play was first produced not by the
Pioneer Players but by the Play Actors.

The techniques used here are amongst those identified by Joanna Russ in *How to
Suppress Women's Writing* (1983):

> She didn't write it. . . . She wrote it, but look what she wrote about. She wrote it but
> 'she' isn't really an artist and 'it' isn't really serious, of the right genre – i.e., really art.
> She wrote it, but she only wrote one of it. (p. 76)

In *Chains*, as often in Baker's plays, the focus of the action is on work: on the low-paid
and monotonous work of the many clerks in the play, on Maggie's hard and hated shop-
work, on Lily's domestic work which is the work we see on stage, and on the possible

alternatives to all this drudgery. All three of the central characters are tied by their gender and class roles in terms of what their possibilities are and what is expected of them. Maggie can work in a shop, or an office, or she can get married. When she considers the excitement of emigrating, it would be to be a cook or a housekeeper. Charley has to work to support his family – any suggestion that he won't, that he would like to emigrate to Australia, produces dismay – but he doesn't earn enough to support them, and Lily takes in lodgers, increasing her domestic work, to increase their income. Lily has to keep Charley there: if he emigrates, her only alternative will be to return to her parents' home. The bleak prospect for Lily is apparent to the audience from the beginning, as we know long before Charley does that she is pregnant, and this must colour the way we interpret her desperation to keep him in his clerk's job. For much of the play the focus is on Charley's indecision, with Maggie, Lily's sister, urging him to emigrate, recognising that this vicarious adventurousness is all that's available to her as a woman. But in the end it is Maggie who breaks out. In deciding to stay working in the hated shop and not marry the boring Foster, she chooses chains she knows she can later reject, rather than the ones of marriage which she knows she won't be able to break. The chains of marriage are shown to us in Charley and Lily: the possibility of taking control of your own life is shown to us in Maggie.

Linda Fitzsimmons

Select Bibliography

Chains (London, Sidgwick and Jackson, 1911)
Miss Tassey (London, Sidgwick and Jackson, 1913)
The Price of Thomas Scott (London, Sidgwick and Jackson, 1913)
Miss Robinson (London, Sidgwick and Jackson, 1920)
Partnership (London, French, 1921)
Bert's Girl (London, Ernest Benn, 1927)

Chains was first performed by the Play Actors at the Court Theatre, London, on 18 April 1909, with the following cast:

Lily Wilson	Miss Gillian Scaife
Charley Wilson	Mr Ashton Pearce
Fred Tennant	Mr Gordon A. Parker
Maggie Massey	Miss Rose Matthews
Morton Leslie	Mr Leonard Calvert
Sybil Frost	Miss Doris Digby
Percy Massey	Mr Harold Chapin
Thomas Fenwick	Mr Sebastian Smith
Alfred Massey	Mr Clive Currie
Mrs Massey	Miss Marion Sterling
Walter Foster	Mr A. K. Ayliff

Produced by Farren Soutar

Act One

Scene: sitting-room at 55 Acacia Avenue. The principal articles of furniture are the centre table, set for dinner for three, and a sideboard on the right. There are folding doors at the back, leading to the front room, partly hidden by curtains; on the left a low French window leading into the garden. On the right is a fire burning; and above it a door into the kitchen.

The furniture of the room is a little mixed in style. A wicker armchair is on one side of the fireplace, a folding carpet-chair on the other. The other chairs, three at the table and two against the walls, are of bent wood. The sideboard is mahogany. The carpet-square over oilcloth is of an indeterminate pattern in subdued colours, dull crimson predominating. Lace curtains at window. Family photographs, a wedding group and a cricket group, and a big lithograph copy of a Marcus Stone picture, are on the walls. There is a brass alarm clock on the mantelpiece and one or two ornaments. A sewing-machine stands on a small table near the window; and on the edge of this table and on the small table on the other side of the window are pots of cuttings. A couple of bookshelves hang over the machine. A small vase of flowers stands in the centre of the dinner table.

Lily Wilson, *much worried, is laying the centre table. She is a pretty, slight woman, obviously young, wearing a light cotton blouse, dark skirt and big pinafore. The front door is heard to close.* **Charley Wilson** *enters. He is an ordinary specimen of the city clerk, dressed in correct frock-coat, dark trousers, carefully creased, much cuff and a high collar.*

Lily Here you are, then. (*She puts up her face and they kiss hurriedly.*) Did I hear Mr Tennant with you?

Charley Met on the step.

Lily *How* funny! Well, that's nice. We can have dinner almost directly.

Charley (*putting down his hat carefully on sideboard, and stretching himself slowly, with evident enjoyment*) Saturday, thank the Lord!

Lily (*laughing prettily*) Poor thing!

Charley (*looking at his silk hat*) I should like to pitch the beastly thing into the river. (*He shakes his fist at it. Then he stretches his neck as if to lift it out of the collar and shaking down his cuffs till he can get a fine view of them, regards them meditatively.*) Pah!

Lily (*anxiously*) What's the matter with them? Are they scorched?

Charley Scorched! No, they're white enough. Beastly uniform!

Lily But you must wear cuffs, dear.

Charley A chap came to the office today in a red tie. Old Raffles had him up, and pitched into him. Asked him if he was a Socialist. Chap said he wasn't, but liked red. 'So do I,' says the Boss, 'but I don't wear a golf coat in the city!' Thought he was awfully smart, and it did make Poppy swear.

Lily Who's Poppy, dear?

Charley Popperwell. He almost left there and then. Said he should wear whatever tie he liked.

Lily It would have been rather silly of him, wouldn't it? He's so sure there.

Charley That's what *he* said. He thought better of it and swallowed it. Well – dinner ready?

Lily Waiting.

Charley (*going out*) I'll be down in a jiffy.

Lily *goes to the fire.* **Tennant** *heard outside whistling a bar of the song 'Off to Philadelphia'. He comes in. He is a broad-shouldered young fellow, a little shy in his manner with women.*

Tennant Nice day, Mrs Wilson.

Lily Beautiful.

Tennant I've brought you home the paper, if you'd like it. It's the *Daily Mirror*.

Lily Oh, thank you. I do like the pictures. Charley is getting so dreadfully serious now in his reading, and won't buy it. He takes the *Daily Telegraph*. He thinks the gardening notes are so good.

Tennant He's luxurious. It's a penny.

Lily Oh, he shares it with somebody. (*Pause.*)

Tennant How goes the garden?

Lily It's rather trying – I should like to give up those peas and things, and have chickens. They would be so useful.

Lily *goes out.* **Tennant** *takes a map out of his pocket and stands studying it.* **Charley** *and* **Lily** *enter together.* **Charley** *has made a wonderful change into a loose, rather creased suit of bright brown, flannel shirt with soft collar, flowing tie and old slippers. A pipe is sticking out of one pocket, and a newspaper out of the other. They sit down, and* **Lily** *tries not to look worried as* **Charley** *laboriously cuts the small joint which she has brought in with her and put before him. He splashes the gravy a little and has to use the sharpener.* **Lily** *serves vegetables.*

Charley I think I shall get one of Robertson's pups.

Lily It would be lovely.

Charley He's got one he'll let me have cheap.

Tennant I saw them last night. They're a good breed. Make fine house-dogs.

Charley That's what you want round here. A quiet neighbourhood like this is A1 for burglars.

Lily You don't think we shall have any, do you?

Charley No. 24 had 'em the other night.

Tennant What were they after?

Lily 24? That's the new people. What a shame!

Charley Wanted the wedding presents.

Lily And Mrs Thompson told me they had real silver at 24.

Charley Trust the burglars for knowing that. They won't risk their skins for electro. So *we* shan't have 'em.

Lily Charley! You forget the biscuit barrel and the tray.

Tennant Where's the Bobby?

Lily There's only one about here.

Charley They don't have Bobbies for burgles in these sort of places, only for rows. And we don't have rows. We're too respectable.

Lily I think it's so mean of burglars to come to people like us.

Charley (*with a burst of laughter*) Let 'em go to Portman Square, you say?

Lily Well, of course, it's wrong to steal at all; but it doesn't seem quite so bad. (*She stops, a little confused.*)

Tennant Of course it isn't.

Charley (*lying back comfortably in his chair*) Going away Sunday?

Tennant No – the fact is –

Lily Maggie is coming round this afternoon. Shall we ask the Leslies for whist tonight?

Charley All right. Don't make it too early,

though. (*Looking out of the French window into the garden.*) I've got to get in my peas.

Tennant Green peas?

Charley Green peas in that patch? My dear chap, don't I wish I could!

Lily (*to* **Tennant**) Have some more?

Tennant No, thanks.

Charley For one thing, there's the soil! It's rotten. Then there're the sparrows. . . .

Lily Some of them are so tame, dear, and they don't seem to care a bit for the cat next door.

Charley (*bitterly*) They don't care for anything. I wish they'd take a fancy to a few snails.

Lily They don't eat snails.

Charley You spoil 'em. She gives 'em soaked bread all through the winter, and then expects me to grow things. Lord!

Lily *collects plates.* **Tennant** *goes out.* **Charley** *lights pipe.* **Charley** *goes to window, where he stands leaning against the post and smoking.*

Lily The baby across the road is such a darling, Charley.

Charley Is it?

Lily The girl was out with it this morning, and I called her over.

Charley What is it?

Lily It's a boy.

Charley *'s replies are without interest and he continues to gaze out into the garden.*

They're going to call him Theodore Clement Freeman. It's rather a lot, isn't it?

Charley What's he got it all for?

Lily After her father and his father and Freeman is a family name.

Charley What did they want to give 'em all to *him* for? They should keep some for the next.

Lily Charley!

Charley It's silly. Still, it's their business.

Lily It might be a girl.

Charley Well – there's the others.

Lily Charley!

Charley My dear girl, why not?

Lily I don't like you to speak like that.

Charley I – (*Stops suddenly, looks at her, and comes over. He takes her face between his hands.*) You silly! (*Kisses her.*)

Lily *goes out with a tray of things singing.* **Charley** *rolls up his sleeves and goes into the garden.* **Tennant** *comes in and looks round.* **Charley** *comes to the window with a spade.*

Tennant You – er – busy?

Charley (*lighting his pipe*) Um! Want a job? There's a nice little lot of squirming devils under that flower-pot that want killing. Take your time over it.

Tennant Thanks. My fancy doesn't lie in gardening.

Charley Filthy soil, this.

Tennant Mrs Wilson would like to keep chickens.

Charley Not if I know it! I'd rather go into a flat. (*Leaning against the door and smoking thoughtfully.*) I could chuck the lot sometimes. These two-penny-halfpenny back yards make me sick.

Pause.

I'd give something for a piece of good land.

Something to pay you for your labour. (*Rousing.*) Well – going out?

Tennant (*uneasily*) Yes – presently.

Charley (*turning to look at him*) What's up?

Tennant I've er – got some news for you.

Charley Anything wrong?

Tennant No – no! The fact is – I'm going to hook it.

Charley (*astonished*) Hook it? Where to?

Tennant I'm sick of the whole show. I can't stand it any longer.

Charley (*trying to realise the situation*) Do you mean you've left Molesey's?

Tennant Yes. I'm going to leave England – and so, you see, I've got to leave here – your place.

Charley Leave England? Got a crib?

Tennant No, nothing.

Charley What are you going for then?

Tennant Because I'm sick of it.

Charley So am I, and so are others. Do you mean you are just going out because you want a change?

Tennant That's about it. I've had enough of grind.

Charley Well, perhaps you'll get grind somewhere else.

Tennant It'll be a change of grind then. That's something.

Charley Canada?

Tennant No, Australia.

Charley Phew! That's a long shot. Got any friends there?

Tennant No.

Charley It's a bit risky, isn't it?

Tennant Of course it's risky. But who wouldn't have a little risk instead of that beastly hole every day for years? Scratch, scratch, scratch, and nothing in the end, mind you?

Charley (*ironically*) You might become a junior partner.

Tennant (*ignoring the remark*) Suppose I stay there. They'll raise the screw every year till I get what they think is enough for me. Then you just stick. I suppose I should marry and have a little house somewhere, and grind on.

Charley (*looking round*) Like me.

Lily *heard singing off* R.

Tennant No offence, old chap. It's all right for some. It suits you. You're used to it. I want to see things a bit before I settle.

Charley *is silent. His pipe has gone out and he is staring at the floor.*

So I thought I'd go the whole plunge. I've got a little cash, of course, so I shan't starve at first, anyhow.

Charley *makes no remark.* **Tennant** *becomes apologetic.*

I'm – I feel a bit of a beast – but the fact is – I – it was decided in a hurry – I – er –

Charley *looks up.*

I'm going on Monday.

Charley On Monday! Why, that's the day after tomorrow.

Tennant Yes, I know. It was like this. I heard of a man who's going Monday – a man I know – and it came over me all at once, why shouldn't I go too? I went to see him Friday – kept it dark here till I'd seen the guv'nor, and now it's all fixed. I'm awfully sorry to have played you like this –

Charley Oh, rot! That's nothing. But I say, it's the rummest go I ever heard of. What did Molesey say?

Tennant Slapped me on the back! What d'ye think of that? I thought he'd call me a fool. He pointed out that I could stay there for ever, if I liked – which was jolly decent of him – but when I said I'd rather not, thanks muchly, he banged me on the back, and said he wished he could do the same and cut the office. He didn't even stop the money for notice.

Charley Did he give you a £5 note?

Tennant (*laughing*) You don't want much. The old chap was quite excited, asked me to write – how's that?

Pause.

(*Rising.*) The thing is – I can't see why I didn't go before. Why did I ever go into the beastly office? There was nobody to stop me going to Timbuctoo, if I liked. I say, will you tell Mrs Wilson?

Charley She's only in the kitchen. Lil! – Lil! (*Shouting.*)

Lily (*from outside*) Yes, dear.

Charley Come here! Here's news.

Lily *enters, wiping her hands on her pinafore and smiling.*

Lily Yes?

Charley (*waving his pipe towards* **Tennant**) What d'ye think *he's* going to do?

Lily (*studying* **Tennant** *seriously*) Do? How –

Tennant (*nervously*) I – I'm going to leave you, Mrs Wilson.

Lily To leave us? (*With enlightenment.*) You're going to be married!

Tennant Good Heavens, no! Not that!

Charley Whatever made you think of that?

Lily What else could he do?

Tennant I'm going abroad.

Going over to garden door.

Charley He's going to seek his fortune. Lucky dog!

Lily Have you got a good appointment, Mr Tennant?

Tennant No, nothing. I'm going on the chance.

Lily Whatever for? Didn't you like Molesey's?

Tennant Oh, they were good enough and all that, but I got sick of the desk. I'm going farming.

Lily And throwing up a good situation?

Tennant I suppose you'd call it good.

Lily It was so sure. You'd have been head clerk in time. I'm sure you would. It does seem such a pity.

Tennant Sounds a bit foolish, I expect.

Lily Of course you must get tired of it sometimes. But to throw it up altogether! I do hope you won't be sorry for it. Charley gets tired of it sometimes – don't you, dear?

Charley (*from the garden door*) Just a bit – now and then.

Lily Everybody does I expect. It would be very nice, of course, to see other places and all that – but you can always travel in your holidays.

Charley How far on the Continong can you go in a fortnight, Lil?

Tennant I don't think you quite understand. It isn't so much that I want to see things – though that'd be jolly – but I want a change of work.

Lily (*sympathetically*) It *is* trying to do the same thing over and over again. But then the hours are not so very long, are they?

Charley Nine to six, with an hour for lunch and tea thrown in. Count your many blessings, Freddy.

Lily (*reproachfully, and crossing to him*) You know, Charley, we've often talked it over, and you've said how regular the hours were.

Charley So they are.

Charley *disappears for a moment into garden, but is now and again to be seen outside the door with a flower-pot or some other thing for the garden.*

Lily And you have the evenings, and they give you Saturday morning at Molesey's as you get on, don't they?

Tennant Yes, it's all true, Mrs Wilson – but I can't stand it. Anybody can have the job.

Charley It's the spring, Freddy. That's the matter with you.

Lily I do hope you won't be sorry for it. It would be so dreadful if you failed, after giving up such a good situation. Of course we are very sorry to lose you, Mr Tennant – you have been so kind.

Tennant (*hastily and with much embarrassment*) Oh, please don't.

Lily And we have always got on so very well together. I'm sure it will be very difficult to get anyone to suit us so well again. But you won't forget us and if we have your address, we can write sometimes –

Charley And if anything striking occurs,

I'll send a cable. The novelty will be worth it. (*Coming just inside the door with the spade in his hand.*) For the rest, I'll describe one day and you can tick it off for the whole lot of the others. Rise at 7, breakfast; catch the 8.30, City –

The door-bell is heard.

Who on earth – !

He goes into the garden.

Lily Maggie, I expect.

She goes out. **Tennant**, *after making a step towards the garden, turns to the door, only to meet* **Maggie Massey** *and* **Lily**. **Maggie** *is of medium height, well-proportioned, good-looking without being pretty.*

Maggie (*shaking hands with* **Tennant**) How do you do?

Lily What *do* you think, Maggie? Mr Tennant is going to leave us. Guess what for!

Maggie He's going to be married?

Charley Good Lord! There's another.

Maggie Hullo, Charles, you there!

Lily He's going to leave England.

Maggie How nice for him!

Lily (*emphatically*) Nice! But he's got nothing to do there!

Maggie (*to* **Tennant**) Are you going to emigrate?

Tennant Yes; I'm going to Australia to try my luck.

Charley Isn't he an idiot?

Maggie Do you think so?

Charley Throwing up a nice snug little place at Molesey's and rushing himself on to the already over-stocked labour market of the Colonies.

Maggie You are really going on your luck?

Tennant Yes.

Maggie How fine!

Lily Maggie! I think of the risk!

Maggie He's a man. It doesn't matter.

Lily If he'd been out of work, it would have been so very different.

Maggie That would have spoilt the whole thing. I admire his pluck.

Lily Well, he's got no one depending on him, so he will suffer alone.

Maggie You're not very encouraging, Lil. I have heard of a married man doing the same.

Charley (*quickly*) Who was that?

Lily How very foolish!

Maggie Oh, he was already out of work.

Lily That is different – although even then –

Maggie His wife went to live with her people again and he went out to the Colonies and made a home for her.

Lily (*sceptically*) How did he do that?

Maggie I don't know. *You* are quite free to do as you like, aren't you, Mr Tennant? How does that feel?

Tennant I have only just started to think about it. Directly the idea came into my head, off I had to go.

Charley, *who has stood listening, turns slowly and walks away.*

Maggie You are lucky to have found it out in time.

Tennant In time?

Maggie Before you got too old to do anything.

Pause.

Charley (*near the garden window but outside*) Climb on to the dustbin, only mind the lid's on tight.

Tennant That's Leslie coming over. I'll go. (*Goes.*)

Enter from the garden **Morton Leslie**, *a big fair man, clean-shaven, lazy and good-natured.* **Charley** *follows.*

Leslie I nearly smashed your husband, Mrs Wilson. . . . Good day, Miss Maggie – and I'm sure I've absolutely killed Mr Wilson's beans.

Charley If you don't the birds will – and if they don't the worms will – and – how can you expect anything to grow in that garden?

Leslie I thought it was such an excellent Small Holding! What about the carrots?

Charley Pah! Carrots! Why not peaches? Come on, Leslie! I've got the papers in the other room.

Charley *lifts the curtain and they go into front room.*

Lily I'm afraid Charley must be tired. He seems quite irritable.

Maggie So am I when I get home from business. (*Throwing out her arms and smiling at* **Lily**.) No more shop for me in a month or two, Lil.

Lily (*excitedly*) You're going to marry Mr Foster?

Maggie *nods.*

Oh, how lovely! How nice for you, dear! I am so glad. What did mother say?

Maggie (*with a little laugh*) Mother is charmed.

Lily Everybody is, of course. He is such a nice man. He will spoil you, Maggie. You lucky girl!

Maggie Yes, I suppose I am.

Lily You don't like to show it, of course, dear.

Maggie Don't I? You should have seen me last night! I took off my shop collar and apron and put them on the floor and danced on them – till mother came to see what was the matter.

Lily You *must* be fond of him, dear.

Maggie No, I'm *not*, particularly.

Lily Maggie!

Maggie (*walking up and down*) That's funny now. I didn't mean to say that. It just came. (*A pause.*) How queer! (*A pause.*) Well, it's the truth, anyway. At least, it's not quite true. When I came here today I was awfully happy about it – I am fond of him at least – I – well – he's very nice – you know. (*Irritably.*) What did you want to start this for, Lil?

Lily (*aggrieved*) *I* start it? I did nothing.

Maggie I was so satisfied when I came.

Lily (*soothingly and taking her sister's hat and coat from her*) You're a little tired, dear. We'll have an early cup of tea. Have you got your ring, dear?

Maggie *holds out her left hand.*

How sweet! Sapphires! He must be rich, Maggie.

Pause.

Maggie I wish I was a good housekeeper, Lil.

Lily (*reassuring*) Oh, you'll soon learn, dear; and his other housekeeper wasn't very good.

Maggie I wasn't thinking of that.

Lily But you talked of housekeeping, dear.

Maggie Yes, but that's quite different from being married. If I could cook decently, I would have left the shop before.

Lily But you *are* going to leave the shop!

Maggie (*unheeding*) Or if I understood anything about the house properly, but I couldn't be even a mother's help unless I could wash.

Lily I don't know what you mean, Maggie. You haven't got to wash. You know Mr Foster can afford to send it all out. (*Sighing enviously.*) That must be nice.

Maggie I heard of a girl the other day, Fanny White – you know her – she's gone to Canada.

Lily Canada! Who's talking about Canada? What's that to do – ?

Maggie I was envious. She used to be with us at the shop.

Lily (*impatiently*) Yes, I know. Well, you've done better than she, anyway, Maggie, if she *is* going to Canada. She'll only be a servant, after all. What else can she do? And then in the end she'll marry some farmer man and have to work fearfully hard – I've heard about the women over there – and wish she had *never* left England. While here are you, going to marry a rich man who's *devoted* to you, with plenty of money and long holidays, and your own servant to begin with! Really, Maggie – !

Maggie (*stretching a little and smiling*) Isn't it gorgeous? (*Shaking herself.*) Well – it must be Mr Tennant's fault. He shouldn't get mad ideas into his head –

Lily And he really is mad. Throwing up a most *excellent* situation. My dear, I call him just stupid!

Charley (*lifting the curtain and coming forward with* **Leslie**) There's no hurry.

Leslie Oh, I'll start on it tonight. My wife's gone away and left me for the day, and I'm a forsaken grass widower.

Lily (*laughing*) Poor Mr Leslie! Won't you come in here tonight? Don't you think it would be very nice, Charley, as Mr Tennant is going so soon –

Leslie Tennant? Where's he going?

Maggie *You'll* never guess.

Leslie He's leaving you? He's going to get married?

Charley (*impatiently*) You're as bad as a woman!

Maggie I thought you more brilliant, Mr Leslie.

Leslie I thought of the happiest thing that could happen to a man, Miss Maggie.

Lily No, it's not marrying. He's going abroad.

Leslie Got a fortune?

Maggie He's just going to try his luck. He's emigrating.

Leslie What a fool! He's got the sack, I suppose?

Maggie No. He's thrown it up.

Leslie Thrown up a safe job? Oh, he's an ass, a stupid ass! You surely don't ask me to come and wish good luck to an ass?

Maggie You can help with a dirge then.

Leslie Much more like it. But, I say, is it really true? He must have got something to go to?

Charley He hasn't. He's got a little cash, of course. He's always been a careful beast.

Leslie And he's going to throw it away! And then I suppose he'll be out of work over there, and we shall be hearing of the unemployment in the Colonies! It's just this sort of thing that makes a man a Conservative. It's what I call getting off the ladder and deliberately kicking it down.

Charley Well, I don't then. I think he's a lucky chap to be able to do something he likes. He's got some pluck.

Lily Why, dear, you know you think it's very silly of him!

Leslie (*laughing*) You must look after your husband, Mrs Wilson, I can see. He'll be running away. Well, so long, old chap! I'll come back later. Just give me a hitch over the wall. You'll be sorry about those beans next week. (*Pause.*)

They go out. A crash is heard.

Charley Hullo! What's up?

Leslie (*in the distance*) Smashed a box of tomato plants. Phew!

Lily, *laughing, goes out with* **Maggie**. *A long whistle –* **Charley** *comes back into the room and stands looking into the fire. Pause.*

Enter **Tennant** R.

Tennant I'm just going round to Carter's. Anything you want? (*Pause.*) I suppose Leslie had something to say about me?

Charley He doesn't want to come *with* you.

Tennant *laughs.*

You don't seem to know much about it, but I suppose you've fixed on a town. Sydney?

Tennant No, Brisbane. (*Pulling out a map.*) The chap I know is cattle raising. Look!

He opens the map on the table: they both lean over it, **Charley**'s *burnt-out pipe still in his hand.*

We're going to Brisbane, then this way (*moving his finger*) across Queensland. He knows something at Merivale – here – see – in the Darling district. Then we shall push on to Maronoa – that's the county – we're going to a tiny place – Terramoa – but of course I mayn't get anything –

Charley (*who is practically lying over the map*) Not fruit-farming then? That's more my line.

Tennant No. If ever you thought of that – see – this is a good district – I heard of a man there once – see – this way – ship to Sydney – vineyards and all sorts – suit you.

Charley U-m! Or one could go this way. (*Pointing with his pipe.*)

Lily's *voice heard calling 'Charley' –* **Tennant** *stands upright.*

Lily (*enters – laughing*) Charley! What are you doing?

Charley *jumps up and* **Tennant** *folds up the map.*

Looking at the plans?

Tennant I'm off.

Goes out.

Lily Finished gardening already, dear?

Charley (*putting on his coat*) Don't feel like it.

Lily (*holding out a newspaper*) Look here, dear, this will do for us, I think.

Charley (*glancing round*) What is it?

Lily An advertisement. (*Reading.*) 'Wanted, by Young Man, board – residence in quiet family within easy reach of city. Western suburb preferred.' I must answer it.

Charley I say – give Tennant a chance to get out first.

Lily But he is going, dear, so there's no risk. And it's such a good chance. Besides, we can ask Mr Tennant for a reference.

Charley (*sharply*) No, don't. Surely we can exist a week without anybody.

Lily Oh, yes! Only I thought – it's a pity to miss – You don't want Mr Tennant to go, do you, dear? He is nice company for you.

Charley He's a nice chap. But you needn't get lodgers to keep me company.

Lily (*laughs*) What an idea! Of course not.

Charley (*going to her and turning her face towards him*) I say, Lil, aren't you ever dull here?

Lily No – well – hardly ever. There's always something to do. What a question!

Charley Don't you ever get sick of it? It's jolly hard work sometimes. (*He takes her hands and looks at them, stroking them as if unconsciously.*) Why they're getting quite rough. (*She pulls them away.*)

Lily It's the washing, dear. It does roughen your hands.

Charley (*taking them again and kissing them*) They weren't rough when we married.

Lily (*she turns away*) You silly boy, of course they weren't. I never did washing at home. What do you think, dear? Maggie is going to be married.

Charley (*with little interest*) To Foster?

Lily Yes. Isn't she lucky? He's quite well off.

Charley So *she* won't do the washing. I shall never be rich.

Lily You'll be head clerk one of these days.

Charley One of these days!

Lily And then we'll have a servant.

Charley Perhaps I shall never be head clerk.

Lily Oh, yes, you will!

Charley I don't know that I'm excited at the idea – a sort of policeman over the other chaps. I'd rather be as I am.

Lily But think of the position – and the money!

Charley *nods gloomily – he walks to garden door.*

Where's your ambition, dear?

Charley Perfectly safe. No fear of that getting lost. The man who built that road (*pointing out of the window*) ought to be hanged.

Lily They're not very pretty, those houses. Mrs Freeman told me this morning that they're going to raise our rents a little.

Charley (*turning round sharply*) What? *That's* because they've brought the fares down. Just like 'em.

Lily I was thinking this morning, dear, that perhaps we could take two boarders. It would help a little. That little room at the back, over the scullery, would do nicely with a single bed.

Charley That's where I keep my cuttings and things.

Lily Yes, dear, but you could have half the coal shed. We never fill it.

Charley I don't want the coal shed. I say – must we have two?

Lily It would make things better, dear.

Charley But it's beastly, choking up your house with a lot of fellers. *You* don't like it, do you?

Lily No, dear, of course not.

Charley You don't seem much put out.

Lily It's no good being cross about it, dear, is it? If it's got to be done, we may as well make the best of it.

Charley Oh, make the best of it. (*Fretfully.*) You might at least seem vexed.

Lily (*patiently*) Of course I don't like it, dear, and of course I'd much rather be alone with you and have all my house to myself – though really the boarders don't worry much, you know. They are always home late and only have meals with us.

Charley Who wants 'em at meals? I don't, if you do!

Lily (*pathetically*) You are very unkind. I never said I wanted them. I'm only doing my best to make things smooth. You might help me, Charley. (*She turns away.*)

Charley (*crossing to Lily and patting her on her hand*) I'll be all right later. But I say it is a bit thick. An Englishman's home is his castle. I like that! Why, the only place where you can be alone is the bedroom. We'll be letting that next. (*He laughs sarcastically.*)

Lily (*shocked*) Charley! What are you saying?

Charley Ha, ha, what a joke! The – well, never mind. The day we let the bathroom, Lil – I'm off to the Colonies. (*He stops, suddenly struck with a thought.*)

Lily You silly boy.

Charley Supposing I did, eh?

Lily We're not going to let the bathroom, so you needn't suppose anything.

Charley (*abstractedly – sitting on a corner of the table*) Why not?

Lily Did you speak, dear?

Charley (*starting*) Eh? – No, no! – nothing.

Lily *goes, closing door.*

Curtain.

Act Two

Scene: sitting-room at 55 Acacia Avenue. The folding doors between front and back parlour are opened, with red curtains looped up. The front parlour, a glimpse of which is visible between curtains, is in full light and a corner of the piano can be seen. The furniture in this room is of the imitation Sheraton variety. There is an ornamental overmantel with photographs and vases, and a marble clock in the middle of the mantelpiece.

*Someone is playing the piano, and **Lily**, standing beside it, is singing in a sweet but rather weak voice, 'Sing me to sleep'. No one is in the back parlour, but through the curtains can be seen **Morton Leslie**, lolling on mantelpiece; **Sybil Frost**, a pretty fair-haired girl, much given to laughing at everything; **Percy Massey**, a good-looking, somewhat weak youth of perhaps twenty-one or twenty-two, sitting very close to **Sybil**, and **Tennant**, standing in the bay window.*

*__Charley__ comes in quietly through the side door into the back parlour during the singing. When **Lily** comes to the refrain of the song, everyone except **Charley** joins in. He stays in the back parlour and sitting down in the shadow, lights a cigarette. **Lily** sits down amid a good deal of clapping and words of admiration.*

Sybil I do love that song.

Percy Now you sing something.

Sybil (*with a giggle*) I couldn't really – you know I couldn't.

Percy Oh, yes, you can – that nice little coon thing you sang at the Richards.

Sybil I've got a cold.

Maggie (*crossing from piano*) Of course you have.

Sybil (*laughing*) But it's quite true. Really. And I couldn't really sing after Mrs Wilson.

Lily Sybil! Do sing, *please*.

Leslie We're all waiting, Miss Frost.

Sybil Oh, please – I can't. Let someone else sing first.

Maggie *comes to the doorway and catches sight of* **Charley**. *She comes in. In the front parlour* **Sybil** *can be seen still resisting, while* **Lily**, **Leslie**, *and* **Percy Massey** *beseech her.*

Maggie You here – all alone?

Charley 'Um.

Maggie What's the matter?

Charley Nothing.

Maggie Why didn't you come into the front room?

Charley I can hear quite as well here.

Maggie Got the hump?

Charley What for? Head's a bit nasty, so I'm smoking it off.

Maggie It isn't that – it's all this about Tennant.

Charley (*irritably*) I'm not grieving over him, if that's what you mean.

Maggie As if I did! and as if you'd confess if you were. Are you sick of everything?

Charley Sick! I'd cut the whole beastly show tomorrow if – (*He stops suddenly.*)

Lily's *voice can be heard distinctly from the front room.*

Lily Well, we'll ask Mr Tennant to sing first.

Sybil Oh, I can't sing, really –

Charley Why doesn't the girl sing when she's asked?

Maggie She says she has a cold. (*She laughs a little.*)

Charley Rot! Affectation, I call it.

Maggie Percy's awfully smitten, isn't he?

Charley (*surprised*) With her?

Maggie Of course. But you haven't noticed that. Lily's been arranging it.

Charley But he's such a kid.

Maggie He's twenty-two.

Charley What's that?

Maggie Lots of men marry at twenty-two.

Charley More fools they! Getting tied up before they've seen anything.

Maggie (*thoughtfully*) I can never understand why a man gets married. He's got so many chances to see the world and do things – and then he goes and marries and settles down and is a family man before he's twenty-four.

Charley It's a habit.

Maggie If I were a man I wouldn't stay in England another week. I wouldn't be a quill-driver all my life.

Charley *gets up and walks restlessly up and down the room.*

If I were a man –

Charley Men can't do everything.

Maggie I say, don't you think it's fine of Mr Tennant to throw up everything and take the risk?

Charley I'd do the same if . . .

Lily (*coming forward a little*) Where's Charley? Oh, never mind, I daresay he's got a lantern and is looking for worms or something. Are you ready, Mr Tennant?

Maggie I wonder what Lil would say if you did!

Charley *stops dead and looks at* **Maggie**.

Charley If I *did*? What are you talking about?

Maggie Why shouldn't you?

Charley Why shouldn't I? Aren't there a thousand reasons?

Maggie There's Lily, certainly – but . . .

Charley She wouldn't understand. She'd think I was deserting her.

A pause.

But that's not all. I might manage her – I don't know – but – you see, I've got a berth I can stay in all my life . . .

Tennant *starts singing the first verse of 'Off to Philadelphia'.*

It's like throwing up a dead cert. And then . . .

Maggie It *would* be a splash.

Charley Yes – and think of all your people? What'd they say? They'd say I was running away from Lil – of course, it would seem like it. . . .

Another pause.

It's impossible. I might never get anything to do – and then –

His voice is suddenly drowned as the front room party sing the chorus 'With my Knapsack', etc. Knock at front door.

I –

Maggie I believe I heard a knock.

She goes out in corridor as **Tennant** *commences the second verse.* **Charley** *sits on the edge of the table watching and listening. The door opens and* **Maggie** *enters, followed by* **Fenwick**. **Fenwick** *is a man of middle age, short and slight, with a quiet, rather crushed manner.*

Maggie Mr Fenwick didn't want to come

in when he heard all the singing. He thought we had a party.

She goes through curtains.

Charley Oh, it's nothing – a sort of family sing-song.

Fenwick Miss Massey would have me come in – but really I'd rather come some other –

Charley Stuff! Sit down. I'll pull the curtains if it's anything special you've come about. I thought it was perhaps over those geranium cuttings. Afterwards, if you feel like it, we'll go and join them. (*Draws curtains and turns up light.*) Freddy Tennant – you know him, don't you – he's going to seek his fortune in the Colonies.

Fenwick Is he?

Charley Yes, and we'll drink his health. What's up?

Fenwick I didn't see you at the train today.

Charley No, you were late. I came on with Malcolm.

Fenwick The chief sent for me.

Charley Wasn't a rise, I suppose?

Fenwick Do I look like it? It's the other thing.

Charley Docking?

Fenwick (*nodding first and then speaking slowly*) He said he'd sent for me as senior of my department. The company has had a bad year and they can't give the usual rises.

Charley None?

Fenwick None. Haven't you had a letter?

Charley No. I say, have I got the sack?

Fenwick No, you haven't. But they're

offering you the same alternative they offered me – stay on at less – or go.

Charley (*walking up and down*) What are you going to do?

Fenwick What can I do? Stay, of course – what else is there?

Charley Sit down under it?

Fenwick What else?

Postman's knock.

Charley There's the postman. Wait a bit.

He goes out R and the voices in the other room can be distinctly heard laughing, while someone is playing a waltz tune very brilliantly. **Charley** *comes back with a letter in his hand, closes door and music dies down.*

Charley Here it is. (*He opens and reads it, then throws it on the table.*)

Fenwick A bit of a blow, isn't it?

Charley I didn't expect it. Did you?

Fenwick Not until last week when Morgan started making enquiries as to salaries, et cetera. Then I guessed.

Charley We can't do anything.

Fenwick Of course not.

Charley But I say, you know, it's all rot about a bad year. Don't expect we've been exactly piling it up, but it's nothing to grumble about.

Fenwick That doesn't affect us, anyway. We've got to do as we're told. I fancy old Morgan is hit, too. He was sugary, but of course he had to obey the instructions of the directors and so on.

Charley It's no good swearing at him.

Fenwick It's no good swearing at anybody. What's a Board? Where is it?

The curtains part and **Lily** *appears in the opening.*

Lily Charley – are you there? Are you never coming back? Oh, Mr Fenwick!

Fenwick *rises; shake hands.*

Fenwick Good evening. I'm afraid I'm an awful nuisance, but I just called to see your husband about a little business.

Lily You'll stay to supper, won't you? You and Charley can sit and talk business the whole time. I'm afraid Charley doesn't like music very much – do you, dear?

Charley Oh, sometimes.

Lily (*big laugh from behind curtains*) You should hear Mr Leslie. He's so funny, he's been giving Mr Tennant advice what to do when he's a lonely bachelor in Australia. He made us *roar* with laughter.

Goes back laughing.

Charley Silly ass!

Fenwick (*startled*) What?

Charley That chap Leslie! It'd do him good to go to Australia for a bit. He'd stick to his berth if they docked his screw to ten bob. He's got no pride in him.

Fenwick Well, we – at least, I – can't say much – I'm going to stay on. You, too, I suppose.

Charley (*with a sort of defiance*) Why should I? What's to hinder me leaving? Why shouldn't I go to Morgan and say, 'Look here – just tell those directors that I won't stand it! I'm not going to be put up or down – take this or that – at their will and pleasure'.

There is a burst of laughter from the inner room.

Fenwick That's all very well – and if you've got something else –

Charley (*fiercely*) I haven't – not an idea of one – but why should that hinder? Look at Tennant, he's chucked his job and no one wanted to take off anything.

Fenwick (*quite undisturbed*) Tennant? Oh, he's going to the Colonies? Very risky. I nearly went there myself once.

Charley Why didn't you quite?

Fenwick Various things. All my people were against it. Oh, well, what was the good of going? It was only a passing fancy, I daresay. Once you leave a place the chances are you won't get another. There are so many of us . . .

Charley Of course, it's safe and it's wise and it's sensible and all that – but it's *damnable.*

Fenwick It's come suddenly to you – I've almost got used to the idea. (*With a little laugh.*) You do, you know, after a little. You're young. . . . (*With sigh.*) Well, there it is. (*A pause.*) But I'd looked for that rise. It'll make a difference. (*Pulling himself together.*) However, it can't be helped. We've got something left and I'm safe, and that's more than a good many people can say. I'm sorry I came tonight, Wilson.

Leslie*'s voice can be heard, shouting out a comic song.*

(*Smiling.*) Life doesn't seem to worry him.

Charley Won't you stay and have supper?

Fenwick Thanks, no. I don't feel exactly sociable.

Charley (*with a short laugh*) Neither do I, old chap. Fact is, I was feeling a bit off when you came.

Fenwick You're a little restless, but it'll work off. Look at me. I felt like that once.

They go out. The curtains are pulled wide and

Leslie *and* **Percy Massey** *enter.* **Tennant** *can be seen in the front parlour.*

Leslie May we interrupt? (*Looking around.*) Empty was the cradle.

Re-enter **Charley**.

Where's the business?

Charley Fenwick's been, but he's just gone.

Leslie Fenwick? Wasn't cheerful company, was he?

Charley (*crossly*) What's the matter with him?

Leslie He never is, that's all.

Charley He isn't exactly boisterous. He nearly emigrated once, he tells me.

Tennant (*coming forward*) Why didn't he quite?

Leslie Not enough devil in him. Hundreds of 'em almost go.

Charley Did you?

Leslie (*with energy*) I'm comfortable enough where I am. I've been telling this chap here he's a fool, but he won't believe me. He says he'd rather be a fool in the Colonies than a wise man here. Don't know what he means quite, but it sounds rather smart. (*Waving his pipe oracularly as he faces the three men.*) I've known lots of chaps who've wanted to go. The guv'nor is unpleasant or there's too much overtime or they get jealous of their girl or something of that sort and off they must go. I've known a few who went – and sorry they were, too. You can't do anything out there. Read the emigration books, read your papers. Failure all along the line. Market overcrowded. Only capitalists need apply – the Colonies don't want you –

Charley Neither does England –

Leslie Of course not but (*waving his arm impressively*) but you're here and got something. That's the whole point. My advice is – stick where you are. Tennant's a stupid ass to give up a decent berth; he deserves to fail. Of course, we should all like to see the world. *I* should –

Tennant It's more than that.

Charley Yes, yes, you don't understand. It isn't the idea of travelling – it's because you want to feel – oh! (*He stretches out his arms.*) I don't suppose you ever feel so –

Leslie Can't say I did.

Tennant Aren't you ever sick of the thing, Leslie?

Charley And don't you ever want to pitch all the ledgers into the dustbin and burn the stools?

Leslie Never – though I've met many that have. I tell you, it's a good thing to have a safe berth nowadays. Many fellows would only be too glad to pick up Tennant's berth – or yours, Wilson. Think of the crowds that will answer the advertisement at Molesey's. Last week our firm wanted a man to do overtime work, and they don't pay too high a rate – I can tell you. They had five hundred and fifteen applications – five hundred and fifteen! Think of that! And that's what would happen to you if you went, Wilson, and that'll be the end of Tennant. Sorry to be unpleasant – but truth –

Tennant But there's room on the land –

Leslie Land! What on earth can a bally clerk do with a spade? He'd be trying to stick it behind his ear –

Shout of laughter from **Percy Massey**.

He's got no muscle – he's got a back that would break if he stooped – he'd always have a cold in his nose –

Charley Shut it, Leslie. You can't call Tennant exactly anaemic. And look at this. (*He strips off his coat and turns back his shirt sleeves to display his arms.*) How's that?

Tennant *looks on with interest.* **Leslie** *comes near and pinches* **Charley**'s *arm, while* **Percy Massey** *looks on smilingly.*

Leslie All right for a back garden. I suppose you think you're an authority on the land question 'cause you grow sweet peas?

Charley (*digging his hands into the pockets without turning down his sleeves again*) I don't think anything of the kind. What I do know is that if I had a chance I could farm land with anybody. *Do* you think I chose this beastly business of quill-driving because it's the best work I know. Do you?

Leslie I don't suppose you chose it at all. Your father chose it for you.

Percy (*to* **Charley**) Well, I say, what's the matter with it?

Charley You wait till you're a few years older.

Leslie Wilson's caught the land fever. Take up an allotment – that'll cure you. Your garden isn't big enough. Have you got that map, Tennant?

Tennant It's in my room. Shall we go up?

Leslie Is there a fire?

Tennant No.

Leslie Bring it down, there's a good chap. I like to take things comfortable. I'll wait down here.

Tennant *goes out* R. **Leslie** *rises; goes back to the front room.*

Percy I say, Charley –

Charley Well?

Percy I've got a rise.

Charley Congratulations – wish I had.

Percy Foster's given me Beckett's job.

Charley And Beckett?

Percy Well, he's got the sack, you know. It's a bit rough on him, but I couldn't help it, could I?

Charley I suppose you're doing it cheaper?

Percy That's about the line. I'm awfully sorry for Beckett. He's not young, and it's awfully hard to get anything when you're middle-aged.

Charley So I believe. Well, anyhow, you're in luck – aren't you?

Percy Yes, it's sooner than I thought.

They sit in silence. **Tennant** *re-enters, and goes into inner room.*

I say, Charley, what did you start on?

Charley Eh? What d'ye mean?

Percy You – and – and Lily – you know.

Charley *looks at him steadily.*

Charley Oh, that's it, is it?

Percy You didn't begin with a house, of course.

Charley You know as well as I do that we had three rooms – and jolly small ones.

Percy Still you were comfortable.

Charley It was warm – winter and summer.

Percy It wasn't very expensive?

Charley You have to choose your housekeeper carefully.

Percy If you're going to chaff –

Charley Don't be an idiot. You've now got ninety, I suppose. You can manage on that.

Percy You really think so?

Charley I know from experience.

Percy You don't ask who the lady is?

Charley Sybil is a pretty little girl.

Percy Well, I suppose you did guess a bit.

Charley Not me! Maggie and Lil did it between them.

Percy Did it?

Charley Made the match – Maggie told me.

Percy (*indignantly*) They did nothing of the kind. I met Sybil here and . . .

Charley 'Um-um!

Percy We just came together – it was bound to be.

There is a sound of laughter outside and **Lily** *and* **Sybil** *are seen carrying in cakes and lemonade.*

Charley She *is* pretty –

Percy Yes, in rather an unusual –

Charley But so are others.

Percy I say, old man.

Charley Well, aren't they? I suppose you won't listen to advice.

Percy What about?

Charley You're too young to marry.

Percy I'm twenty-three. So were you when you married.

Charley I was too young.

Percy Do you mean . . .

Charley (*impatiently*) Oh, don't look so scandalised. No, I'm not tired of Lily. It's not that at all – but, are you satisfied to be a clerk all your life?

Percy I say, Tennant's upset you. Of course I'm satisfied to be a clerk.

Charley But *are* you?

Percy (*impatiently*) Don't I say so?

Charley Have you ever felt a desire to kick your hat into the fire? Have you?

Percy No! Not yet!

Charley Not yet. There you are – but you will. Don't you ever want to see anything more of the world – did you ever have that feeling?

Percy (*a little thoughtfully*) Well, I did once. I wanted to go out with Robinson. But the dad wouldn't consent. It was a bit risky, you know, and this job came along – and so I wouldn't go.

Charley Did Robinson come back?

Percy No, he's got a decent little place out there.

Charley They don't all fail, then?

Percy Of course not – but lots do. I might be one of those.

Charley Well, the thing is if you ever thought of doing anything now's your time. You can't do it afterwards. Take my tip and don't get engaged yet. You're too young to decide such an important question.

Percy No younger than you were – and I must say . . .

Charley Don't be so touchy – can't you see I'm talking to you for your good?

Percy I think you're crazed.

Charley (*sharply*) Why am I crazed, as you call it? Isn't it because I know a little what your life is going to be? Haven't I gone backwards and forwards to the city every day of my life since I was sixteen and am I crazed because I suggest it's a bit monotonous? (*Going close to* **Percy** *and putting his hand on his shoulder solemnly.*) I'm not saying she isn't the right girl for you – I'm only suggesting that perhaps she isn't! She's pretty and she's handy . . .

Percy I say! I won't have that.

Charley Don't. Pass it over. It's just this – think – and don't marry the first pretty girl and live in three rooms because your brother-in-law did it.

Percy She wasn't – the first pretty girl . . .

Sybil (*appearing at opening and smiling demurely*) Mrs Wilson says – Oh, Mr Wilson, have you been fighting?

Charley (*suddenly remembering that he has his coat off*) I beg your pardon. (*He pulls it on hastily.*) (*To* **Percy**.) Remember!

Percy (*with his eyes on* **Sybil**) Rot! (*Goes back with* **Sybil**.)

Lily (*coming towards him*) Who said anything about fighting? Now I suppose you've been arguing with everybody and shouted at them. You do get so cross when you argue – don't you, dear? Supper is quite ready. I sent Sybil to tell you. . . .

Charley Sybil's feeding Percy. She's got all her work cut out.

Lily How rude you are! Do you know, I'm quite angry with you. You've hardly been in the whole evening.

Charley Fenwick . . .

Lily Yes, I saw him. He looks so lifeless, don't you think?

Charley He says I shall grow like him.

Lily What an idea! Why, how could you?

The **Company** *move about the two rooms, the* **Men** *handing refreshments to the* **Women** *– they all come more forward.*

Leslie What do you think – ? I lost the 8.15 this morning!

Charley Should have thought it would have waited for you.

Leslie I left the house at the usual time and there was a confounded woman at the station with about five trunks and a paper parcel, who took up the whole doorway.

Much laughing from **Sybil** *and an encouraging smile from* **Lily**.

By the time I got over the train was gone. Never did such a thing in my life before.

Lily *You* haven't sung to us, Charley, dear.

Maggie He's tired.

Lily Not too tired for that, are you?

Sybil Oh, do, Mr Wilson, I know you sing splendidly. Per – Mr Massey told me so.

Percy S'sh! don't give me away – he's my brother-in-law.

Charley Not tonight, Lil – I – I'm a little hoarse.

Lily That's being out in the garden at all hours.

Leslie Don't say that, Mrs Wilson. Your husband wants to go as a farmer in the Colonies – and you'll discourage him.

Lily You silly man, Mr Leslie. (*To* **Charley**.) You must have something hot when you go to bed, dear.

Leslie I love being a little ill. My wife's an awfully good nurse.

Sybil I believe you put it on sometimes, Mr Leslie.

Leslie Well, do you know – I believe I do.

Ladies won't put their pretty fingers round your neck for nothing. But if you have a little hoarseness – not too much to be really unpleasant – or a headache is a very good thing – it is delightful – I always say to myself:
'O woman – in our hours of ease –
Uncertain, coy and hard to please,
When pain and anguish wring the brow,
A ministering angel thou.'

Lily We ought to have 'Auld Lang Syne' –

Tennant Please don't.

Lily It would be so nice for you to remember. (*Going up* L.) Yes, we must. Come. (*She puts out her hands and makes them all form a ring, with hands crossed and all round table.*)

Tennant *and* **Charley** *join most reluctantly and are not seen to sing a note.*

There! That's better.

Sybil Now I must go, Mrs Wilson.

Lily Must you really? Come and get your things.

They go out. A tapping is heard at the window in the near room – **Maggie** *runs and opens it.*

Voice Is my husband there, Mrs Wilson?

Leslie Y – es. I'm here. Coming, darling.

Sybil *and* **Lily** *re-enter* R.

Leslie My wife has sent for me home, Mrs Wilson.

Maggie Are you going over the wall?

Sybil Oh, do, Mr Leslie – I should love to see you.

Leslie If it will give you any pleasure it shall be done, though I am not at my best on the fence.

They all crowd round – he shakes hands, smiling profusely, and disappears through the window.

Voice Mind the flower-pot. No – not there – that's the dustbin. Not the steps.

There is a great shout to announce his safe arrival.

Leslie Safe!

Sybil I do think he is so funny!

Lily Yes, isn't he? Are you going by 'bus?

Percy *I'm* going Miss Frost's way.

Sybil (*much surprised*) Are you really?

Maggie How extraordinary!

Much kissing between **Sybil**, **Lily** *and* **Maggie**. **Sybil** *and* **Percy** *go out.*

Lily She's so sweet, isn't she? And Percy's so awfully gone.

Maggie (*as they start clearing away the dishes*) Very. So he was over Daisy Mallock and Ruby Denis – and who's the other girl with the hair?

Lily The hair? What do you mean?

Maggie The one with the hair all over her eyes – nice hair, too.

Lily Gladys Vancouver? Poor Percy – I'm afraid he is a little bit of a flirt.

Maggie He's got nothing else to do with his evenings.

Lily And then people like Mr Tennant think it's a dull life.

Maggie Well, good night all. No, don't come out, Mr Tennant – I'm quite a capable person.

Tennant Oh, but I shall – if you'll allow me.

Maggie I'd rather you didn't – still, if you will. (*They go out with* **Lily**.)

Charley *looks round and sighs with relief – he walks round, looks out of the window, then at the* *garden – he takes up the paper, but after trying in vain to settle to it, throws it on the floor – he re-fills his pipe and lights it. Re-enter* **Tennant**.

Tennant Well. (*He pauses, but* **Charley** *does not stir.*) I say, Wilson, I never thought you'd take it like this.

Charley *does not answer, but only shifts restlessly.*

I thought you'd think I was a fool too. In fact I was half ashamed to say anything about it. It wouldn't do for most people, you know. I'm in an exceptional position, and even in spite of that they call me an ass. I've got a little cash, too.

Charley (*quickly*) So have I.

Tennant Yes, but the cases are different. I can rough it.

Charley Let me have the chance to rough it.

Tennant You're married.

Charley *does not reply.*

You're settled. Your friends are here. I've got nothing and nobody to worry about.

They both smoke in silence.

I say, don't sit up and think. Go to bed.

Charley I'm going soon. Don't stay up, old chap.

Tennant You'll get over it.

He goes out. Enter **Lily** *– she pulls down blind and fastens catch of window.*

Lily I'm going up now. Don't be long. You look so tired.

Charley (*irritably*) Oh, don't fret about me. I'm a little worried, that's all.

Lily (*timidly*) Did Mr Fenwick bring bad news? He looked miserable enough.

Charley (*looking at her steadily*) Yes, I'm not going to have that rise.

Lily Oh, dear – what a shame! Why?

Charley Lots of reasons – but that's all.

Lily Of course, you're worried. Still – it might have been worse. You might have been sent away.

Charley Yes.

Lily It's very disheartening – after all we'd planned to do with it. You won't be able to have the greenhouse, now, will you, dear?

Charley (*with a short laugh*) What's the good of a greenhouse in that yard. It isn't that.

Lily (*a little timidly*) But we can manage very well, dear. We – you remember what I said this morning – about the other lodger.

Charley Oh, don't, for heaven's sake. It isn't losing the cash I mind; it's having to give in like this. I want to go to them and tell them to do their worst and get somebody else.

Lily But dear, you might lose your place.

Charley I should.

Lily But that – we couldn't afford that, could we? Why, we can manage quite well as we are. I can be very careful still –

Charley I'm tired of going on as we've been going.

Lily What do you want to do?

Charley I – I want to go away. (*Pause.*)

Lily And leave me?

Charley (*suddenly remembering*) Oh – er –

Lily It's just that horrid Mr Tennant –

Charley It's nothing to do with him – at least . . .

Lily I said it was. He wants you to go with him – and you want to go – you're tired of me –

Charley (*going up to her and trying to speak gently but being very irritated – his voice is sharp*) Oh, don't cry . . . you don't understand. Look, Lil, supposing I went and you came out afterwards.

Lily You want to go without me.

Charley I couldn't take you, dear, but I would soon send for you; it wouldn't be long.

Lily You want to go without me. You're tired of me.

Charley Oh, don't cry, Lil. I didn't say I was going. Of course I don't want to leave you, dear. You mustn't take any notice. (*Attempting to take her in his arms.*)

Lily (*turning away from him, sobs*) But you do . . .

Charley I don't want to go because I want to leave you . . .

Lily But you said . . .

Charley Never mind what I said. (*He kisses her and pets her like a child.*) Come, go to bed. It's the news – and the excitement about Tennant – and all that. Come, go to bed and I'll be up in a few minutes.

Charley *leads her to the door and coaxes her outside and stands at the door a few seconds, then he comes back into the room, stands still, looking round. He goes to the front parlour and hunts over the chairs and the piano as if in search of something. Finally he picks up a paper off the floor and brings it to table – it is the map of Australia. He opens it on the table and leans over it, his pipe unnoticed burning out in his left hand.*

Curtain.

Act Three

*Scene: the sitting-room at 'Sunnybank',
Hammersmith. There is no centre table, but there
are various small ones against the wall and in the
window. There is a piano, a tall palm in the
window, and one or two wicker chairs that creak.
The rest of the furniture is upholstered in
saddlebags with antimacassars over the sofa head
and armchairs. Gramophone in the corner. Big
mirror over mantelpiece. Gilt clock in glass case
and lustres.*

    Mrs Massey *is sleeping in one armchair.* **Mr
Massey** *is asleep on sofa, pulled across centre.*
Maggie *sits reading at small table.* **Maggie**
*softly rises and goes to fire. She pokes it and a
piece of coal falls out.* **Mrs Massey** *turns her
head.*

Maggie I'm so sorry, Mother, I tried to
poke it gently.

Mrs Massey I was hardly asleep, my dear.

Maggie Mother! – you've been sleeping for
half an hour!

Mrs Massey It didn't seem like it, dear.
Why, your father's asleep.

Maggie Isn't that extraordinary!

Mrs Massey (*admiringly*) How soundly he
sleeps! What's the time?

Maggie Four o'clock.

Mrs Massey I should have thought they'd
have been here now.

Maggie Not Percy and Sybil, I hope. You
don't expect *them*, until the last minute, do
you?

Mrs Massey No, dear – of course not.

Maggie I wouldn't walk the streets this
afternoon for any man.

Mrs Massey I don't suppose they find it
cold.

Maggie Oh, I daresay they're sitting in the
Park.

Mrs Massey I hope they won't be late for
tea. I shall want mine soon.

Maggie I'll put on the kettle now and
when Lil and Charley come, we will have
tea and not wait for the others. We'll have
it cosily in here. (*She goes out, returning with
kettle, which she puts on fire. Sits close to* **Mrs
Massey**.)

Maggie Mother!

Mrs Massey Yes.

Maggie Mother, did you love father when
you married him – very much, I mean,
very, very much!

Mrs Massey (*much astonished*) What a
question! Of course.

Maggie More than any other man you'd
ever seen?

Mrs Massey Of course!

Maggie More than everything and
everybody?

Mrs Massey *Of course!*

Maggie Well, there's something wrong
with me, then – or else with Walter. I don't
feel a bit like that. There's no 'of course'
with me. I wouldn't go and sit in the Park
with him this afternoon for anything.

Mrs Massey I suppose you've quarrelled?

Maggie No, we haven't. I wish we had.

Mrs Massey Maggie! Don't talk like that.

Maggie But I do. He wants me to marry
him next month.

Mrs Massey And a very good thing too.

Maggie He says he's found a house, and
wants me to go and look at it. *I* don't want
to see it.

Mrs Massey What's come over you lately? You used to be satisfied. Walter is very nice and attentive – in fact, quite devoted.

Maggie Yes, I know. Just like he was to his first wife, I expect.

Mrs Massey You've such an absurd prejudice against widowers, Maggie. You're jealous.

Maggie I'm not. Not a bit. But I do wish he would do something, and not worry about getting married.

Mrs Massey The poor man is doing something, I should think, running after you every spare minute, and house hunting.

Maggie I would much rather he went to Australia – or somewhere.

Mrs Massey That's that absurd Tennant man again. You're not in love with *him*, I hope?

Maggie (*promptly*) Not a scrap! I find him rather dull.

Mrs Massey Then what is it?

Maggie I should like Walter to go out and seek his fortune instead of getting it in a coal merchant's office.

Mrs Massey He mightn't come back.

Maggie (*thoughtfully*) Perhaps he wouldn't.

Click of gate.

Mrs Massey There's the gate, Maggie.

Maggie *goes out* R. *She comes back in a moment, followed by* **Lily**. **Lily** *goes to her mother and kisses her. She looks at her father.*

Lily Father asleep?

Maggie What a question. Shall I take your hat and coat?

Lily *takes them off and hands them to* **Maggie**.

You're shivering! Sit close to the fire. Aren't you well?

Lily (*in a pathetic voice*) Yes, I'm well, thank you.

Mrs Massey Are you alone?

Lily Charley is coming on. He's gone to the station with Mr Tennant.

Mrs Massey To see him off?

Lily No – Mr Tennant goes tomorrow.

Maggie *goes out with hat and coat. She brings back with her a tray, with cloth etc., and prepares for tea on a small table.*

Mrs Massey Have you got another lodger?

Lily No. We – we've got to have two.

Mrs Massey Two? What for?

Maggie *stops to listen.*

Lily They've reduced Charley's salary.

Mrs Massey (*sitting up energetically*) Reduced it? What for?

Lily I don't know – I . . . oh, I'm so miserable. (*She suddenly covers her face with her hands and sobs.*)

Maggie (*stooping over her*) Lil, dear, you're not crying over *that*, are you?

Lily (*sobbing*) Oh, no, no! It doesn't matter. We can make room for two lodgers quite well. I don't mind the work.

Maggie Then what is it?

Mrs Massey I suppose you and Charley have quarrelled?

Maggie Tell us, dear.

Lily Charley – wants – to go away – and leave me.

Mrs Massey What? What's this?

Lily (*looking apprehensively round at the sleeping figure*) Hush! don't wake father!

Maggie He won't wake till the tea-cups rattle. Charley wants to leave YOU!

Mrs Massey I *knew* they'd quarrelled.

Lily We haven't – not exactly – but he's been so *funny* ever since Mr Tennant said he was going to Australia. He wants to go too.

Mrs Massey What next? Charley ought to be ashamed of himself. Go to Australia indeed! He forgets he is married.

Lily I don't want him to stay just because he's married, if he wants to leave me.

Maggie You are quite *wrong*, I'm sure, Lil. He doesn't want to leave you at all. He wants to leave his work.

Mrs Massey Perhaps he does. So do other people very often. Suppose we all stopped work when we didn't like it? A pretty muddle the world would be in. Charley is forgetting there is such a thing as duty.

Lily He's very unhappy – and I – I can't make him happy.

Mrs Massey So he ought to be miserable with such ideas in his head. I never heard of such a thing! The sooner Mr Tennant goes the better. He's been putting Charley up to this, I suppose?

Maggie You don't know Mr Tennant, Mother. He's not that sort.

Mrs Massey Then what made Charley think of it at all?

Maggie It's just a feeling you get sometimes, Mother. You can't help it. Office work is awf'lly monotonous.

Mrs Massey Of course it is. So is all work. Do you expect work to be pleasant? Does anybody ever like work? The idea is absurd. Anyone would think work was to be pleasant. You don't come into the world to have pleasure. We've got to do our duty, and the more cheerfully we can do it, the better for ourselves and everybody else.

Lily I – I didn't mean to tell you.

Mrs Massey He ought to be talked to.

Lily Don't say anything, please – not yet. Perhaps after tea we can all talk about it, and it may do him good.

Maggie *goes out.* **Lily** *starts to arrange the tea-cups.* **Mr Massey** *rouses. Re-enter* **Maggie** *with tea-pot.*

Massey Tea?

Maggie Yes, Daddy.

Massey In here? There's no room.

Maggie It's cosy. I'll bring yours to the sofa.

Massey Where am I to put it? – on the floor?

Maggie I'll bring up a table for you if you must have one. You wouldn't do for a Society gentleman. Can't you balance a cup on your knee?

Massey I don't mean to try. Hope you haven't got out those finnicky little cups. I want my own.

Maggie I've got your own – here. (*She holds up a very big breakfast cup, plain white with gilt band.*)

Massey I didn't hear you come in, Lil. Where's Charley?

Lily Coming on.

Massey What've you done with Foster, Mag?

Maggie He's not coming.

Maggie *takes tea round.*

Massey Gone away for the weekend?

Maggie (*taking a cup for herself and sitting down beside* **Lily**) Oh, no! He's not coming. That's all. Lily and I are grass widows. It's a very nice feeling.

Massey It's all right about you, but Lil looks a bit off. You've got a cold. Your eyes are red.

Lily Yes, Father.

Mrs Massey You've dropped some bread and butter on the carpet, Alfred.

Massey (*irritably*) Of course I have! I knew I should.

Maggie (*running to pick it up*) Percy hasn't come back with Sybil yet, Dad. We expect they're sitting in the Park.

Massey (*his attention taken from his grievance*) What, in this weather?

Maggie The seats will be dry and they sit close together, you know. I've often seen them do it.

Massey (*chuckling*) You have, have you? And what about yourself? What about yourself? You! Lord! what a nest of turtle doves it is – nothing but billing and cooing!

Maggie Especially Percy.

Massey P'raps so. He's young at it. Well, he'll be the next, I suppose. And you, too, Mag?

Maggie I'm in no hurry.

Mrs Massey (*a little impatiently to* **Maggie**) Don't talk like that, my dear.

Massey Of course she says she isn't. She's a modest young woman – I never heard *you* say you were in a hurry, my dear.

Mrs Massey Of course I shouldn't – to you.

Massey Ha, ha! You put on the shy business then. Lord! these women. (**Maggie** *moves towards table.*) Come, now, Mag, confess! You think of it sometimes.

Maggie I think of it a lot.

Massey There you are! There you are! What did I say?

Maggie And what do you think I think about it?

Massey How should I know. Wedding, I suppose. I bet you never think of anything else after the wedding day.

Maggie (*slowly*) I think of the wedding dress, and the bridesmaids, and the pages. Shall I have pages, Mum?

Mrs Massey Maggie!

Maggie I suppose I shan't. I think of the house I'm going to have, Daddy – and the furniture, and I'm going to have a cat and a dog –

Massey (*slyly*) Nothing else, of course. Just a cat and a dog. Ha, ha!

Mrs Massey Alfred, don't suggest. It isn't nice.

Massey A cat and dog – ha, ha, ha!

Maggie Don't laugh, Daddy. I'm telling you the solemn truth – I think most of all that I shall never, never, never have to go into a shop again.

Massey I wish old Foster could hear you.

Maggie Why?

Massey He'd say – 'And where do I come in?'

Maggie Well, of course he'll be there. I wish –

Mrs Massey Maggie, my dear – I should

like a little more tea! Have you got some more hot water?

Maggie I'll get some. (*Goes out.*)

Massey It's all very well for her to chaff, but she ain't quite natural about this affair of hers. She ought to be more pleased – excited like.

Mrs Massey I think they've had a little quarrel. People often do. She's a little bit down about it. We've had a talk about it.

Massey Well, she can't have any quarrel about him himself. *He's* all right, and got a jolly soft job, too. He'll make her a good husband. He's insured for £500.

Mrs Massey Is he? That's very nice. If anything happened to him she'd be all right.

Massey He's a thoughtful sort of chap. Of course he's not exactly young, but he's steady.

Mrs Massey The poor child is jealous of his first wife.

Massey You don't say so? Jealous, is she? That's all right – that's a healthy feeling. I'm glad she's jealous, but she'll get over it once she's married. Jealous! Lord! Fancy, Mag too – I wouldn't have thought it. He'll be head clerk, one of these days – he can stay at Whitakers all his life. He told me.

Lily Do you think he'll ever get tired of it?

Mrs Massey What an idea!

Massey (*roaring*) Tired! Tired of what? A good job? Why ever should he be? He couldn't have anything better – Ten to half-past five every day of his life, except Saturdays, and then it's *one* – and three weeks' holiday. Think of that?

Lily But, I –

Enter **Maggie** *with hot water. The door-bell is heard.*

Mrs Massey Let them in, Lily, my dear – it's Percy and Syb.

Lily *goes out* R. *Re-enter* **Lily** *a moment after, followed by* **Percy** *and* **Sybil**.

Sybil *kisses* **Mrs Massey** *and* **Maggie**.

Sybil Aren't we dreadfully late, Mrs Massey? I'm *so* sorry!

Percy Awfully sorry, but my watch is –

Maggie Don't blame the poor thing – it's all right.

Massey The watch, was it? Come here, my girl!

Sybil *goes to him with giggling shyness. He takes her face between his hands.*

Was it the watch? Not a bit of it! It was this – (*He pats her cheek.*) these roses. Lucky young dog! Percy! (*He kisses her.*)

Maggie Rather cold in the Park, isn't it?

Percy Not very.

Maggie There's a northeast wind. Still, you can find a sheltered seat.

Percy Just beyond the glass house thing.

Maggie What did I tell you? (*Looking triumphantly round.*)

Sybil (*covering her cheeks*) What a tease you are, Maggie!

Massey Don't listen to her!

Percy You're only giving yourself away, Mag. What do you know about sheltered seats and glass houses?

Maggie It wasn't exactly guess work. (*Click of gate.*)

Mrs Massey There's Walter.

Maggie What?

Massey Isn't she surprised? Now isn't she surprised? Fancy! Walter!

Maggie He said he wasn't coming. (*She looks out of the window.*) Charley is with him.

Lily Will you open the door, Maggie?

Maggie (*almost at the same moment*) Go to the door, Percy.

Percy Well, you're two dutifully loving young women, I must say.

Maggie You forget – we're used to it. (**Percy** *goes out.*) Come, Sybil, and take off your things.

Exeunt **Sybil** *and* **Maggie**. *Enter* **Walter Foster**, *a man of about 35, prosperous looking, rather stout of build, and fair.* **Charley** *also enters, and* **Percy**.

Foster (*looking round for* **Maggie**) Good afternoon. (*Shakes hands with* **Mrs Massey** *and* **Massey**.)

Mrs Massey She's gone up with Sybil, Walter.

Foster Oh! I was afraid she was out, perhaps.

Massey Well, Charles, you're not looking spry.

Charley I'm a bit seedy – nothing much.

Massey And when's that madman lodger of yours going, eh?

Charley Tomorrow.

Massey Of all the fools he's the biggest I know.

The door opens, and **Sybil** *and* **Maggie** *come back.*

Maggie I was just telling Sybil, Percy, that tea is laid in the sitting-room. We didn't know when you'd be in.

She crosses up to **Foster** *and lifts her face to be kissed.*

Sybil Isn't she dreadful?

Massey Well, you won't be alone, don't you worry. Charley here wants some tea, and Lil will have to see he gets it, won't you, Lil?

Lily Yes, Dad.

Maggie (*to* **Foster**) Have you had tea?

Foster Yes, thanks.

Exeunt all, except **Massey**, **Maggie** *and* **Foster**.

Massey (*finally he looks at the two, then at the clock; poking the fire, then humming a little*) Have you seen the *Argus*, Mag?

Maggie In the kitchen. I'll get it. (*Makes a move to the door.*)

Massey No, no, I'm going out.

Goes.

Maggie Father calls that tact.

Foster (*coming over to her*) What?

Maggie Didn't you notice? He doesn't want the *Argus*, really.

Foster (*just understanding*) You mean he's left us together?

Maggie Yes.

Foster Awfully kind of him! I say, Maggie, you don't mind my coming, do you? I really had to. We – hadn't made arrangements about Tuesday.

Maggie *laughing a little sadly.*

Maggie And you couldn't write them? You are very good to me, Walter.

Foster Don't talk like that.

A pause.

Maggie, I – you haven't kissed me yet.

Maggie I did – when you came in.

Foster No – I kissed *you*.

Maggie I'm sorry – I – I don't care for kissing in front of people.

Foster (*getting bolder*) There's no one here now.

Maggie *rises, turns, and looking at him very straight, then lifts her face – pause – and going to him, kisses him on the lips. He keeps her close to him till she gently moves herself away.*

I've got something here – you said the other day you wanted – you would like one of those Dutch brooches.

He puts his hand in his coat pocket and brings out a little parcel.

Here it is!

Maggie (*unfastens it*) It *is* good of you! You are so thoughtful!

She looks at him.

I suppose – (*She kisses him again.*)

Delighted, he keeps hold of her hand. She looks at him and then at her hand imprisoned in his, and then away at the fire.

Foster What's the matter, dear?

Maggie (*impatiently drawing her hand away*) It's still the mood. I can't help it. I don't feel like love-making.

Foster All right, dear – I won't bother you.

Maggie Perhaps if you did bother – no, never mind. You know I asked you not to come today.

Foster Yes.

Maggie Well, I had no reason, except that I didn't feel like it. But I ought to feel like you always, didn't I?

Foster You're different from me. I always feel like you.

Maggie Walter, I don't want to settle down. I want to go and – and do things.

Foster What things, dear?

Maggie Oh, I don't know. (*A pause.*) Did you ever go abroad?

Foster Yes, to Paris, once at Easter.

Maggie Oh! just for a holiday. Wouldn't you just love to go out and try your luck? Have a change? – Do something with your hands? Aren't you ever tired of what you are doing?

Foster I can't say I am, really. Why should I? The work is not too hard, but you like change. I have a good salary, you know, dear. When we are married you can go about a lot, you'll be quite free.

Maggie No, I shan't.

Foster But you can have a servant and all that, you know.

Maggie Oh, yes – yes – I understand.

Foster If I went abroad – suppose it, for instance – I shouldn't have you, should I?

Maggie No, and a good thing for you. You deserve something better. You know – you *know*, Walter, that I don't love you half or a quarter as you love me.

Foster Yes, I know that. But you don't love anybody else.

Maggie No. Have you ever thought that I'm really marrying you to get out of the shop?

Foster Of course not. Of course you are glad to leave the shop because you don't like it. You are so tied.

Maggie I should love to be absolutely

independent, quite – altogether free for a whole year. Oh!

Foster (*a little hurt*) You will be free when you are married to me, Maggie. You can do anything you like.

Maggie (*looking at him despairingly for a moment, then suddenly going up to him*) You are a dear! – you are, really! Marry me quick, Walter!

He takes her in his arms delightedly.

Quick – or – or –

Foster Or what? (*Very tenderly.*)

Maggie Or I shall run away.

Foster And where would you run to?

Maggie Perhaps if I'd known where to run to – I should have gone before.

Foster Dearest, don't talk like that!

Maggie (*turning away a little*) But I don't! I'm safe!

Massey *is heard outside the door, coughing and making a noise. Enters.*

I'm afraid you've caught a cold in the kitchen, Daddy. I thought you went for the *Argus*?

Massey So I did. (*He looks down at it.*)

Maggie And you've brought the *Family Herald*. (*She takes it from him.*) *Enter* **Mrs Massey**, **Charley**, **Lily**, **Percy** *and* **Sybil**.

Mrs Massey Play something, Lily.

Lily *goes to piano and picks out some music.* **Sybil** *and* **Percy** *occupy one big chair between them.* **Charley** *stands idly at window, turning over an album.*

Percy Going to church, Mother?

Mrs Massey No, dear, it's a very nasty night. Such a cold wind.

Percy Last Sunday it was the rain – and the week before it was foggy, and the week before –

Sybil Don't be such a very rude boy!

She puts her hand over his mouth and he takes it and holds it.

Mrs Massey (*complacently*) You're a bad boy to make fun of your old mother. I went to church this morning.

Percy You're getting a oncer, Mother.

Mrs Massey Well, I should only go to sleep if I went.

Percy Think of the example you set if you put in an appearance.

Mrs Massey Yes, dear; I have thought of that, but it wouldn't do for them to see me asleep.

Foster (*who always has the effect of trying to smooth things over*) I'm sure it is better for you to rest, Mrs Massey, than walk such a distance twice a day!

Mrs Massey Yes, it is rather a long way. It's quite a quarter of an hour's walk, and I don't care to ride on Sundays.

Lily *plays, choosing the mournful hymn, 'Abide with me'.* **Charley** *fidgets, goes to the piano and then back again to the window.*

Massey Can't you find a seat, Charles? You look uncomfortable.

Charley Plenty, thanks. Sybil only has half a one.

Sybil Oh, Mr Wilson. (*She fidgets away from* **Percy**, *who pulls her back again.*)

Lily *has played the tune through. She stops.*

Mrs Massey That's such a nice tune, don't you think, Walter?

Foster Very! – *rather plaintive, but soothing.*

Lily *starts another – this time 'Sun of my Soul'.*

Charley For heaven's sake, Lil, play something cheerful.

Lily *stops, turns undecidedly on the stool, looks round imploringly at* **Charley**, *turns a few pages and then rises and goes out of the room hurriedly.*

Sybil She's crying!

Massey What?

Mrs Massey You've hurt her, Charley, speaking like that. There was nothing to get cross about. She came this afternoon crying.

Charley I've done nothing! I –

Exit **Mrs Massey** *in much indignation.*

Massey Had a tiff?

Charley A tiff – we don't tiff.

Massey Well, then, don't shout at her like that. (*To* **Sybil**.) Here – are you sure she was crying?

Sybil Yes, quite.

Massey That's queer. She didn't use to.

Charley She's been worrying, I expect. Women worry so quick.

Massey What's she got to worry about? A bit hysterical, perhaps.

Re-enter **Mrs Massey**.

Massey Is she better?

Mrs Massey She's got a headache, she says. But it isn't that; I know what's the matter. When she came today she could hardly speak –

Charley (*interrupting*) Is she worrying over me?

Massey What's she got to worry over you about?

Charley I happened to say – I got the hump, I think . . . I feel a bit restless . . .

Mrs Massey (*hotly*) You know what it is well enough. You want to go away with that Tennant man and leave your wife –

Massey (*shouting*) What!

Sybil *looks shocked,* **Percy** *astonished, while* **Foster** *tries to pretend he didn't hear.*

Mrs Massey The poor child's breaking her heart because she says he wants to leave her.

Charley I never said anything of the kind – I never thought of such a thing, I –

Mrs Massey *Do* you want to go away with that man?

Massey I should think you're mad, both of you, to talk about it. Go with who? What for? What're you talking about?

Mrs Massey Lily told me distinctly this afternoon that Charley wanted to go to Australia. She nearly cried her eyes out. Of course that means he wants to leave her. What else could it mean? She said he'd been funny and she was miserable. I said Charley ought to be ashamed of himself to want to go away like that, and so I think so.

Massey (*sitting up very straight and looking angry*) What's all this, Charley? What . . .

Foster *on tiptoe slowly goes to door.*

Charley Don't go, Foster. Let's have all the family in. You're going to be part of it some day.

Foster (*sitting down again*) I'm quite ready to go.

Charley No, don't. Let's have it out. You may as well know, all of you.

Mrs Massey (*with a resignation of despair*)
Then you do want – to go and leave her?
It's disgraceful!

Charley (*angrily*) What stuff you all talk!
I –

Mrs Massey Do you or do you not want to
go?

Charley Yes, I do!

General consternation.

Mrs Massey There! I said so.

Enter **Maggie.**

How's the poor dear?

Maggie She says her head is better and she
will come down in a minute. What's the
matter?

Mrs Massey Charley wants to go to
Australia and leave his wife. He's *told* us so.

Charley Well, suppose it was true,
wouldn't it be better than going without
telling you? But it isn't true.

Massey Do you want to take Lil with you?

Charley How could I?

Enter **Lily** – *all mutter words of encouragement.
General movement towards her. Everybody offers
chairs in sympathy. She sits by her father.*

Charley Look here now, just listen! It's
quite true I want to go. I want to do as
Tennant's done, chuck everything and try
my luck in the Colonies. As soon as I had a
fair start Lil would come out.

Massey (*interrupting*) Yes, and suppose you
failed? You should have thought of that
before you married. You can't run off when
you like when you've a wife.

Charley (*excitedly*) But why not?

Mrs Massey (*interrupting*) Why not? – just
hear him.

Charley It's that I'm just sick of the office
and the grind every week and no change! –
nothing new, nothing happening. Why, I
haven't seen anything of the world. I just
settled down to it – why? – just because
other chaps do, because it's the right thing.
I only live for Saturday –

Percy So do I! – so does everybody!

Charley But they shouldn't –

Percy You don't mean to suggest, I hope,
that we ought to *like* our work, do you?

Massey Do you suppose I like plumbing?
Do you think I ever did? No, but I stuck to
it, and now look at me, got a nice little bit
in the bank and bought my own house.
(*Looks proudly round.*) Of course, I hated it,
just as you do.

Maggie Then why didn't you try
something else, Daddy?

Massey I like that! What could I do? I was
taught plumbing. We don't have choice.
Your grandfather put me to it, and of
course I stuck to it.

Maggie But why didn't you ask for a
choice?

Massey Me! Why should I do such a
thing? Father was a plumber, and if it was
good enough for him, it was good enough
for me. Suppose I had thrown it up and
gone to Canada for a lark? A *nice* thing for
my family. (*To* **Maggie**.) You wouldn't
have had the education you've had, my
girl. We've got to live somehow, and if you
get a good job stick to it, say I – none of
your highty flighty notions. Live 'em down!

Foster (*gently*) We all have moments of
discontent, I fancy, but we get over them.

Maggie (*turns to* **Foster**) Did you ever have
any?

Foster A long time ago, but I'm quite safe
now, dear.

Maggie *shrugs her shoulders and turns half away impatiently.*

Charley I never said you couldn't live them down. I never said, did I, that I was going away? I only said I should like to. Did I ever say more, Lil?

Lily (*meekly*) No, dear.

Mrs Massey But you shouldn't want to. It's ridiculous.

Charley It wasn't till Tennant started about his going –

Mrs Massey I knew it was that man Tennant –

Charley . . . that I thought of it. But if he threw up his job, I thought, why shouldn't I?

Massey Because he's a fool, you needn't be another.

Maggie He's not a fool, and I wish Charley could go, too.

Lily Maggie, how can you?

Maggie (*crossing to fireplace*) Why should a young man be bound down to one trade all his life? I wish I were a man – I'd –

Mrs Massey Well, you're not, so it doesn't matter.

Charley Of course it must make a difference my being married.

Massey Remember your wife's here and don't talk as if you were sorry about it.

Charley (*turning on them fiercely*) For heaven's sake, can't you listen fair? My wife needn't go to her father for protection from me! I'm not a scoundrel just because I've got an idea, am I?

A pause – nobody answers.

But I'll tell you what, marriage shouldn't tie a man up as if he was a slave. I don't want to desert Lily – she's my wife and I'm proud of it – but because I married, am I never to strike out in anything? People like us are just cowards. We seize on the first soft job – and there we stick, like whipped dogs. We're afraid to ask for anything, afraid to ask for a rise even – we wait till it comes. And when the boss says he won't give you one – do we up and say, 'Then I'll go somewhere where I can get more'? Not a bit of it! What's the good of sticking on here all our lives? Why shouldn't somebody risk something sometimes? We're all so jolly frightened – we've got no spunk – that's where the others get the hold over us – we slog on day after day and when they cut our wages down we take it as meek as Moses. We're not men, we're machines. Next week I've got my choice – either to take less money to keep my job or to chuck it and try something else. You say – everybody says – keep the job. I expect I shall – I'm a coward like all of you – but what I want to know is, why can't a man have a fit of restlessness and all that, without being thought a villain?

Foster But after all, we undertake responsibilities when we marry, Mr Wilson. We can't overlook them.

Charley I don't want to. But I don't think we ought to talk as if when a man gets married he must always bring in just the same money.

Foster If you have the misfortune to have your salary reduced, nobody would blame you.

Charley I don't know. I felt a bit of a beast when I had to tell Lil about that.

Maggie (*suddenly*) If you went away, Lily could come and live with us.

Mrs Massey (*scandalised*) How could she?

Everybody would think she was divorced or something.

Foster Live with *us*, dear?

Maggie (*impatiently*) No, here, I meant.

Charley I've got a little cash put by that she could live on. *Don't* cry, Lil, for heaven's sake! Can't any of you see my point – or won't you?

Massey I suppose you're a Socialist.

Charley Doesn't anybody but a Socialist ever have an idea?

Massey They're mostly mad, if that's what you mean. And they're always talking about the wickedness of the boss and the sweetness of the working man.

Charley I never said anything about either, and I'm not a Socialist.

Percy You'll be better when Tennant's gone.

Charley (*viciously*) Just you wait till you're two years older, my boy.

Foster You see it isn't as if you had any prospects in the Colonies. Has Mr Tennant?

Charley He's got an introduction to a firm.

Massey What's the good of that?

Lily (*tearfully*) Perhaps I could go with Charley. I'm quite willing to – rough it a little.

Maggie You'd help him more by staying here.

Mrs Massey He doesn't want her. He said so.

Lily (*still tearfully*) If Charley really means it – I think – I –

Mrs Massey My dear, don't think anything about it. It's worrying you and

making you ill – you want nursing, not frightening. (*This with a glare of indignation at* **Charley**.)

Lily I'm all right.

Charley (*suddenly dropping his defiance*) Oh, let's go home, Lil. You're tired.

Mrs Massey Have you just noticed that?

Maggie Mother!

Mrs Massey She's my child, and if her husband won't think of her, I must.

Lily Mother, dear, Charley means all right. I'm sure he does. Yes, dear – I'm quite ready to go.

Foster (*with the air of pouring oil on troubled waters*) Well, at any rate, it needn't be settled tonight. Perhaps after a night's rest –

Maggie (*vehemently*) I like impulse.

Massey I expect you do. You don't know what's good for you.

Maggie Well, at any rate, Daddy, you can't say I have much. There's not much chance at Jones & Freeman's.

Percy So you've caught it, too, Mag.

Sybil Don't tease.

Enter **Lily**, *dressed for going out, also* **Mrs Massey**. **Lily** *goes round, kissing and shaking hands, with a watery smile and a forced tearful cheerfulness.*

Charley (*without going all round and calling from the door*) Good night, all!

Exeunt **Lily** *and* **Charley**.

Mrs Massey Well, I must say –

Percy Oh, let's drop it, Mother. Play something, Maggie.

Maggie I don't want to.

Mrs Massey Walter would like to hear something, wouldn't you, Walter?

Foster If Maggie feels like it.

Maggie She doesn't feel like it.

Massey Be as pleasant as you can, my girl – Charley's enough for one evening.

Maggie *goes to the piano and sitting down plays noisily with both pedals on, the chorus 'Off to Philadelphia'.*

Mrs Massey Maggie, it's Sunday!

Maggie I forgot!

Mrs Massey You shouldn't forget such things – Sybil, my dear –

Sybil I don't play.

Massey Rubbish! Come on!

Sybil *goes to the piano and* **Percy** *follows her.*

Percy (*very near to* **Sybil** *and helping to find the music*) Charley is a rotter! What d'ye think he was telling me the other day?

Sybil I don't know.

Percy Told me to be sure I'd got the right girl.

Sybil Brute!

Percy What do you think I said? Darling!

Kisses her behind music.

Massey (*looking round*) Take a bigger sheet.

Sybil *sits at piano quickly and plays the chorus to 'Count your many Blessings'.*

To which they all sing –

Count your blessings, count them one by
    one,
Count your blessings, see what God has
    done.
Count your blessings, count them one by
    one,

And it will surprise you what the Lord has
    done.

Curtain.

Act Four

Scene: sitting-room at 55 Acacia Avenue. Early morning.

Lily *discovered, cutting sandwiches. Ring at door.*
Lily *admits* **Maggie**, *who is dressed for the shop.*

Lily (*rather nervously*) You, Maggie! How early. What is it?

Maggie I've come to help Mr Tennant off, Lil. Where's Charley? Is he up?

Lily Oh, yes. (**Maggie** *goes to the garden door and stands looking out.*) He's been up a long while.

Maggie So the great day has come. (*Turning.*) Is Charley going, or isn't he, Lil?

Lily (*nervously and avoiding* **Maggie**'*s eyes*) No, of course not.

Maggie Why not?

Lily Because – why, how can he? (*Tearfully.*) Don't speak in that tone, Maggie.

Maggie He would have decided to go, if you had encouraged him.

Lily I *did* encourage him. You heard me last night. I told him – and I told him again after we got home – 'If you want to go, I'll never stand in your way'.

Maggie Yes, I heard. Is that how you told him last night?

Lily It doesn't matter how I said it. He'll get over it. Everybody says he will – except you. And how could he go? It's just an idea he's got over Mr Tennant.

Maggie (*angrily*) Of course it's Mr Tennant. Everybody speaks as if Mr Tennant was a wicked person going round tempting poor husbands to desert their wives. 'It's all that Mr Tennant.' 'What a blessing when that man goes,' etc., etc., as if he had a bad character. The truth is, that he's done a jolly good thing. He's stirred us all up. He's made us dissatisfied.

Lily What's the good of that? Nobody can make things different if they wanted to.

Maggie Don't talk nonsense. Hasn't he made things different himself? (*Getting a little heroic.*) Heaps of fellows in London go on doing the same old thing, in the same old way, only too glad if it's safe. Look how everybody runs for the Civil Service. Why? Because it's safe, of course, and because they'll get a pension. Look at the post-office clerks and Somerset House and lawyers' clerks and bank clerks –

Lily Bank clerks don't get pensions –

Maggie I know they don't, but once in a bank, always in a bank. Is there anything to look forward to – and aren't they all just – exactly *alike*? I once went past a lot of offices in the city – I don't know what sort of offices they were. But the windows had dingy drab blinds, and inside there were rows and *rows* of clerks, sitting on high stools, bending over great books on desks. And over each there was an electric light under a green shade. There they were scribbling away – and outside there was a most beautiful sunset. I shall never, never forget those men.

Lily They don't have long hours.

Maggie (*promptly*) Nine to six.

Lily I always thought it was ten to four.

Maggie Don't you believe it. That's what I thought once. You're thinking of the bank clerks, of course. My dear, the doors close at half-past three or four – but the clerks – why, they never see the daylight.

Lily In the summer they do.

Maggie (*impressively*) I don't care what you say, or what anybody says, it's not right. And if the men have got used to it, it's all the worse. They want stirring up – and it's the women who've got to do the stirring.

Lily Whatever can *they* do?

Maggie Lots. It's the women who make the men afraid. In the old days the women used to help the men on with their armour and give them favours to wear, and send them forth to fight. That's the spirit we want now. Instead of that we say to the men: – 'I shouldn't trouble, my dear, if I were you. You're safe here. Do be careful.'

Lily You're very unjust. Look at the Boer War, and how brave the women were then.

Maggie That isn't the only kind of war. Is a soldier to be the only kind of man, that a woman's going to encourage? Can't she help the man who wants to make a better thing of life? Oh, what a lovely chance you had and didn't take it, Lil!

Lily How can you talk like that! What a fuss you're making over a little thing.

Maggie It wasn't a little thing. Here is Charley, with all sorts of 'go' in him and fire and energy. Why couldn't you go to him and say, 'I'm proud of you. Throw up the horrid business and go and seek your fortune.' It was all he wanted, I do believe. Instead of which, he's got every blessed person against him – wife, mother-in-law, father-in-law, and all his friends and relations, and everything he can have. Everybody thinks him mad.

Lily *You* ought to have married him, I should think!

Maggie Don't get spiteful, Lil!

Lily Wait till you're married yourself to Walter –

Maggie I'm not going to marry Walter.

Lily (*struck with astonishment*) You're not going to marry Walter? Maggie!

Maggie I've broken it off. I did it last night.

Lily Whatever for? Did you quarrel? You were a little touchy last night, I thought – but Walter is so good tempered.

Maggie I'm sure it's very good of him, but I don't wish to be forgiven and taken back. It was all through Mr Tennant.

Lily (*anxiously*) You don't love *him*?

Maggie (*exasperated*) No, I'm not in love with *anybody*; but all last week I was thinking and thinking, and it wasn't till last night that I found I was just marrying – to get away from the shop!

Lily But he was *devoted* to you and so kind.

Maggie I don't want kindness. My shopwalker is very kind where I am, and I don't see any need to change.

Lily How extraordinary you talk!

Maggie Well, when I heard Charley talking last night, I thought what a fool I was to throw up one sort of – cage – for another.

Lily But you *are* free when you're married –

Maggie Nobody is – more especially the woman. But the thing is, I shouldn't want to be, if I loved the man. But I don't love Walter, only his house. Now, I can leave the shop any day, when I've saved enough – and run away. But I couldn't run away from Walter.

Lily (*horrified*) Run away –

Maggie (*suddenly beginning to laugh*) Can you see me? Running away from Walter? *Walter!* Oh! (*She laughs, but* **Lily** *looks very grave.*)

Lily You don't take the matter seriously.

Maggie It shows how seriously I do take it. Have you ever heard of any girl, throwing up a good match, who wasn't dead serious?

Tennant *enters.*

Tennant Good morning. Oh, good morning, Miss Massey.

Lily You're ready for breakfast, aren't you?

Goes out.

Maggie Aren't you surprised to see me here? I wanted to give you a send off.

Tennant Awfully good of you.

Maggie You're quite a hero in my eyes, you know, and I feel I must cheer or do something extra. (**Lily** *comes in with porridge.*)

Lily You'll have some, won't you, Maggie?

Maggie Thanks. Here, I'll pour out the tea.

Lily *goes out.*

(*To* **Tennant**.) Aren't you just frightfully excited?

Tennant Can't say I am.

Maggie (*sighing and looking admiringly at him*) I should be *wild*, absolutely wild, if I were going.

Tennant I'm going to chance it, you know. There's no fortune waiting for me.

Maggie That's the point of it. You know it's awfully unsettling, all this talk about Australia. You've made me so dissatisfied. I don't feel I can go back to the shop.

Tennant (*easily*) You'll get over that.

Maggie Oh, I suppose so.

Lily *enters with toast and puts it down beside him.*

Tennant (*turning*) Please don't bring anything else, Mrs Wilson. I can't eat it.

Lily But it's such a journey to the boat.

Tennant Oh, that's nothing – besides, I've got these sandwiches. (*Laying his hand on the package near him.*)

Lily Are you sure there are enough? I can soon cut some more.

Tennant Heaps, thanks. (*Earnestly.*) Really, I shan't know what to do with them.

Lily I'll put you an apple or two in.

Tennant No, don't –

Lily Oh, but they won't take up much room.

Tennant (*resignedly*) Thanks very much.

Charley *enters.*

Lily Oh, there you are. You'll have breakfast now, dear, won't you?

Charley I'll have it later. You here, Mag?

Maggie Of course. Do you think this great event could go off without me?

Lily *and* **Maggie** *go out.*

Tennant (*smilingly*) Miss Massey seems to think it's a sort of picnic.

Charley (*absently*) Does she?

Tennant She'd marry well out there, I daresay.

Charley Would she?

Tennant She looks strong and healthy. Her sort get snapped up in no time.

Charley You're catching the 10.15, aren't you?

Tennant (*surprised*) Yes. Why? Coming to the station?

Charley There's another just after twelve –

Tennant, *who has been swinging his chair backwards, comes to a pause as* **Charley** *comes up to him.*

Tennant Is there? I don't know. But what –

Charley (*lowering his voice*) Look here, old chap, suppose I come too?

Tennant What!

Charley (*who keeps his voice rather low the whole time, though visibly excited*) Don't shout! I haven't told anybody – but I mean it. I want you to look out for me at Plymouth.

Tennant But, Wilson – I say – you –

Charley Don't! It's all settled. There's no use arguing. I've made up my mind. I'm going to leave here as usual and come on by the second train and pick you up at Plymouth. Don't stare like that – I've thought it all out –

Tennant But your wife – your people here – you can't do it. When I've gone, you'll get over it.

Charley Get over it? I'm not going to get over anything. I've been a coward, see? – and now I'm going to cut and run. It's no good telling *Lil* – she wouldn't understand – but when I'm out there and get something and making a tidy little place for her, she'll be all right. She's nervous – the women are like that, you know – they can't help it – and her people, too – well, they're old, and when you're old, you're afraid.

Tennant (*interrupting*) You mean to go! Today?

Charley Why not? Why not? If I put it off, I'll never go. It wants a bit of doing, and if

you don't do these things at the time, well, you give in. I've packed a bag with some things – I did it this morning.

Tennant That's why you were up so early –

Charley I have written a note to Lil. (*Argumentatively.*) It's the only thing to do – there's no other way – I say, Freddy, you'll stand by me? It's easy for chaps like you –

Morton Leslie *crosses behind sitting-room window.*

Tennant (*uneasily*) Well – you know best –

Charley Of course – it's the only thing –

The door opens and voices can be heard outside, laughing.

Who's this coming? It's that ass . . .

He rises as **Maggie**, **Lily** *and* **Morton Leslie** *enter.*

Leslie (*a little short of breath*) Where's that fool? Thought I'd come and give you a goodbye kiss, old fellow. I would cry, but I've only brought one handkerchief.

Maggie Lily will lend you one of Charley's. But won't you miss the 8.15? Do be careful.

Leslie Miss Maggie, I'll tell you a great, an awful secret. (*He goes to her and says in a loud whisper.*) I mean to miss it.

Maggie I don't believe it – you couldn't do such a thing.

Leslie (*to* **Charley**) Well, Wilson, how is it? You look –

Charley (*curtly*) I'm all right. You don't expect me to laugh all the time, do you?

Leslie Certainly not. I'm afraid you're still pining for the flesh pots – or is it coconuts –

Charley No, it's gourds –

Tennant Tin mugs, you mean.

Leslie Take my word for it, before a week's out, you'll be thankful you're sitting opposite your own best tea service, on a Sunday afternoon.

Charley I say, it's about time you were off, Freddy.

Tennant (*looking at his watch*) So it is.

Lily You're sure you've got everything. (*To* **Tennant**.)

Leslie *Don't* forget to write, please – and *do* let us know what boat you're coming back by.

Tennant (*laughing*) Shut up! Where did I put my cap?

They all make a rush for the cap, and **Maggie** *brings it from the hall.*

Charley (*picking up a paper off the table*) Here, is this yours?

Tennant Another map – it doesn't matter. Burn it.

Charley Australia!

Tennant (*looking at* **Charley**) Put it in the fire.

Charley (*defiantly*) It might be useful. (*He opens it and fixes it with a pin against the wall.*)

Lily Now we shall be able to follow your travels, shan't we?

Leslie The time has come! Well, goodbye – old man. Allow me to prophesy you'll soon be back – remember what I said –

Maggie (*from the door*) It's a most glorious morning! The sun is shining for you, Mr Tennant – and there's not a cloud in the sky.

Leslie I hope you won't lose *all* your money –

Maggie The sea will be all beautiful with the dearest little ripples.

Leslie And if by any wonderful stroke of luck you do make anything, let us know. Goodbye.

Maggie All the men are running off to the city – but *you're* going to Australia.

Tennant *is rushed out.* **Lily** *and* **Charley** *follow him.* **Maggie** *runs in quickly and opens the sitting-room window, through which* **Tennant** *can be seen shaking hands again and again with* **Charley** *and* **Lily**.

Maggie Good luck!

Leslie (*shouting through window*) Give my love to What's-his-name, the Prime Minister!

Maggie (*sings*) 'For I've lately got a notion for to cross the briny ocean.'

Leslie (*joining*) 'And I'm off to Philadelphia in the morning.'

Leslie *drawls out the last word, bursts out laughing and turns away.*

Maggie Anybody would think you were excited.

Leslie If a man *will* be a fool, Miss Maggie, he may as well go away a happy fool. A cheer costs nothing. So much for *him*. Now it's me.

Maggie How many trains *have* you missed?

Leslie (*seriously*) Quite two, I should think. But I promise you it shan't happen again.

Goes out. **Charley** *and* **Lily** *enter.*

Lily (*wiping her eyes*) So he's gone. Poor man, I do hope he'll get on all right.

Charley (*easily and in a brighter tone*) He'll be all right. He can stand a little roughing.

Lily It was such a pity you couldn't get the time to go and see him off, dear.

Charley Oh, that's nothing.

Lily I'll have breakfast ready for you soon.

Goes out.

Charley There's no hurry.

Maggie *is looking at the map.*

Maggie It's a big place.

Charley Um. A chance to get some fresh air there.

Maggie (*turning*) So you're not going after all?

Charley Oh – er – how can I, Mag?

Maggie It means such a lot, of course.

Charley Courage or cheek – I don't know which. Of course, it's quite a mad idea – any fool can see that.

Maggie You're not a fool. It's the others who're fools. If only you could hold out a little longer. Lil would be all right. She might fret a little at first – but she's the clinging sort –

Charley But think what everybody would say!

Maggie You're getting over it already!

Charley What else can I do? I – I – shall settle down.

Maggie Settle down! Charley – why should you? *I've* refused to settle down. Why can't you?

Charley What do you mean? What's it got to do with you?

Maggie (*triumphantly*) I've refused to marry Walter.

Charley (*surprised, but not particularly interested*) What on earth for?

Maggie It was all through Mr Tennant –

Charley Tennant? You're –

Maggie (*impatiently*) Oh, dear, NO. I'm not pining for him. But I found out, when there was all this talk about Mr Tennant, that I was marrying Walter because I wanted to be safe and was afraid of risk. Then I made up my mind I wouldn't do that. I tell you because – if a girl can risk things – surely a man –

Charley There wasn't any risk for you with Walter. I can't see it.

Maggie A woman isn't tested in the same way as a man. It's the only way I have –

Charley Well, you know best, and if you don't like him – but everybody thought you did. I must say you've been rather hard on Foster. You led him on. I should have thought it was rather a good thing for you. Still . . .

Maggie (*sighing*) So it's no good, then, saying anything?

Charley (*uneasily*) No – er – (*Turning to her.*) Mag! What would you really think of me if I did?

Maggie What? (*Looks at him for a second.*) Charley – will you – after all?

Charley Supposing I don't give in – supposing I did go –

Maggie Do you mean it?

Charley Are you sure about Lil – I'm ready to throw up everything –

Maggie I would look after her – she would be all right in a week – I would do anything –

Charley But if I go it must be at once – at once, you understand.

Maggie Yes, yes . . .

Charley And if Lil thinks me a brute beast for leaving her like this – in this way – you'll explain – you'll stick up for me –

Maggie This way? I don't –

Charley I'm going today, Mag. I've arranged everything. I couldn't stand it. I had to go. I've written to Lil. She'll be all right for money – I've thought of that and I shall soon send for her. I know I shall, and then she'll be glad I did it. I look a brute, but, Mag, it's got to be. (*Postman's knock on front door.*) Hush! Here comes Lil – don't breathe a word –

Maggie Today!

Lily *enters with letters.*

Lily Here's the post. Two for you, dear. (*Gives letters to* **Charley** *who, however, doesn't look at them, but goes up to map.*)

Maggie (*quickly*) I'll call back for you, to go to the station.

Charley All right.

Maggie *goes out hurriedly.*

Lily I'm sure you're ready for breakfast now, dear – and you won't have very much time.

Charley I'm not very hungry.

Lily It was so nice of Mr Leslie to come in like that, wasn't it?

Charley Yes. He means all right.

Lily (*as he eats*) They're very nice neighbours. I think we're very lucky to have them.

Charley Um. You were up very early. You'll be tired tonight.

Lily These things don't often happen, do they, and I can keep better hours in future. We generally go along so regularly, don't we?

Charley (*suddenly turning from his breakfast*) Yes.

Lily I've been thinking, dear, that we shall feel a little dull tonight without Mr Tennant. Shall we go to the theatre? – something light –

Charley Oh – no – I don't think so –

Lily Shall we ask the Leslies for whist?

Charley (*rising*) No – not them – it doesn't matter, Lil – unless you'd rather.

Lily Oh, I shall be quite happy at home, by ourselves. I am so glad you would prefer that, dear. (*She goes up to him.*)

Charley I haven't been up to much in the company line lately, have I?

Lily You'll be better now, dear. What time shall you be home?

Charley Oh – er – you know my usual –

Lily Yes, dear. Don't be late. I've got something to tell you – which will please you, I think.

Charley Have you?

Lily Would you like to hear it now?

Charley Is it important?

Lily *Is* it important? You'll have to be such a good man soon, dear – you'll have to set a good example.

Charley (*uneasily*) What do you mean?

Lily Can't you guess? How dull you are! Bend down and let me tell you. (*She pulls down his face and whispers.*)

Charley (*pulling himself away*) What! God! (*Taking her by the arms.*)

Charley (*turning away a second, and then turning back*) Is that true?

Lily Yes, dear.

Charley Lil – I . . .

Lily You *are* pleased! But of course you are.

Charley Of course, dear.

Lily Isn't it lovely to think of! And can't you imagine mother as grandmamma! Won't she be a fuss! Why, you're quite overcome. There! Go away and get ready. You didn't open your letters. There's the door. I suppose it's Maggie back.

Lily goes out, and re-enters a moment after with **Maggie**. *They meet* **Charley** *going out, and* **Maggie**, *looking at him almost stops him.*

Maggie What have you been saying to Charley, Lil?

Lily Why?

Maggie I thought he looked a little – upset . . .

Lily He is rather. He's quite overcome, in fact. But then he would be, of course.

Maggie *closes door, still looking at* **Lily**.

Maggie What about?

Lily What could I tell him, that would make him more pleased than anything else?

Maggie I'm sure I don't know.

Lily What generally happens when people are married?

Maggie That! (*Pause.*) Lily!

Lily Charley is delighted.

Maggie (*unconsciously speaking her thought*) So you've *got* him after all.

Lily (*indignant*) Maggie!!

Maggie Why did you tell him *now*?

Lily *goes out, a little indignant.* Charley *enters from kitchen, dressed for the office.*

Maggie Charley!

Charley What's up? Don't rot, Mag!

Maggie And now –

Charley Oh, let's drop it. I was a fool all along – a bit of a beast, too – it's done with . . .

Maggie But –

Charley What's the good of talking? Don't make me out more of a brute than I am! No, the thing was meant to be! I was mad. After all, a man can't do just what he likes! It's better as it is. If this hadn't happened I should have done it – and a pretty mess, I daresay, I'd have been in – and dragged her in, too –

Maggie If –

Lily *enters.*

. . . I don't think I can wait for you, after all, Charley.

Charley Don't trouble.

Maggie Goodbye.

She goes.

Lily You didn't open your letters, dear.

Charley What are they?

Lily (*tearing one open*) About the new lodger – very quick replies . . .

Charley (*hastily*) Oh, leave them over.

Lily Ready?

Charley (*moving his neck uneasily in the high collar*) Yes – this beastly collar.

Lily It's a pity they make you wear such things.

Charley I've got a short neck. I suppose you shouldn't be a clerk, if you've got a short neck. It doesn't fit the collars.

Lily What an idea!

Charley *stands looking at the map a moment.*

Suddenly he tears it down and throws it into the fire.

Charley Goodbye, Lil. (*He kisses her.*)

Lily Goodbye, dear.

He picks up his silk hat and gloves and puts the hat on as he reaches the door. **Lily** *runs to the door.*

Goodbye.

Charley (*from outside*) Goodbye.

There is a sound of the front door slamming. **Lily** *starts chorus of hymn:*

Count your blessings, count them one by
    one.
Count your blessings, see what God has
    done, etc.

Curtain.

Rutherford and Son

Githa Sowerby

Githa Sowerby (1876–1970)

Rutherford and Son was first performed in John Leigh's matinée season at the Court Theatre on 31 January 1912 and the three subsequent afternoons. It then transferred to the Little Theatre on 18 March and to the Vaudeville on 22 April where, with only two changes in the cast, it was performed for the rest of the season: a total of 133 performances. It was performed at the Little Theatre in New York in December 1912, with several members of the same cast, 'staged' by Norman McKinnel who played Rutherford to great acclaim. It was revived by Mrs Worthington's Daughters in June 1980 and again by Southern Lights at New End in September 1988.

The play was very well received in 1912, being hailed in the press as 'a remarkable play' of 'unmistakeable, if undisciplined, power' (unidentified cuttings, British Theatre Association library) and described in the *English Review* as a play which has 'astonished London' and which 'in many ways is the most virile work we have seen for some years' (May 1912). Several reviewers compared it to *Chains*, John Palmer in the *Saturday Review* writing of both plays being 'the work of an aesthetic puritan. . . . The conscientiousness and hard logic of a woman applied to the theatre are able to go surprising lengths. These plays of Miss Elizabeth Baker and Miss Sowerby are really astonishing examples of what can be done in a modern theatre by keeping strictly to the point' (30 March 1912). Much emphasis was placed on Sowerby's being a new playwright; in the *Athenaeum* she was described as 'a playwright of uncommon promise' (3 February 1912), and *The Times* wrote of *Rutherford and Son* that, 'For a first play it is a marvel' (19 March 1912). When it transferred to the Vaudeville in April 1912, according to *The Times*, 'the audience treated the occasion as if it were a first night, and went on calling for the author until Miss Sowerby showed herself . . . Seldom does so gloomy a play receive, and deserve, so much success' (23 April 1912). Sowerby was acclaimed as being 'now in the very first rank of our playwrights' (unidentified cutting, BTA library). Several reviewers wrote of looking forward to her future work:

> It is to be hoped that Miss Sowerby will find encouragement in her success to give us something more, and the sooner the better (*The Times*, 19 March 1912)

and:

> We shall await with interest the future work from the pen of Miss K. G. Sowerby. . . . We hope to see more of Miss Sowerby as a maker of plays . . . which seem sure to have plenty of power behind them. (Unidentified cuttings, BTA library)

Along with this acclaiming her as a new writer went an emphasis on her youth: the reviewer in the *Westminster Gazette* described Sowerby as 'young, charming and modest' (2 February 1912), although she was thirty-five when *Rutherford and Son* was produced. It was her first performed play, but she had by then published eleven books for children, several of them in verse, and most of them together with her sister, Millicent, a successful illustrator. Children's books continued to be her main literary output, the last of them being *The Wise Book* in 1921.

She followed the enormous success of *Rutherford and Son* with a one-acter, *Before Breakfast*, which opened on 2 May 1912 as a curtain-raiser at the Playhouse, where it had sixty-three performances. As in *Rutherford and Son*, Sowerby is concerned with cross-class relations, here comically treated, when George Linton, 'the only son of a well-known baronet', decides he has made a mistake in forming 'an alliance [with] a charming recruit to the Variety Stage'. George's hypocrisy is exposed, and Jinny, the kitchen-maid, is shown to have integrity and honesty. John Palmer in the *Saturday Review* wrote enigmatically of it that it was 'a play . . . well written and not empty of idea, of which the author of *Rutherford and Son* has reason to be proud' (11 May 1912). Her next play, *Sheila*, was first produced at the St James's on 7 June 1917, and was given nineteen performances. The comments by the licenser, in the copy in the Lord Chamberlain's Collection, describe the play as being 'marked by [Miss Sowerby's] characteristics of thoughtfulness and sincerity'. The play's central character, Sheila, like Mary in *Rutherford and Son*, is an office worker – in her own words 'a common little thing' – who marries her boss and finds herself patronised and excluded from the family. It was not enthusiastically received by the critics, J. T. Grein describing it in the *Era* as 'not very exhilarating' (13 June 1917), and the *World* writing of it as a 'slender sentimental play on conjugal misunderstanding . . . The motive for the said misunderstanding is too feminine or too far-fetched for the mere man' (12 June 1917). *The Stepmother*, her last play as far as I can discover, was given one performance by the Play Actors at the New Theatre on 13 January 1924. The critic in the *Era*, who described the play as 'full of strong dramatic situations' displaying 'a masterly knowlege of stagecraft and dialogue', recognised that Sowerby seems in the play to have posed an alternative to the stereotype of the wicked stepmother:

> Perhaps Miss Githa Sowerby considers that there has never been an adequate retort to Strindberg's indictment of women in *The Father*, or she may have met some despicable men in her time. Anyhow, *The Stepmother* is a smashing blow at the male sex. (16 January 1924)

While *Rutherford and Son* met with great critical acclaim, it was only the feminist press that recognised its feminist analysis. The Women's Freedom League's newspaper, *The Vote*, wrote of it:

> No play has ever been written that in the truest, strongest sense was so really a 'Suffrage' play, although the word is never uttered and the thought never enters the minds of the people portrayed. (20 July 1912)

Its affinity with the suffrage movement consists in its condemnation of a patriarchy which destroys those it has power over, and in its showing the way forward as being through the self-empowerment of women. In the course of the play, Rutherford attacks, degrades and rejects each of his children in turn. But whereas John is shown to be irresponsible and worthless, and Dick to be weak and biddable, Janet matches her father's rejection of her with a forceful condemnation of him and his values. At the same time she rejects Martin, her lover, who has not the strength to stand up against Rutherford, but has become enthralled to 'the Master' (the play's original title). When Janet leaves the family home she sees Rutherford's banishing of her as a release from prison. Before she leaves, her sisterhood with Mary is firmly established, when Mary offers her help whenever she should need it. Mary spends most of the play as near-silent observer, ignored by Rutherford because he disapproves of his son's having married beneath his class. She is the carrier of the play's positive values. Janet recognises Mary's arrival as the beginning of a new hope:

> It came to me that this was what we'd been making for ever since you came without knowing it, that we were to win through to happiness after all.

She has learnt from Mary to see Rutherford for the tyrant he is, as she explains to Martin:

> You didn't see through him. . . . You were too near to see, like I was till Mary came.

And Janet only approached Martin once Mary had arrived in the house. Mary, then, signifies for Janet a hope for change and freedom; at the end of the play Mary secures the future for herself and her son. She has dismissed her husband, herself suggesting that he leave alone, and then she bargains with Rutherford. In offering him her son as inheritor of the glass works, she takes on the responsibility of providing for her son – a prime responsibility for Edwardian feminism – but also ensures that the future of the house and the firm will be influenced and changed by her enlightened views. Rutherford will not be allowed to interfere with Tony's upbringing until he is ten years old, during which time Mary will have control of his education and so of the future. The play is about the ending of patriarchal tyranny and the development of better ways of living:

> The Rutherfords are bound by time, by the eternal forces of change. Their influence on human life is indeed terrible. Notwithstanding it all, however, they are fighting a losing game. They are growing old, already too old to make anyone afraid. Change and innovation are marching on, and the Rutherfords must make place for the young generation knocking at the gates. (Emma Goldman, *The Social Significance of Modern Drama*, 1914, p. 137)

Linda Fitzsimmons

Select Bibliography

The Bumbletoes, illustrated by Millicent Sowerby (London, Chatto and Windus, 1907)

Little Plays for Little People, illustrated by Millicent Sowerby (London, Henry Frowde and Hodder and Stoughton, 1910)

Rutherford and Son (London, Sidgwick and Jackson, 1912)

Before Breakfast (London, Lacy, 1912)

The Bonnie Book, illustrated by Millicent Sowerby (London, Humphrey Milford, 1918)

Rutherford and Son was first performed at the Court Theatre, London, on 31 January 1912, with the following cast:

Ann	Agnes Thomas
Mary	Thyrza Norman
Janet	Edyth Olive
John	Edmund Breon
Richard	Frank Randell
John Rutherford	Norman McKinnel
Martin	A. S. Homewood
Mrs Henderson	Agnes Hill

Produced by John Leigh

Scene: living room in John Rutherford's house.

Two days elapse between Acts One and Two. One night between Acts Two and Three.

Act One

John Rutherford's *house stands on the edge of the moor, far enough from the village to serve its dignity and near enough to admit of the master going to and from the Works in a few minutes – a process known to the household as 'going across'. The living room, in which the family life has centred for generations, is a big square room furnished in solid mahogany and papered in red, as if to mitigate the bleakness of a climate that includes five months of winter in every year. There is a big table in the middle of the room covered with a brown cloth at which the family take their meals. An air of orderliness pervades the room, which perhaps accounts for its being extremely uncomfortable. From above the heavy polished sideboard the late* **John Rutherford** *looks down from his frame and sees the settle and arm-chair on either side of the fire, the marble clock on the mantelpiece, the desk with its brass inkstand and neatly arranged bundles of papers precisely as he saw them in life.*

On this particular evening in December **Ann Rutherford** *is sitting by the fire alternately knitting and dozing. She is a faded, querulous woman of about sixty, and wears a black dress with a big flat brooch and a cap with lilac ribbons.* **Mary Rutherford**, *a gentle delicate-looking woman of twenty-six, is seated on the settle opposite to her making a baby's cap; she is bending forward to catch the light of the fire on her work, for the lamp has not yet been brought in.*

Presently **Janet** *comes in carrying a silver basket and a pair of carpet slippers. She is a heavy dark woman, some ten years older than*

Mary, *with an expressionless tired face and monotonous voice. All her movements are slipshod and aimless, and she seldom raises her eyes. She is dressed in a dark dress of some warm material with white collar and cuffs.*

Janet (*glancing at the clock*) He's not back yet.

Ann No. . . . If you mean your father.

Janet (*folding up the brown cloth preparatory to laying the table*) Who else should I mean?

Ann You might mean any one. . . . You always talk about he and him, as if there was no one else in the house.

Janet There isn't.

Ann Answer me back, that's the way. (**Janet** *makes no reply. She puts the silver basket on the table and comes to the fire with the slippers.*) There – put his slippers down to warm. The Committee room's cold as ice, and he'll come in like the dead.

Mary (*looking up from her work for a moment*) I believe it's going to freeze tonight – the chimneys are flaring so.

Janet *drops the shoes one by one on to the hearthrug without stooping.*

Ann They'll never warm there! I never seed sic a feckless lass. (*Stoops laboriously and sets them up against the fender.*) Is the dinner all right?

Janet Susan's let the pie get burnt, but I've scraped the top off – he won't notice. The girdle cake's as tough as leather. She'll have to do a fresh one – if there's time.

Ann You might ha' seen to things a bit.

Janet I have. There wouldn't ha' been a pie at all if I hadn't. The oven damper's gone wrong.

Ann Answer me – answer yer aunt! You

and your dampers – and there you are a-laying the table and ye know weel enough yer father's forbid you to do things like a servant.

Janet What else is there to do? I can't sit and sew all day.

Ann I'm sure I'm never done finding fault from morning to night with one thing and another.

Janet Don't then.

Ann And a nice thing if I didn't! Nothing ever done in the house unless I see to it – that's what it comes to.

Janet (*spreading the cloth*) You'll drop your stitches.

Ann You never stir yourself, nor Mary neither, for that matter.

Mary I can't do much else with Tony to look after, Miss Rutherford.

Janet There's no need for her to do anything. It's not her business.

Ann Nor anybody's business, it seems to me. (*Subsiding.*) I don't know what's come to Susan nowadays, she's that daft – a head like a sieve, and that clumsy-handed.

Janet Susan's got a man.

Ann Well, I never!

Janet That's what she says. It's one of the men at the Works. He hangs about on his way home from the night shift – when she ought to be doing the rooms. . . . Susan's happy . . . that's why she forgot to take the milk out of the can. There's no cream for the pudding.

Ann And he's so particular about his cream.

Janet He'll have to do without for once. And what with the pie burnt – and the girdle cake like leather, if he comes in before the other's ready – I should think we'll have a fair evening.

She leaves the room.

Ann Eh, dearie – dearie. Sic doings!

Mary (*absorbed in her cap*) Never mind, Miss Rutherford.

Ann Never mind! It's well for you to talk.

Mary Janet'll see that it's all right. She always does, though she talks like that.

Ann Her and her sulky ways. There's no doing anything with her of late. She used to be bad enough as a lass, that passionate and hard to drive. She's ten times worse now she's turned quiet.

Mary Perhaps she's tired with the long walks she takes. She's been out nearly two hours this afternoon in the rain.

Ann (*turning to her knitting*) What should she have to put her out – except her own tempers.

Mary (*trying to divert her attention*) Miss Rutherford, look at Tony's cap; I've nearly finished it.

Ann (*still cross*) It's weel enough. Though what he wants wi' a lot o' bows standing up all over his head passes me.

Mary They're butterfly bows.

Ann Butterfly bows! And what'll butterfly bows do for 'n? They'll no keep his head warm.

Mary But he looks such a darling in them. I'll put it on tomorrow when I take him out, and you'll see.

Ann London ways – that's what it is.

Mary Do north-country babies never have bows on their caps?

Ann Not in these parts. And not the Rutherfords anyway. Plain and lasting – that's the rule in this family, and we bide by it, babies and all. But you can't be expected to know, and you like a stranger in the hoose.

Janet comes in carrying a lamp and a loaf on a trencher, which she puts on the table.

Mary I've been here nearly three months.

Ann And this very night you sit wasting your time making a bit trash fit for a monkey at a fair. A body would think you would ha' learned better by now.

Janet (*quietly*) What's the matter with Mary now?

Ann We can talk, I suppose, without asking your leave?

Janet It was you that was talking. Let her be.

Ann And there you've been and put the loaf on as if it was the kitchen – and you know weel enough that gentlefolk have it set round in bits.

Janet Gentle folk can do their own ways.

She goes out to fetch the knives.

Ann (*she gets up laboriously and goes to the table*) I'll have to do it myself as usual.

She cuts the bread and sets it round beside the plates.

Mary (*who has gone to the window and is looking out at the winter twilight*) If I'm a stranger, it's you that makes me so.

Ann Ye've no cause to speak so, lass. . . . I'm not blamin' you. It's no' your fault that you weren't born and bred in the north country.

Mary No. I can't change that. . . . I wonder what it's like here when the sun shines!

Ann (*who is busy with the bread*) Sun?

Mary It doesn't look as if the summer ever came here.

Ann If ye're looking for the summer in the middle o' December ye'll no' get it. Ye'll soon get used to it. Ye've happened on a bad autumn for your first, that's all.

Mary My first.

Ann Ye're a bit saft wi' livin' in the sooth, nae doubt. They tell me there's a deal of sunshine and wickedness in them parts.

Mary The people are happier, I think.

Ann Mebbees. Bein' happy'll make no porridge.

She goes back to her chair.

Mary I lived in Devonshire when I was a child, and everywhere there were lanes. But here – it's all so old and stern – this great stretch of moor, and the fells – and the trees – all bent one way, crooked and huddled.

Ann (*absorbed in her knitting*) It's the sea-wind that does it.

Mary The one that's blowing now?

Ann Aye.

Mary (*with a shiver*) Shall I draw the curtains?

Ann Aye.

Mary *draws the curtains. After a silence she speaks again gently.*

Mary I wonder if you'll ever get used to me enough to – like me?

Ann (*with the north-country dislike of anything demonstrative*) Like you! Sic a question – and you a kind of a relation.

Mary Myself, I mean.

Ann You're weel enough. You're a bit slip of a thing, but you're John's wife, and the mother of his bairn, and there's an end.

Mary Yes, that's all I am!

She takes up her work again.

Ann Now you're talking.

Mary (*sewing*) Don't think I don't understand. John and I have been married five years. All that time Mr Rutherford never once asked to see me; if I had died, he would have been glad.

Ann I don't say that. He's a proud man, and he looked higher for his son after the eddication he'd given him. You mustn't be thinking such things.

Mary (*without bitterness*) Oh, I know all about it. If I hadn't been Tony's mother, he would never have had me inside his house. And if I hadn't been Tony's mother, I wouldn't have come. Not for anything in the world. . . . It's wonderful how he's picked up since he got out of those stuffy lodgings.

Ann (*winding up her wool*) Well, Mr Rutherford's in the right after all.

Mary Oh yes. He's in the right.

Ann It's a bitter thing for him that's worked all his life to make a place i' the world to have his son go off and marry secret-like. Folk like him look for a return from their bairns. It's weel known that no good comes of a marriage such as yours, and it's no wonder that it takes him a bit of time to make up his mind to bide it. (*Getting up to go.*) But what's done's done.

Young **John Rutherford** *comes in while she is speaking. He is delicate-looking and boyish in speech and manner – attractive, in spite of the fact that he is the type that has been made a gentleman of and stopped half-way in the process.*

John (*mimicking her tone*) So it is, Aunt Ann. Dinner's late, isn't it?

Ann He's not back yet. He's past his time. I'm sure I hope nothing's happened.

John What should have happened?

Ann Who's to tell that he hasn't had an accident. Things do happen.

John They do indeed. He may have jumped into a furnace.

Ann Ah, you may joke. But you never know. You never know.

She wanders out, with the vague intention of seeing to the dinner.

John Cheery old soul, Aunt Ann. No one's ever five minutes late but she kills and buries them. (*Pause.*) What's she been saying to you?

Mary (*sewing*) She's been talking about – us.

John I should have thought that subject was about threadbare by now. (*Pause.*) What's she say?

Mary The usual things. How angry your father still is, and how a marriage like ours never comes to good –

John Oh, rot. Anyway, we needn't talk about it.

She looks quickly up at him and her face changes.

Mary Someone's always talking about it.

John Who is?

Mary Miss Rutherford – any of them. Your father would, if he ever spoke to me at all. He looks it instead.

John Oh, nonsense; you imagine things. The Guv'nor's like that with us all – it's always been so; besides, he doesn't like women – never notices them. (*Trying to* *make it all right*.) Look here, I know it's rather beastly for you just now, but it'll be all right in time. Things are going to change, so don't you worry, little woman.

Mary What are we going to do?

John Do? What should we do?

Mary Anything. To get some money of our own. To make some sort of life for ourselves, away from here.

John You wait till I get this invention of mine set going. As for getting away, please remember it was you who insisted on coming. I never wanted you to.

Mary I had to come. Tony was always ailing in London.

John You never left me alone till I'd crawled to the Guv'nor and asked to come back.

Mary What else was there left to do? You couldn't find work –

John If you'd had patience and waited, things would have been all right.

Mary I've waited five years. I couldn't go on earning enough when Tony came.

John (*sulkily*) Well, you couldn't expect me to ask the Guv'nor to keep us all three. And if I had stayed in London with you instead of coming back when he gave me the chance, what good would it have done? I'd have missed the biggest thing of my life – I know that. . . . Anyway, I do hate this going back over it all. Beastly, sordid –

Mary (*looking before her*) I couldn't go on. I'd done it so long – long before you knew me. Day after day in an office. The crowded train morning and night – bad light – bad food – and because I did that my boy is small and delicate. It's been nothing else all along – the bare struggle for life. I sometimes think that it's the only reality in the world.

John (*ill-humoured*) Whether it's the only reality or not, I call it a pretty deadly way of looking at things.

Mary It is deadly. I didn't know how deadly till I began to care for you and thought it was going to be different.

John The old story.

Mary No, no, we won't look back. But oh, John, I do so dreadfully want things for Tony. (**John** *begins to move about the room*.) I didn't mind when there was only ourselves. But when he was coming I began to think, to look at the other children – children of people in our position in London – taught to work before they'd had time to learn what work means – with the manhood ground out of them before ever it came. And I thought how that was what we had to give our child, you and I. . . . When your father forgave you for marrying me, and said you might come here, it seemed like a chance. And there's nothing, nothing – except this place you call home.

John Hang it all –

Mary Oh, I know it's big – there's food and warmth, but it's like a prison! There's not a scrape of love in the whole house. Your father! – no one's any right to be what he is – never questioned, never answered back – like God! And the rest of you just living round him – neither children, nor men and women – hating each other.

John (*turning to look at her with a sort of wonder*) Don't exaggerate. Whatever has set you off talking like this?

Mary Because I'm always thinking about it.

John You've never had a home of your

own, and you don't make excuses for family life – everybody knows it's like that more or less.

Mary And you've lived with it always – you can't see it as I do.

John I do see it. And it's jolly unpleasant – I'm not arguing about that –

Mary Don't you see that life in this house is intolerable?

John Well, frankly, no, I don't. That is, I don't see why you should find it so. It's all very well to abuse my people, and I sympathise with you in a way – no one dislikes them more than I do. I know Janet's got a filthy temper, and Aunt Ann – well, she hasn't moved on with the rest of us, poor old soul, that's the long and the short of it. As for the Guv'nor – it's no use beginning to apologise for him.

Mary Apologise!

John Well, that's about what you seem to expect. I've told you I quite see that it isn't over pleasant for you, and you might leave it at that, I think. You do drive at one so . . . and you seem to forget how ill I've been.

Mary I don't forget. But don't you see we may go on like this for twenty years doing nothing?

John Do you suppose I wouldn't have done something? Do you suppose I didn't mean to do something, if I hadn't been knocked over just at the critical moment? (*Injured.*) Do you suppose I wouldn't rather have been working than lying on my back all these weeks?

Mary (*quietly*) How about all the other weeks?

John Good heavens, what more could I do than I have done? Here have I hit on a thing worth thousands – a thing that any glass-maker would give his ears to have the working of. And you talk to me about making money – and a life of our own. Good Lord! We're going to be rich – rich, once it's set going.

Mary (*unimpressed*) Have you told Mr Rutherford about it?

John Yes. At least, I've told him what it is. . . . I haven't told him how it's done – naturally. . . . He won't listen to me – it's like talking to a lump of granite. He'll find he'll have to listen before long. . . . I've set Martin on to him.

Mary Why Martin?

John Because he helped me to work it out. And because he happens to be the one person in the world the Guv'nor ever listens to.

Mary (*looking up*) He trusts Martin, doesn't he? Absolutely.

John Oh, Lord! Yes. Martin can do no wrong. The Guv'nor'll listen to him all right.

Mary (*resuming her work*) When is he going to tell him?

John Oh, directly he gets a chance. He may have done it already.

Mary (*putting down her sewing*) Today? Then Martin really believes there's something in it?

John (*indignantly*) Something in it! My dear Mary, I know you don't mean to be, but you are most fearfully irritating. Here have I told you over and over again that I'm going to make my fortune, and because someone else agrees with me you're kind enough to believe what I say. One would think you had no faith in me.

Mary (*giving it up as hopeless*) I'm sorry. We won't talk of it any more. I've said it all so often – said it till you're sick of hearing it, and it's no good.

John Molly, don't be cross. . . . I don't mean to be a brute, but it is a bit disappointing, isn't it? when I really have found the right thing at last, to find you so lukewarm about it. Because it really is this time. It'll change everything; and you shall do what you like and enjoy yourself as much as you want to – and forget all about those filthy years in Walton Street. (*He comes to her and puts his arm round her.*) There, don't be a little fool. What are you making?

Mary A cap for Tony.

John Dear little beggar, isn't he?

Mary Yes. . . . Don't say things to please me, John.

John I'm not. I do think he's a dear little beggar. (*Pleased with himself.*) We'll be as happy as kings by and by.

Mary As happy as we were at first?

John Happier – we'll have money.

Mary We couldn't be happier. (*She sits with her hands in her lap, her mouth wistful.*) What a pair of babies we were, weren't we?

John Oh, I don't know.

Mary What – blunderers! I thought it was so different – and I dare say you did, too, though you never said so. I suppose it's really true what they think here – that we'd no business to marry and have a child when we'd nothing to give him when he came.

John What a little worrit you are.

Mary I do worry, John – you don't know how much.

John But what about?

Mary Tony.

John You funny little thing. Surely there's time enough to think about Tony; he's just four months old.

Mary Yes, but to me – I suppose every woman thinks about her baby like that – till he's a boy and a man and a child all in one – only he never grows old. (*In a practical tone.*) How long will it take?

John How long will what take?

Mary Your invention. (*Looks up quickly.*) I mean – don't be cross – will it be months – or years before it pays?

John (*moving away*) I really can't say – it depends. If the Guv'nor has the sense to see things my way – it depends.

He takes a cigarette.

Mary I see. You will work at it, won't you? Make it go?

John (*striking a light*) There's no work to be done. All I've got to do is to sit down and let someone pay for it.

Mary Sit down? It seems so much to us, doesn't it? Everything –

John (*who has burnt his finger*) It means my getting the whip-hand of the Guv'nor for once in my life. (*Irritably.*) And it means my getting away from your incessant nagging at me about the kid – and money.

Mary John!

John (*sharply*) After all, it isn't very pleasant for me having you dependent on the Guv'nor and being reminded of it every other day. I don't choose this kind of life, I can tell you. If you're sick of it, God knows I am.

While he is speaking **Ann** *drifts into the room again.*

Ann There you are – smoking again; and

you know what the doctor said. Mary, tell him he's not to.

Mary John must do as he likes.

John I must have something; my nerves are all on edge.

Ann Weel, ye can't expect to be right all of a sudden. When I think o' the Sunday night ye was so bad, I never thought to see ye standin' there now.

John (*injured*) I shouldn't worry about that. I don't suppose anyone would have been much the worse if I had pegged out.

Ann Whatever makes you say a thing like that?

John Mary. Yes, you do, Mary. To hear you talk one would think I was no good. How do you suppose I've made an invention if I were the rotter you think me?

Mary I didn't say that – I didn't say that.

Ann An invention's weel enough if you're not mistaken.

John Mistaken!

Ann Ah, but older people nor you make mistakes. There was old Green – I mind him fiddlin' on wi' a lot of old cogs and screws half his time, trying to find oot the way to prevent a railway train going off the line. And when he did find it and took it to show it to some one as knawed aboot such things, it was so sartin sure not to go off the line that the wheels wouldn't turn roond at all. A poor, half-baked body he was, and his wife without a decent black to show herself in o' Sundays.

John I'll undertake that my wheels will go round.

Ann If it's such a wonderful thing, why hasn't someone thought of it afore? Answer me that.

John You might say that of any new idea that ever came into the world.

Ann Of course, if you set up to know more about glass-making than your father that's been at it ever since he was a bairn . . .

John It isn't a case of knowing. I've a much better chance because I don't know. It's the duffers who get hold of the best things – stumble over them in the dark, as I did. It makes my blood run cold to think how easily I could have missed it, of all the people who must have looked straight at it time after time, and never seen it. (*Contemptuously.*) Hullo, Dick!

Richard Rutherford *has come in from the hall. He wears the regulation clergyman's clothes and looks older than* **John**, *though he is in reality the younger by a couple of years. He is habitually overworked, and his face has the rather pathetic look of an overweighted youth that finds life too much for its strength. His manner is extremely simple and sincere, which enables him to use priggish phrases without offence. He comes to the table while* **John** *is speaking, looks from him to* **Ann**, *then at the butter, sugar, and bread in turn.*

Dick (*very tired*) Dinner?

John (*mimicking him*) Not imminent.

Dick Will it be long?

Ann (*crossly*) Ye'll just have to bide quiet till it comes.

Dick (*gently*) Ah! . . . In that case I think I'll just –

He takes a piece of bread and moves towards the door.

Ann You look fair done.

Dick I've had a tiring day. (*To* **Mary**.) Where is Janet?

Mary In the kitchen. (*She looks at him intently.*) Why did you ask? Do you want her?

Dick (*uncertainly*) No, no. I thought she might have gone out. It's best for her not to go out after dark.

Ann You can't sit in your room i' this cold.

Dick I'll put on a coat. It's quiet there.

John You'll have time to write your sermon before he comes in, I dare say.

Dick (*simply*) Oh, I've done that, such as it is.

He leaves the room, eating his bread as he goes.

John (*irritably*) This is a damned uncomfortable house. I'm starving.

Ann It's Committee day.

John He'll be having the whole Board on his toes as usual, I suppose.

Ann That Board'll be the death of him. When I think of the old days when he'd no one to please but himself!

John He's stood it for five years. I wouldn't – being badgered by a lot of directors who know as much about glass-making as you do.

Ann That's all very well. But when you borrow money you've got to be respectful one way and another. If he hadn't gone to the Bank how would Rutherford's ha' gone on?

John (*who has taken up the newspaper and is half reading it as he talks*) Why should it go on?

Ann (*sharply*) What's that?

John Why didn't he sell the place when he could have made a decent profit?

Ann (*scandalised*) Sell Rutherford's? Just you let your father hear you.

John I don't care if he does. I never can imagine why he hangs on – working his soul out year after year.

Ann (*conclusively*) It's his duty!

She resumes her knitting.

John Duty – rot! He likes it. He's gone on too long. He couldn't stop and rest if he tried. When I make a few thousands out of this little idea of mine I'm going to have everything I want, and forget all about the dirt and the ugliness, the clatter and bang of the machinery, the sickening hot smell of the furnaces – all the things I've hated from my soul.

Ann (*who has become absorbed in a dropped stitch*) Aye weel . . . there's another strike at Rayner's, they tell me.

John Yes. Eight hundred men. That's the second this year.

Ann You don't think it'll happen here, do you?

John I can't say. They're smashing things at Rayner's.

Ann It'll no' come here. The men think too much of your father for that.

John I'm not so sure.

Ann There was the beginnings of a strike once, years ago, and he stopped it then. The men at the furnaces struck work – said it was too hard for 'n. And your father he went doon into the caves and took his coat off afore them all, and pitched joost half as much coal again as the best of 'em – now!

John Yes, that's the sort of argument they can see – it catches hold of the brute in them. If the Guv'nor had sat quietly in his office and sent his ultimatum through the usual channels, he would have been the owner of Rutherford's, and the strike would have run its course. Shovelling coal in his shirt with his muscles straining, and the sweat pouring off him, he was 'wor John' – and there's three cheers for his fourteen stone of beef and muscle. That was all very well – thirty years ago.

Ann And what's to hinder it now?

John Oh, the Guv'nor was a bit of a hero then – an athlete, a runner. The men who worked for him all the week crowded to see him run on Saturday afternoons, Martin's told me. But when all's said and done, Rutherford's is a money-making machine. And the Guv'nor's the only man who doesn't know it. He's getting old.

Ann (*crossly*) To hear you talk, a body would think we were all going to die tomorrow. Your father's a year younger nor me – now! And a fine up-standing man forbye.

John (*who is looking at himself in the glass above the mantelpiece*) Oh, he knows how to manage a pack of savages.

Ann There's not one of 'em today or thirty years ago but'll listen to him.

John He'd knock anyone down who didn't.

Janet *comes in with a tray and begins to set cups and saucers on the table.*

Ann They all stood by him when the trouble came, every one of 'em. And he's climbed up steady ever since, and never looked ahint him. And now you've got your invention it'll no be long now – if it's all you think it. Ah, it 'ud be grand to see Rutherford's like old times again.

John Rutherford's . . . (*He speaks half seriously, half to tease* **Ann**.) Aunt Ann, have you ever in your life – just for a moment at the back of your mind – wished Rutherford's at the bottom of the Tyne?

Ann *gazes at him in silence. When she speaks again it is as to a foolish child.*

Ann Are you taking your medicine reg'lar?

John Yes. But have you ever heard of Moloch? No. – Well, Moloch was a sort of a god – some time ago, you know, before Dick and his kind came along. They built his image with an ugly head ten times the size of a real head, with great wheels instead of legs, and set him up in the middle of a great dirty town. (**Janet**, *busy at the table, stops to listen, raising her eyes almost for the first time.*) And they thought him a very important person indeed, and made sacrifices to him – human sacrifices – to keep him going, you know. Out of every family they set aside one child to be an offering to him when it was big enough, and at last it became a sort of honour to be dedicated in this way, so much so, that the victims gave themselves gladly to be crushed out of life under the great wheels. That was Moloch.

There is a silence. **Janet** *speaks eagerly.*

Janet Where did you get that?

John Get what?

Janet What you've been saying.

John Everybody knows it.

Janet Dedicated – we're dedicated – all of us – to Rutherford's. And being respected in Grantley.

Ann Talk, talk – chatter, chatter. Words never mended nothing that I knows on.

John (*who is tired of the subject*) Talk – if I hadn't you to talk to, Aunt Ann, or Mary, I think I'd talk to the door-post.

Janet (*who has slipped back into her dull listlessness*) And just as much good would come of it, I dare say.

Ann And who are you to say it? You got no book-learning like him – and no invention neither.

Janet (*who is laying forks round the table*) How do you know he's got an invention?

Ann Because he says so, o' course – how else? It's a secret.

Janet John always had a secret. He used to sell them to me when we were little. And when I'd given him whatever it was he'd taken a fancy to, there was no secret. Nothing worth paying for, anyway.

John Oh, shut up.

Ann (*as if they were children*) Now, now. Don't quarrel.

Janet We're not quarrelling.

John Yes, we are. And you began it.

Janet I didn't. I only said what anyone can see. (*Scornfully.*) You make an invention. Likely.

John A lot you know about it.

Janet If you did, you'd muck it somehow, just as you do everything.

Ann (*querulously*) Bairns! Bairns! One would think you'd never growed up.

John (*angrily to* **Janet**) I wish you'd keep quiet if you can't say anything decent. You never open your mouth except to say something disagreeable. First there's Mary throwing cold water, then you come in.

Janet I'm not any more disagreeable than anyone else. We're all disagreeable if it comes to that. All except Susan.

Ann Susan's not one of the family! A common servant lass.

Janet Like me.

Ann (*using the family threat*) Just you let your father hear you.

Janet We do the same things.

Ann Susan's paid for it. Whoever gave you a farthing?

Janet (*bitterly*) Aye!

Ann Has she made another girdle cake?

Janet I didn't notice. She's probably talking to her young man at the gate.

John Susan with a young man!

Ann Yes, indeed – a nice thing, and her turned forty.

John Ugliest woman I ever saw bar none. Who is it? Not Martin surely! (**Janet** *stops suddenly and looks at him.*) I've noticed he's been making excuses to come about lately, and he's taken the cottage at the Tarn.

Janet (*with a sudden stillness*) It isn't Martin.

John Well, if it is, the Guv'nor would soon put a stop to it.

Janet Put a stop to what?

John Martin getting married – if it's that he's after.

Janet What right's he to interfere?

John Right – nonsense. Martin practically lives at the Works as it is. If he had a wife he'd get to be just like the other men – hankering after going home at the proper time, and all that.

Ann (*preparing to leave the room*) You and your gossip – and the dinner spoiling every minute. (*With a parting shot at* **Janet**.) It's a good thing nobody's married you – a nice hoose you'd make without me to look to everything.

She fusses out.

John Married! Cheer up, Janet! Thirty-five last birthday, isn't it?

Mary John!

Janet (*her voice hard*) No, it isn't. It's thirty-six.

John You'll make a happy home for someone yet. No one's asked you so far, I suppose?

Janet Who's there been to ask me?

John Oh, I don't know. I suppose you have been kept pretty close. Other girls manage it, don't they?

Janet I don't know other girls.

John Mary caught me.

Janet I don't know anybody – you know that. No one in Grantley's good enough for us, and we're not good enough for the other kind.

John Speak for yourself.

Janet Oh, we're all alike; don't you fret. Why hasn't young Squire Earnshaw invited you to shoot with him again? He did once – when none of his grand friends were there.

John *pretends not to hear.*

Janet I know why.

John Oh, you know a lot, don't you?

Janet It was because you pretended – pretended you knew the folk he talked about, because you'd shown them over the Works once when father was away. Pretended you said 'parss' for pass every day. I heard you. And I saw the difference. Gentlemen are natural. Being in company doesn't put them about. They don't say 'thank you' to servants neither, not like you do to Susan.

John Oh, shut up, will you?

Janet I wouldn't pretend, whatever I did – mincing round like a monkey.

Ann (*coming in from the kitchen*) Now, now. That's the door, isn't it?

They all listen. A voice is heard outside, then the outer door opens.

John Father.

Janet Martin.

There is the sound of a stick being put into the umbrella stand; then **John Rutherford** *comes in, followed by* **Martin.** *He is a heavily-built man of sixty, with a heavy lined face and tremendous shoulders – a typical north countryman. There is a distinct change in the manner of the whole family as he comes in and walks straight to his desk as if the door had scarcely interrupted his walk.* **Martin** *is a good-looking man of the best type of working man. Very simple in manner and bearing – about forty years of age. He touches his forelock to the family and stands beside the door with nothing servile in either action.*

Rutherford (*talking as he comes in*) . . . and it's got to be managed somehow. Lads are wanted and lads'll have to be found. Only six out of the seventeen shops started the first shift o' Monday.

Martin Grey couldn't start at all last week for want o' lads.

Rutherford What's got them? Ten years ago you could have had fifty for the asking, and taken your pick. And now here's the work waiting to be done, and half the hands we want to do it lounging about Grantley with their hands in their breeches pockets, the beggars. What do they think they're bred for?

Martin There's too many of 'em making for the towns, that's it. It's lighter work.

Rutherford Just remind me to give the men a word o' wages time o' Saturday. They got to keep their lads at home as long as they're wanted at Rutherford's. (*Turning papers and a bunch of keys out of his pocket on to the desk.*) The new lear man's shaping all right then.

Martin Dale? Knows as much aboot a pot-arch as I knows aboot a flying-machine.

Rutherford Why didn't you tell me before?

Martin I thought I'd wait to give him a trial. I took a look at the flues myself to make sure it wasn't them at fault. He can't get the heat up properly, and the pots are put into the furnaces afore they're furnace heat. They'll all be broke one o' these days.

Rutherford We'd better take on Ford.

Martin He finishes at Cardiff Saturday.

Rutherford He'll do, I suppose?

Martin (*feeling in his pocket and pulling out a leather purse or bag*) You couldn't get a better man for the job in all Tyneside. There's the ten pound young Henderson had out o' the cash-box.

He counts it out on the desk.

Rutherford What! He's given it up?

Martin Aye. Leastways, I took it off him.

Rutherford Has he owned to it?

Martin Sure enough. Said he hadn't gone for to do it. Cried like a bairn, he did.

John (*from his arm-chair by the fire*) Henderson? Has he been stealing?

Martin Aye, Mr John. I caught him at it i' the office – at dinner-time when there's nobody much aboot – wi' his hands i' the box.

John Dirty little sweep! Have you kicked him out?

Rutherford (*pausing with his hand on his cash-box*) I suppose there's no doubt he's a bad 'un?

Martin Bred and born.

Rutherford No use giving him another chance.

Martin Throwed away on the likes o' him.

Rutherford (*locking the box and putting it in a drawer*) Ah. . . . Well, if he comes back, turn him away. Everything ready for the pot-setting in the morning?

Martin Aye, sir. The night shift'll set four when they stop, and the other shift'll set the others a bit later.

Rutherford You'll be there to see them do it?

Martin Surely.

Rutherford (*with a curious softening in his voice*) When'll you get your rest?

Martin Plenty o' time for that, sir.

Rutherford (*crossing to the fire*) We'll have you on strike one o' these days, Martin.

Martin (*turning to go*) Not me, sir. When you begin to spare yourself you can begin to think about sparing me. And next week things'll go easier. . . . Is that all for the night, sir?

Rutherford (*wearily*) Aye. Goodnight to ye. (*He has taken his pipe from the rack above the mantelpiece and is filling it.*) You've further to go now ye're in the Tarn Cottage.

*There is a slight pause before **Martin** replies.*

Martin Aye. A bit, mebbee.

Rutherford (*lighting his pipe*) I – should ha' – thought you'd had done better to stick to your old one – near at hand; but you know your own business best.

Martin It's weel enough.

Ann Now Martin's here, can he no take a look at the range? Susan canna get the oven to go.

Janet (*to* **Ann**) The oven's all right.

Rutherford (*with a complete change of voice and manner*) Now what's that got to do with Martin?

Ann (*subsiding*) He could tell Baines to send up a man i' the mornin'.

Rutherford That's not Martin's business – you must send word to Baines himself.

Martin I could easy take a look at it while I'm here, sir. It 'ud save you sending.

Rutherford (*wearily*) Oh, all right. If you want a job.

Ann Janet, go and show Martin.

Martin *turns at the door and looks for her to pass out before him.*

Janet (*standing motionless*) Susan can show him.

Martin *goes, closing the door.*

Rutherford Any letters?

Ann (*flurried*) Yes. They're somewheres. Janet –

Rutherford (*with the sudden irritation of a tired man*) Bless me, can't I have a simple thing like that done for me? How often have I said to put them in one place and stick to it? (**Janet** *discovers the letters on the small table by the door and brings them to him. He sits on the settle and stretches out his legs.*) Here, take them off for me. I'm dead beat.

After a moment's silent revolt she kneels and begins to unlace his boots. He looks at her bent sullen face.

Ah! sulky, are ye?

She makes no answer.

'Ud like to tell me to take them off myself, I dare say. And I been working the day long for you. (*Getting irritated at her touch.*) Spoilt

– that's what you are, my lass. (*Opening a letter.*) What's this? A polite letter from the vicar, eh? Damn polite – a new organ – that's his trouble – thinks I'd like to help pay for it. (*He throws it across the hearthrug to* **John**.) There's a job for you – you're idle enough. Write and tell His Reverence to go to the devil and ask him for an organ. Or mebbee Richard'll like to do it, as he's his curate. (*To* **Janet**.) Let be, let be.

He takes his boots off painfully one with the other.

Ann (*plaintively*) I'm sure the vicar came in pleasant enough not a week gone, and asked for 'ee –

Rutherford Asked for my money, you mean. They're civil enough when they want anything, the lot of them. (*To* **Janet** – *sarcastically, as she carries the boots away.*) Thank 'ee kindly.

He gets up and puts his slippers on. **Ann** *speaks in a flurried whisper to* **John**.

Ann John, you've got your father's chair.

John (*gets up*) Sorry.

Rutherford (*drags the chair up to the table, and sits down as if he were tired out. He looks at* **John** *with a curiously interested expression as he lounges across.*) Feeling better?

John (*uneasy and consequently rather swaggering*) Oh, I'm still a bit shaky about the knees.

Rutherford You'll be coming back to work, I suppose. There's plenty to be done. How's the little lad?

John I don't know – all right, I suppose. Isn't he, Mary?

Mary Mr Rutherford asked you.

John But I don't know.

Rutherford *looks at* **Mary**, *she at him; there is a pause.*

Rutherford (*busy with his letters*) I thought Gibson had forbidden you to smoke?

John *rebels for a moment, then throws his cigarette into the fire, with an action like a petted child.*

John I must do something.

Rutherford What have you been busy with today? . . . This – metal o' yours? Eh?

John (*evasively*) Aunt Ann's been talking about it.

Ann (*meaning well*) We've joost been saying how it'll all come right now – all the bother. John'll do it – Rutherford's 'll be itself again.

Rutherford Martin tells me you've hit on a good thing – a big thing. . . . I've got to hear more about it, eh?

John If you like.

Rutherford What's that?

He looks up slowly under his eyebrows – a long curious look, as if he saw the first possibility of opposition.

John (*going over to the fireplace*) Can't we have dinner?

Ann You're getting back your appetite. That's a good sign.

Rutherford Dinner can wait. (*He sweeps a space clear on the table and puts his letters down.* **Janet** *presently sits down resigned to a family row.* **Mary** *listens throughout intently, her eyes constantly fixed on* **John**.) I'm a business man, and I like to know how I stand. (*Launching at* **John**.) Now – what d'ye mean?

John I don't understand you, sir.

Rutherford What's there to understand?

John (*his manner gradually slipping into that of a child afraid of its father*) Well, I've been

away from the Works for two months. Before we begin to talk about the other thing, I'd like to know what's doing.

Rutherford What's that got to do with it? You never have known what's doing.

John I think I ought to be told – now.

Rutherford Now! That's it, is it? You want a bone flung to your dignity! Well, here it is. Things are bad.

John Really bad?

Rutherford For the present. These colliery strikes one on top of another, for one thing. Rayner's drew the ponies out of the pit this afternoon.

John It'll about smash them, won't it?

Rutherford Mebbee. The question is how it affects us.

John Oh! We get coal from them?

Rutherford I should have thought you'd ha' picked up that much – in five years.

John Stoking isn't my business.

Rutherford You might have noticed the name on the trucks – you see it every day of your life. Well, yes – we get our coal from them. . . . What then?

John Well – what's going to happen? How bad is it?

Rutherford I said – bad for the present. The balance-sheet for the year's just been drawn up and shows a loss of four thousand on last year's working. It's not a big loss, considering what's been against us – those Americans dumping all that stuff in the spring – we had to stop that little game, and it cost us something to do it. Then the price of materials has gone up, there's a difference there. (*Irritably, answering his own thoughts.*) It's not ruin, bless us – it's simply a question of work and sticking together;

but the Bank's rather more difficult to manage than usual. There's not one of 'em would sacrifice a shilling of their own to keep the old place going – they want their fees reg'lar. That's their idea of the commercial enterprise they're always talking about. It's the pulse they keep their finger on – when it misses a beat, they come crowding round with their hands up like a lot of damned old women. . . . Well, well! Something's wanted to pull things together. . . . Now – this idea of yours. Martin tells me it's worth something.

John (*nettled*) Worth something? It's worth thousands a year to anyone who works it properly.

Rutherford (*with his half smile*) Thousands! That's a fair margin. (*Drily.*) What's your calculation in figures?

John That depends on the scale it's worked on.

Rutherford (*as to a child*) Yes – so I supposed. What's your preliminary cost?

John (*getting nervous*) Nothing – as far as I know. I can't say for certain – something like that.

Rutherford Something like nothing; and on something like nothing you're going to show a profit of thousands a year on a single metal. (*Drily.*) Sounds like a beautiful dream, doesn't it? About your cost of working now – that should run you into something?

John (*who is getting annoyed*) Thirty per cent less than what you're working at now.

Rutherford Indeed. . . . May I ask where and how you've carried out your experiments?

John (*uneasily*) I didn't mention it to you. A year ago I got a muffle furnace. I've worked with it from time to time, in the old pot-loft.

Rutherford Paid for it by any chance?

John Not yet.

Rutherford How did you manage for coals now?

John I – took what I wanted from the heap.

Rutherford Ah, and your materials – I suppose you took what you wanted of those too? Well, I've no objection, if you can make it good. (*Suddenly.*) What's your receipt?

John I haven't – I'm not prepared to say.

There is a silence. **Ann** *lowers her knitting with an alarmed look.*

Rutherford (*heavily*) A week or two ago in this room you told me it was perfected – ready for working tomorrow.

John Yes – I told you so.

Rutherford (*suppressed*) What d'ye mean? . . . Come, come, sir – I'm your father, I want an answer to my question – a plain answer, if you can give one.

John (*in a high-pitched, nervous voice*) I – I'm a business man, and I want to know where I stand.

Rutherford *breaks into a laugh.*

Oh, you turn me into an impudent schoolboy, but I'm not. I'm a man, with a thing in my mind worth a fortune.

Ann John! (*Asserting her authority.*) You must tell your father.

John (*very excited*) I shan't tell him till I've taken out my patent, so there!

There is a pause – **Rutherford** *stares at his son.*

Rutherford (*heavily*) What d'ye mean?

John I mean what I say. I want my price.

Rutherford Your price – your price? (*Bringing his fist down on the table.*) Damn your impudence, sir. A whippersnapper like you to talk about your price.

John (*losing his temper*) I'm not a whippersnapper. I've got something to sell and you want to buy it, and there's an end.

Rutherford To buy? To sell? And this to your father?

John To any man who wants what I've made.

There is a dead silence on this, broken only by an involuntary nervous movement from the rest of the family. Then **Rutherford** *speaks without moving.*

Rutherford Ah! So that's your line, is it? . . . This is what I get for all I've done for you. . . . This is the result of the schooling I give you.

John (*with an attempt at a swagger*) I suppose you mean Harrow.

Rutherford It was two hundred pound – that's what I mean.

John And you gave me a year of it!

Rutherford And a lot of good you've got of it. . . . What ha' you done with it? Idled your time away wi' your books o' poetry when you should ha' been working. Married a wife who bears you a bairn you can't keep. (*At a movement from* **Mary**.) Aye – hard words mebbe. What will you do for your son when the time comes? I've toiled and sweated to give you a name you'd be proud to own – worked early and late, toiled like a dog when other men were taking their ease – plotted and planned to get my chance, taken it and held it when it come till I could ha' burst with the struggle. Sell! You talk o' selling to me, when everything you'll ever make couldn't pay back the life I've given to you!

John Oh, I know, I know.

Ann You mustn't answer your father, John.

John Well, after all, I didn't ask to be born.

Rutherford Nor did the little lad, God help him.

John (*rapidly*) Look here, Father – why did you send me to Harrow?

Rutherford Why? To make a gentleman of you, and because I thought they'd teach you better than the Grammar School. I was mistaken.

John They don't turn out good clerks and office boys.

Rutherford What's that?

John I've been both for five years. Only I've had no salary.

Rutherford You've been put to learn your business like any other young fellow. I began at the bottom – you've got to do the same. There'll not be two masters at Rutherford's while I'm on my legs.

John That's it, that's it. You make a servant of me.

Rutherford What do you suppose your work's worth to Rutherford's? Tell me that.

John What's that matter now? I've done with it. I've found a way out.

Rutherford A way out – of what?

John (*rather taken aback*) Well – you don't suppose I'd choose to live here all my life?

Ann (*taking it personally*) And why not, pray?

Rutherford Your father has lived here, and your grandfather before you. It's your inheritance – can't you realise that? – what you've got to come to when I'm underground. We've made it for you, stone by stone, penny by penny, fighting through thick and thin for close on a hundred years.

John Well, after all, I can't help what you and grandfather chose to do.

Rutherford Chose to do! There's no chose to do. The thing's there. You're my son – my son that's got to come after me.

John Oh, it's useless. Our ideas of life are utterly different.

Rutherford Ideas of life! What do you know about life?

John Oh, nothing, of course.

Rutherford If you did, you'd soon stop having ideas about it. Life! I've had nigh on sixty years of it, and I'll tell you. Life's work – keeping your head up and your heels down. Sleep, and begetting children, rearing them up to work when you're gone – that's life. And when you know better than the God who made you, you can begin to ask what you're going to get by it. And you'll get more work and six foot of earth at the end of it.

John And that's what you mean me to do, is it?

Rutherford It's what you've got to do – or starve. You're my son – you've got to come after me.

John Look here, Father. You tell me all this. Just try and see things my way for once. Take the Works. I know you've done it all, built it up, and all that – and you're quite right to be proud of it. But I – I don't like the place, that's the long and the short of it. It's not worth my while. After all, I've got myself to think of – my own life. If I'd done that sooner, by Jove! I'd have been a jolly sight better off. I'd not have married, for one thing. (*With a glance at* **Mary**.) Not

that I regret that. You talk about what you did when you were young. You've told me the sort of time you've had – nothing but grind, grind, since the time you could do anything. And what have you got by it? What have you got? I have myself to think of. I want a run for my money – your money, I suppose it is – other fellows do. And I've made this thing myself, off my own bat – and – and – (*ending lamely*) – I don't see why I shouldn't have a look in. . . . On my own account . . .

There is an uncomfortable silence.

Rutherford (*in a new tone*) You're going to take out a patent, you say?

John (*taking this as friendly*) Yes.

Rutherford Know anything about Patent Law?

John Well, no – not yet.

Rutherford It's very simple, and wonderfully cheap – three pound for three years. At the end of three years, you can always extend the time if you want to – no difficulty about that.

John Oh, no.

Rutherford But you can't patent a metal.

John I don't see why not.

Rutherford What's the use if you do?

John It's the same as anything else. I take out a patent for a certain receipt, and I can come down on anyone who uses it.

Rutherford And prove that they've used it?

John They have to find out what it is first. It's not likely I'm going to give the show away. (*Pause.*)

Rutherford But you want to sell, you say.

John Yes.

Rutherford How are you going to do that without giving it away? . . . Suppose you go to one of the big chaps – Miles of Cardiff, for example. 'Here you are,' you say. 'I've got an idea worth a fortune. Give me a fortune and I'll tell you what it is.' He's not going to buy a pig in a poke any more than I am. People have a way of thinking they're going to make their fortunes, d'ye see? But those people aren't generally the sort you let loose in your glasshouse.

John Of course, I shall make inquiries about all that. I can't say till I know.

Rutherford Do you remember a little thing of mine – an invention you would call it. Did ye ever happen to see it?

John Yes. Martin showed it to me once.

Rutherford What's your opinion of that now – as a business man?

John Of course, it had the makings of a good thing – anyone could see that.

Rutherford Nobody did. I was nineteen at the time – a lad. Like you, I hadn't the money to run it myself. Clinton, the American people, got hold of it, and sold seven hundred thousand the first six months in New York alone. (*He gets up and addresses the room, generally.*) Dinner in ten minutes.

John Surely you could have got some one to take it up – an obvious thing like that?

Rutherford (*drily*) That's how it worked out in my case. (*He moves slowly to the door.*)

John You don't believe I can do what I say.

Rutherford I can't tell – nor can you.

John (*high-handed*) Oh, very well then. What are we talking about?

Rutherford You undertake to produce ordinary white metal at a third of the usual cost – that's it, isn't it? You've worked this out in a muffle furnace. My experience of muffle furnaces is that they're excellent for experimenting in a very small way. A child can hit on an idea for a metal – provided he's materials at his command, and knows a bit about chemistry. But no man living can estimate the cost of that idea until it's worked out on a big scale. Your receipt, as it stands, isn't worth the paper it's written on.

As **Rutherford** *moves again towards the door* **John** *makes a movement to stop him.*

John Father, look here. Here's an offer.

Rutherford Thank you kindly.

John If you'll let me have a pot in one of the big furnaces for a trial – I swear to you, on my honour, I'll let you see the result without touching it, after I've put in the materials. You can clay the pots up – seal them, if you like. Let me do it tomorrow; I can't stand hanging on like this.

Rutherford Tomorrow! Impossible.

John Why not?

Rutherford You can't come down to the Works in this weather. You'd catch cold, and be laid up again.

John The day after then – next week – or, why not? – let Martin do it.

Rutherford Martin? (*He turns to look at* **John**, *struck by a new thought.*)

John Why not? He can do it as well as I can.

Rutherford Martin? . . . He knows then?

John (*surprised*) Why, he talked to you about it, didn't he?

Rutherford Yes, yes. But – he's got the receipt?

John Yes – there's no difficulty at all. Let him mix the metal and clay her up, and you can open her yourself. Then you'll see. You'll take Martin's word for it, I suppose? Only, for Heaven's sake, give me a fair chance.

Rutherford (*moving suddenly*) Fair chance be damned, sir. You've said your say, and I've said mine. Think it over!

He goes out, leaving **John** *standing staring after him.*

John (*under his breath as the door closes*) Oh, go to the devil!

Ann For shame to speak so. Just let him hear you. And there, dinner'll be as dry as a bone, and I've waited so long I don't feel as if I could touch a morsel. You might keep your business till we'd had something to eat, I think. (*She hurries out.*)

Janet (*with a sort of admiration*) Now you've done it.

John Done it! I've jolly well let him know what I think – and high time, too. (*Brokenly.*) It isn't fair – it isn't fair. Old bully. What am I going to do?

Janet (*dropping into her usual tone*) What you've always done, I suppose.

John What's that?

Janet Say you're sorry. It's the soonest way back.

John I'm not going back. Sooner than give in, I'll starve. I don't care. I'll go to London, Canada, anywhere. He shan't have me, to grind the life out of me by inches – and he shan't have my metal. If he thinks he's going to pick my brains and give me nothing for it, he'll find himself jolly well mistaken. I don't care. Once and for all, I'm going to make a stand. And he can jolly well go to the devil.

Mary *speaks for the first time, in a low voice.*

Mary What are you making a stand for?

John (*stopping to look at her*) Good Lord, Mary, haven't you been listening?

Mary Yes, I've been listening. You said you wanted your price. What is your price?

Janet All the profits and none of the work – that's John's style. (*She sits on settle, her chin on her hands.*)

John A lot you know about it.

Mary *speaks again.*

Mary If you get your price, what will you do with it?

Janet He won't get it.

John (*to* **Janet**) Do you suppose I'm going to sit down under his bullying?

Janet You've done it all your life.

John Well, here's an end of it then.

Janet No one ever stands out against father for long – you know that – or else they get so knocked about they don't matter any more. (*She looks at* **Mary**, *who has made an involuntary movement.*) Oh, I don't mean he hits them – that's not his way.

John Oh, don't exaggerate.

Janet Exaggerate – look at mother! You were too young – I remember – (*To* **Mary**.) You've been here nigh on three months. If you think you're going to change this house with your soft ways, you're mistaken. Nothing'll change us now – nothing. We're made that way – set – and we've got to live that way. (*Slowly.*) You think you can make John do something. If ever he does it'll be for fear of father, not for love of you.

John What do you mean? (*In a high voice.*) If you think I'm going to give in –

Janet You've said that three times. I know you're going to give in.

John Well, I'm not – so there.

Janet What will you do then?

John That's my business. Curse Rutherford's! Curse it!

Janet (*to* **Mary**) That's what he'll do. That's what he's been doing these five years. And what's come of it? He's dragged you into the life here – and Tony – that's all. . . . I knew all the time you'd have to come in the end, to go under, like the rest of us.

Mary (*quickly*) No, no –

Janet Who's going to get you out of it? . . . John? . . . You're all getting excited about this metal. I don't know whether it's good or bad, but anyway it doesn't count. In a few days John'll make another row for us to sit round and listen to. In a few days more he'll threaten father to run away. He can't, because he's nothing separate from father. When he gives up his receipt, or whatever it is, it'll go to help Rutherford's – not you or me or any one, just Rutherford's. And after a bit he'll forget about it – let it slide like the rest of us. We've all wanted things, one way and another, and we've let them slide. It's no good standing up against father.

John Oh, who listens to you? Come along, Mary. (*Moving to the door.*) Disagreeable old maid!

He goes out. **Mary** *stands in the same place looking at* **Janet.**

Mary Oh, Janet, no one's any right to be what he is – no one's any right.

John (*calling from the hall*) Mollie! I want you. (*Irritably.*) Mollie!

Mary Coming! (*She follows him.*)

Janet *remains in the same attitude – her chin on her hands, staring sullenly before her. Suddenly she bows her face in her arms and begins to cry.* **Martin** *comes in from the kitchen on his way out. As he reaches the door leading to the hall, he sees her and stops.*

Martin (*in a whisper*) My lass!

She starts and gets up quickly.

Janet Martin! Martin!

He blunders over to her and takes her in his arms with a rough movement, holding her to him – kisses her with passion and without tenderness, and releases her suddenly. She goes to the fireplace, and leans her arms on the mantelpiece, her head on them – he turns away with his head bent. They stand so.

Martin (*as if the words were dragged from him*) Saturd'y night – he's away to Wickham – at the Tarn. . . . Will ye come?

Janet Yes.

Martin *goes to the door at back. As he reaches it* **Rutherford** *comes into the room with some papers in his hand. In crossing between the two, he stops suddenly as if some thought had struck him.*

Martin Good night, sir.

Rutherford Good night. (*He stands looking at* **Janet** *till the outer door shuts.*) Why don't you say good night to Martin? It 'ud be more civil – wouldn't it?

Janet I have said it.

Their eyes meet for a moment – she moves quickly to the door.

I'll tell Susan you're ready.

Rutherford *is left alone. He stands in the middle of the room with his papers in his hand – motionless, save that he turns his head slowly to look at the door by which* **Martin** *has gone out.*

Act Two

It is about nine o'clock in the evening. The lamp is burning on the large table. Bedroom candlesticks are on the small table between the window and door.

Rutherford is sitting at his desk. He has been writing, and now sits staring in front of him with a heavy brooding face. He does not hear Dick as he comes in quietly and goes to the table to light his candle – then changes his mind, looks at his father, and comes to the fire to warm his hands. He looks, as usual, pale and tired. Rutherford becomes suddenly aware of his presence, upon which Dick speaks in a gentle, nervous tone.

Dick I should rather like to speak to you, if you could spare me a minute.

Rutherford What's the matter with you?

Dick The matter?

Rutherford You're all wanting to speak to me nowadays – what's wrong with things? . . . (*Taking up his pen.*) What's the bee in your bonnet?

Dick (*announcing his news*) I have been offered the senior curacy at St Jude's, Southport.

Rutherford Well – have you taken it?

Dick (*disappointed*) I could not do so without your consent. That's what I want to speak to you about – if you could spare me a minute.

Rutherford (*realising*) Ah! that means you're giving up your job here?

Dick Exactly.

Rutherford Ah. . . . Just as well, I dare say.

Dick You will naturally want to know my reasons for such a step. (*He waits for a reply and gets none.*) In the first place, I have to consider my future. From that point of view there seems to be a chance of – of more success. And lately – I have had it in my mind for some time past – somehow my work among the people here hasn't met with the response I once hoped for. . . . I have done my best – and it would be ungrateful to say that I had failed utterly when there are always the few who are pleased when I drop in. . . . But the men are not encouraging.

Rutherford I dare say not.

Dick I have done my best. Looking back on my three years here, I honestly cannot blame myself; and yet – failure is not the less bitter on that account.

Rutherford (*almost kindly*) Well – perhaps a year or two at a Theological College wasn't the best of trainings for a raw hell like Grantley. It always beats me – whenever a man thinks it's his particular line to deal with humanity in the rough, he always goes to school like a bit of a lad to find out how to do it.

Dick Ah! you don't understand.

Rutherford You mean I don't see things your way – well, that's not worth discussing. (*He goes back to his writing.*)

Dick I have sometimes wondered if your not seeing things my way has had anything to do with my lack of success among your people. For they are your people.

Rutherford What d'ye mean?

Dick (*sincerely*) Not only the lack of religious example on your part – even some kind of Sunday observance would have helped – to be more in touch – but all through my ministry I have been conscious of your silent antagonism. Even in my active work – in talking to the men, in

visiting their wives, in everything – I have
always felt that dead weight against me,
dragging me down, taking the heart out of
all I do and say, even when I am most
certain that I am right to do and say it. (*He
ends rather breathlessly.*)

Rutherford (*testily*) What the devil have
you got hold of now?

Dick Perhaps I haven't made it clear what
I mean.

Rutherford (*deliberately*) I've never said a
word against you or for you. And I've
never heard a word against you or for you.
Now! . . . As for what you call your work, I
don't know any more about it than a bairn,
and I haven't time to learn. I should say
that if you could keep the men out of the
public-houses and hammer a little decency
into the women it might be a good thing.
But I'm not an expert in your line.

Dick (*bold in his conviction*) Father – excuse
me, but sometimes I think your point of
view is perfectly deplorable.

Rutherford Indeed! Frankly, I don't
realise the importance of my point of view
or of yours either. I got my work to do in
the world – for the sake o' the argument, so
have you – we do it or we don't do it. But
what we think about it either way, doesn't
matter.

Dick (*very earnestly*) It matters to God.

Rutherford Does it. – Now run along –
I'm busy.

Dick This is all part of your resentment –
your natural resentment – at my having
taken up a different line to the one you
intended for me.

Rutherford Resentment – not a bit. Wear
your collar-stud at the back if you like, it's
all one to me. You can't make a silk purse
out of a sow's ear – you were no good for

my purpose, and there's an end. For the
matter o' that, you might just as well never
ha' been born – except that you give no
trouble either way. . . . Where's John?

Dick I don't know. His candle is here . . . I
am still absolutely convinced that I chose
the better part.

Rutherford Probably. There are more
ways than one of shirking life, and
religion's one of them. If you want my
blessing, here it is. As long as you respect
my name and remember that I made a
gentleman of ye, ye can go to the devil in
your own way.

Dick Then I have your consent to accept
St Jude's?

Rutherford (*writing*) Aye. Just ring the
bell before you go. I want my lamp.

Dick *does so, depressed and disappointed. On his
way to his candle he hesitates.*

Dick By the way – I'm forgetting – Mrs
Henderson wants to see you.

Rutherford And who is Mrs Henderson?

Dick William's mother.

Rutherford William? . . . The chap who's
been pilfering my money? Oh, that matter's
settled.

Dick Oh! . . . Yes.

Rutherford Good night. Did you ring?

Dick Yes. I rang. Good night. (*There is a
silence, broken by the scratching of
Rutherford*'s pen. **Dick** summons up his
courage and speaks again.*) I'm afraid I told
Mrs Henderson she might call tonight.

Rutherford Did ye now?

Dick Yes.

Rutherford And what the devil did ye do
that for, if one may inquire?

Dick She is one of my parishioners – in my district. She came to me – asked my help.

Rutherford Told you the usual yarn, I suppose. More fool you, to be taken in by it. I can't see her.

Dick We don't know that it isn't true. The boy has been led astray by bad companions to bet and gamble. It's a regular gang – George Hammond's one, Fade's another.

Rutherford I know them. Two of the worst characters and the best workers we've got.

Dick However that may be, the mother's in great grief, and I promised to intercede with you to give her son another chance.

Rutherford Then you'd no business to promise anything of the kind. The lad's a young blackguard. Bless my soul – look at the head he's got on him! As bad an egg as you'll find in all your parish, and that's saying a good deal.

Dick I'm afraid it is – God help them. But –

A series of slow heavy knocks on the outer door are heard, ending with a belated single one.

I'm afraid that is Mrs Henderson.

Rutherford (*going on with his writing*) Aye, it sounds like her hand. Been drowning her trouble, mebbee.

Dick (*after another knock*) Well. She's here.

Rutherford You'd better go and tell her to go away again.

Dick Yes. (*He makes an undecided move towards the door; stops.*) The woman ought to have a fair hearing.

Rutherford (*losing patience*) Fair hearing! She's badgered Martin till he's had to turn her out, and on the top of it all you come blundering in with your talk of a fair

hearing. (*He gets up and swings to the door, pushing* **Dick** *aside.*) Here – let be.

Dick (*speaking with such earnestness that* **Rutherford** *stops to look at him*) Father – one moment. . . . Don't you think – don't you think it might be better to be friendly with her. To avoid unpleasantness? And gossip afterwards –

Rutherford What? God help you for a fool, Richard. One would think I'd nothing to do but fash myself about this young blackguard and speak soft to his mother. (*He goes out into the hall and is heard opening the door.*) Now, Mrs Henderson – you've come about your lad. You've had my answer.

Mrs Henderson *is heard speaking apparently on the mat.*

Mrs Henderson Oh, if you please, sir – if you could just see your way to sparin' me a minute I'd take it kindly, that I would. And I come all the way from home on me two feet – and me a poor widder woman.

She drifts imperceptibly just inside the room. She is a large and powerful woman with a draggled skirt and a shawl over her head, and she is slightly drunk. **Rutherford** *follows her in and stands by the open door, holding the handle.*

Rutherford Well, then, out with it. What ha' ye got to say?

Mrs Henderson It's my lad Bill as has been accused o' takin' your money –

Rutherford Ten pounds.

Mrs Henderson By Mr Martin, sir.

Rutherford What then?

Mrs Henderson And not another living soul near to say the truth of it.

Rutherford Martin's my man, Mrs Henderson. What he does, he does under my orders. Besides, Martin and your son both say he took it. They've agreed about it.

Mrs Henderson Aye, when he was scared out of his life he owned to it. I'm not denying he owned to it –

Rutherford Oh, that's it, is it? He wants to go back on it? Why did he give up the money?

Mrs Henderson He was that scared, sir, o' being sent to the gaol and losing his place and all, what wi' Mr Martin speaking that harsh to him, and all, and him a bit of a lad –

Rutherford I see. In that case I owe him ten pounds?

Mrs Henderson Eh?

Rutherford I've took ten pounds off him, poor lad, all his honest savings mebbee. Good night, Mrs Henderson.

Mrs Henderson Ah, Mr Rutherford, sir, don't 'ee be hard on us – don't 'ee now. We all got summat to be overlooked – every one on us when ye get down to it – and there's not a family harder working nor more respected in Grantley. Mr Richard here'll speak for us.

Rutherford Speak for them, Richard.

Dick I . . . I do believe they are sincerely trying to do better.

Rutherford Just so – better not rake up bygones. My time's short, Mrs Henderson, and you've no business to come up to the house at this time o' night, as you know well enough.

Mrs Henderson Aye, sir, begging your pardon. I'm sure I'd be the last to intrude on you and the family if it warn't for –

Rutherford I dare say. What did Martin say to you when you intruded into the glass-house?

Mrs Henderson What did he say to me?

Rutherford (*impatiently*) Aye.

Mrs Henderson (*fervently*) Far be it from me to repeat what he did say. God forbid that I should dirty my mouth wi' the words that man turned on me! before the men too, and half of 'em wi' their shirts off and me a decent woman. (*Violently.*) 'Hawd yer whist,' I says to 'n. 'Hawd yer whist for a shameless – '

Rutherford That'll do, that'll do – that's enough. You can take what Martin said from me. The matter's ended.

Dick *makes an appealing movement.*

Five years ago your son was caught stealing coppers out o' the men's coats – men poorer than himself. Don't forget that. I knew about it well enough. I gave him another chance because he was a young 'un, and because you ought to ha' taught him better.

Mrs Henderson Me? Taught him better! That I should ever hear the like!

Rutherford I gave him another chance. He made the most of it by robbing me the first time he thought he was safe not to be caught. Every man's got a right to go to the devil in his own way, as I've just been telling Mr Richard here, and your son Bill's old enough to choose his. I don't quarrel with him for that. But lads that get their fingers in my till are no use to me. And there's an end!

Dick Father! If you talk to her like this –

Rutherford It's you that's brought her to hear me – you must take the consequences.

Dick No one is wholly bad – we have no right to say the lad is past hope, to condemn him utterly.

Mrs Henderson Thank'ee kindly, Mr

Richard, sir – it's gospel truth every word of it. My son's as good a son as ever a lone woman had, but he's the spittin' image of his father, that easily led. And now to have him go wrong and all through keeping bad company and betting on the racing – just as he might ha' laid a bit on you, sir, in your young days and won his money too, sir, along o' your being sartain sure to win.

Rutherford Well, I would have done my best to get him his money. But if I'd lost he'd ha' had to take his beating and pay up like a man and no whining about it. You take an interest in running?

Mrs Henderson (*fervently*) Aye, sir, and always has done ever since I was a bit lass. And many's the Saturday me and my old man's gone down to the ground to see you run.

Rutherford You don't happen to have heard who's won the quarter-of-a-mile at Broughton, do you?

Dick Father!

Mrs Henderson I did hear as it was Dawson, sir, as I was passing.

Rutherford Ah. Shepherd was overtrained. What time did he do – Dawson?

Mrs Henderson I don't know, sir.

Rutherford I made him a shade worse than six under at his trial. Shepherd should have been that.

Dick Father, please! Do let us talk this matter out seriously.

Rutherford Seriously? What more?

Dick You see, it is as I said. I am sure Mrs Henderson will answer for her son's good conduct if you will consent to take him back – won't you, Mrs Henderson? Just this once. Your kindness may make all the difference, reform him altogether, who knows? He's had his lesson and I hate to preach, but – there is such a thing as repentance.

Rutherford (*drily*) That's all right. You say what you think! And don't misunderstand me. I've no objection to Bill Henderson repenting, but I won't have him doing it in my Works, d'ye see? There's nothing spreads so quick as a nice soft feeling like that, and – who knows – we might have half-a-dozen other young blacklegs at the same game? Now, Mrs Henderson, go home like a sensible woman and send your lad away from Grantley. He'll soon find his feet if he's a mind to go straight. Keep him clear o' the pit towns – put him on a farm somewhere, where there aren't so many drinks going. And if I were you (*looking at her*), why not go with him yourself?

Mrs Henderson (*after a pause, suddenly truculent*) Me? Me leave Grantley? Me go to a place where I'm not respected and not a friend to speak for me? In Grantley I was born and in Grantley I'll live, like yourself. And beggin' your pardon, though you are the master, I'll joost take the liberty o' choosin' my own way.

Rutherford Quite right – quite right. When you've lived and had your bairns and got drunk in a place you're apt to get attached to it. I'm that way myself. But it's just as well to change your drinks once in a while. It's only a friendly word of advice I'm giving you. Take it or leave it.

Mrs Henderson (*bridling*) And so I will take it or leave it. Much obliged to 'ee.

Rutherford And now go home, like a good woman.

Mrs Henderson (*tossing her head with an unsteady curtsey*) And so I will, and a lot I got for my trouble – thank 'ee for nothing.

Rutherford Thank me for not prosecuting your son, as I might ha' done.

Mrs Henderson (*working herself up*) Prosecute! Prosecute my son! And why didn't ye do it? Ye darena' – that's why. You're feared o' folks talkin' – o' things said i' the court. And ye took and hided him and him a bit of a lad, and not a decent woman in Grantley but's crying shame on ye!

Rutherford (*good-humouredly*) Now, Richard, this is where you come in. You brought her here.

Mrs Henderson (*very shrill*) You let him off easy, did you? You give him another chance, did you? My lad could ha' had you up for assault – that's what he'd ha' done if he'd had a mind, and quite right too. It's him that's let you off, mind that. And you may thank your devil's luck you're not up afore the magistrate this next Assizes that ever is, and printed in the paper for all the countryside to mock at.

Rutherford Go on, Richard. She's your parishioner. Turn her out.

Mrs Henderson Him turn me out? A bit of a preaching bairn no stronger nor a linty – him with his good noos and his sojers-o'-Christ-arise! Whee was it up and ran away from old Lizzie Winter like a dawg wi' a kettle tied to his tail?

Rutherford (*quietly without turning*) We'll have all your secrets in a minute. Are you going, Mrs Henderson?

Mrs Henderson I'll go when it pleases me, and not afore!

Rutherford Are you going –

He gets up and moves towards her in a threatening manner.

Mrs Henderson (*retreating*) Lay hands on me! Lay hands on a helpless woman! I'll larn ye! I'll larn ye to come on me wi' yer high ways. Folks shall hear tell on it, that they shall, and a bit more besides. I'll larn ye, sure as I'm a living creature. . . . I'll set the police on ye, as sure as I'm a living woman. . . .

Rutherford (*to Dick, contemptuously*) Hark to that – hark to it.

Mrs Henderson You think yourself so grand wi' your big hoose, and your high ways. And your grandfather a potman like my own. You wi' your son that's the laughing-stock o' the parish, and your daughter that goes wi' a working man ahint your back! And so good night to 'ee.

The outer door bangs violently. There is a pause.

Dick *speaks in a voice scarcely audible.*

Dick What was that? . . . She said something – about Janet.

Rutherford (*impatiently*) Good God, man – don't stand staring there as if the house had fallen.

Dick (*shaking*) I told you to be careful – I warned you – I knew how it would be.

Rutherford Warned me! You're fool enough to listen to what a drunken drab like that says!

Dick She's not the only one –

Rutherford (*looking at him*) What d'ye mean? What's that?

Dick People are talking. I've – heard things. . . . It isn't true – it can't be – it's too dreadful.

Rutherford Heard things – what ha' ye heard?

Dick It isn't true.

Rutherford Out with it.

Dick Lizzie Winter that time – called out

something. I took no notice, of course. . . . Three nights ago as I was coming home – past a public-house – the men were talking. I heard something then.

Rutherford What was it you heard?

Dick There was his name, and Janet's. Then one of them – George Hammond, I think it was – said something about having seen him on the road to the Tarn late one evening with a woman with a shawl over her head – Martin!

Rutherford Martin!

Dick (*trying to reassure himself*) It's extremely unlikely that there is any truth in it at all. Why, he's been about ever since we were children. A servant, really. No one's ever thought of the possibility of such a thing. They will gossip, and one thing leads to another. It's easy to put two and two together and make five of them. That's all it is, we'll find. Why, even I can recall things I barely noticed at the time – things that might point to its being true – if it weren't so utterly impossible.

Rutherford (*hoarsely*) Three nights gone. In this very room –

Dick What? (*Running on again.*) They've seen some one like Janet, and started the talk. It would be enough.

Rutherford (*speaking to himself*) Under my roof –

Dick After dark on the road with a shawl – all women would look exactly alike. . . . It's a pity he's taken the Tarn Cottage.

Rutherford (*listening again*) Eh?

Dick I mean it's a pity it's happened just now.

Rutherford A good mile from the Works.

Dick You can't see it from the village.

Rutherford A good mile to walk, morn and night.

Dick No one goes there.

Rutherford A lone place – a secret, he says to himself. Martin . . .

He stands by the table, his shoulders stooped, his face suddenly old. **Dick** *makes an involuntary movement towards him.*

Dick Father! Don't take it like that, for heaven's sake – don't look so broken.

Rutherford Who's broken. . . . (*He makes a sign to* **Dick** *not to come near.*) Him to go against me. You're only a lad – you don't know. You don't know.

John *comes into the room, evidently on his way to bed.*

John (*idly*) Hullo! (*Stops short, looking from one to the other.*) What's the matter?

Rutherford (*turning on him*) And what the devil do you want?

John Want? – nothing. . . . I thought you were talking about me, that's all.

Rutherford About you, damn you – go to bed, the pair o' ye.

Dick Father –

Rutherford Go to bed. There's men's work to be done here – you're best out o' the way. (*He goes to his desk and speaks down the tube.*) Hulloh there – Hulloh!

Dick Wouldn't it be better to wait to talk things over? Here's John – you may be able to settle something – come to some arrangement.

Rutherford Who's that? Gray – has Martin gone home? Martin! Tell him to come across at once – I want him. Aye – to the house – where else? Have you got it? Tell him at once.

John (*suspicious*) I rather want a word with Martin myself. I think I'll stay.

Rutherford You'll do as you're bid.

John What do you want Martin for at this time of night?

Rutherford That's my business.

John About my metal –

Rutherford Your metal! What the devil's your metal got to do with it? (*Breaks off.*)

John (*excited*) Martin's got it. You know that. You're sending for him. Martin's honest – he won't tell you.

Dick Here's Janet.

Janet *has come in in answer to the bell and stands by the door sullen and indifferent, waiting for orders.*

Janet Susan's gone to bed. (*As the silence continues, she looks round.*) The bell rang.

Dick (*looking at* **Rutherford**) Some time ago. The lamp – father wanted his lamp.

She goes out.

John (*rapidly*) It's no use going on like this, settling nothing either way. Sooner or later we've got to come to an understanding. . . . (**Dick** *makes a movement to stop him.*) Oh, shut up, Dick!

He breaks off at a look from **Rutherford**.

Rutherford I want to have it clear. You heard what I said, three days past?

John Yes, of course.

Rutherford You still ask your price?

John I told you – the thing's mine – I made it.

Rutherford (*to* **John**) You've looked at it – fair and honest.

Dick Oh, what is the use of talking like this now? Father! you surely must see – under the circumstances – it isn't right – it isn't decent.

John It's perfectly fair and just, what I ask. It benefits us both, the way I want it. You've made your bit. Rutherford's has served its purpose – and it's coming to an end – only you don't see it, Guv'nor. Oh, I know you're fond of the old place and all that – it's only natural – but you can't live for ever – and I'm all right – if I get my price. . . .

Rutherford So much down for yourself – and the devil take Rutherford's.

John You put it that way –

Rutherford Yes or no?

John Well – yes.

A knock is heard at the outer door.

Dick That's Martin, Father –

John I'll stay and see him – I may as well.

Rutherford Tomorrow – tomorrow I'll settle wi' ye.

John *looks at him in amazement;* **Dick** *makes a sign to him to come away; after a moment he does so.*

John (*turning as he reaches the door*) Thanks, Guv'nor – I thought you'd come to see things my way.

They go out.

Rutherford Come in.

Martin *comes in, cleaning his boots carefully on the mat – shuts the door after him and stands cap in hand.* **Rutherford** *sits sunk in his chair, his hands gripping the arms.*

Martin I came up as soon as I could get away.

Pause.

Rutherford (*as if his lips were stiff*) You've stayed late.

Martin One o' the pots in Number Three Furnace ran down, and I had to stay and see her under way.

Rutherford Sit down. . . . Help yourself.

Martin Thank 'ee, sir. (*He comes to the table and pours out some whisky, then sits with his glass resting on his knee.*) Winter's setting in early.

Rutherford Ay –

Martin There's a heavy frost. The ground was hardening as I came along. . . . They do say as Rayner's'll be working again afore the week's out.

Rutherford Given in – the men?

Martin Ay – the bad weather'll have helped it. Given a fine spell the men 'ud ha' hung on a while longer – but the cold makes 'em think o' the winter – turns the women and bairns agin them.

Rutherford Ah!

Martin I thought you'd like to hear the coal 'ud be coming in all right, so I just went over to have a word wi' White the Agent this forenoon. (*He drinks, then as the silence continues, looks intently at* **Rutherford**.) You sent for me?

Janet *comes in carrying a reading-lamp. She halts for a moment on seeing* **Martin**. *He gets up awkwardly.*

Martin (*touching his forelock*) Evenin'.

Janet Good evening.

She sets the lamp on the desk. **Rutherford** *remains in the same position till she goes out, closing the door. There is a moment's silence, then*

Martin *straightens himself, and they look at each other.*

Martin (*hoarsely*) You're wanting summat wi' me?

Rutherford I want the receipt of Mr John's metal.

Martin (*between amazement and relief*) Eh?

Rutherford You've got it.

Martin Ay –

Rutherford Then give it me.

Martin I cannot do that, sir.

Rutherford What d'ye mean?

Martin It's Mr John's own – what belongs to him – I canna do it.

Rutherford On your high horse, eh, Martin? You can't do a dirty trick – you can't, eh?

Martin A dirty trick. Ye'll never be asking it of me – you never will –

Rutherford I am asking it of ye. We've worked together five and twenty years, master and man. You know me. You know what there is'll stop me when I once make up my mind. I'm going to have this metal, d'ye understand. Whether Mr John gives it me or I take it, I'm going to have it.

Martin It's Mr John's own; if it's ever yourn, he must give it to ye himself. It's not for me to do it. He's found it, and it's his to do what he likes wi'. For me to go behind his back – I canna do it.

They look at each other; then **Rutherford** *gets out of his chair and begins to pace up and down with his hands behind him. He speaks deliberately, with clumsy gestures and an air of driving straight to a goal.*

Rutherford Sit down. . . . Look how we stand. We've seven years' losing behind us, slow and sure. We've got the Bank that's poking its nose into this and that, putting a stop to everything that might put us on our legs again – because o' the risk. . . . Rutherford's is going down – down – I got to pull her up somehow. There's one way out. If I can show the directors in plain working that I can cover the losses on the first year and make a profit on the second, I've got 'em for good and all.

Martin That's so – and Mr John'll see it, and ye'll come to terms –

Rutherford Mr John's a fool. My son's a fool – I don't say it in anger. He's a fool because his mother made him one, bringing him up secret wi' books o' poetry and such-like trash – and when he'd grown a man and the time was come for me to take notice of him, he's turned agin me –

Martin He'll come roond – he's but a bit lad yet –

Rutherford Turned agin me – agin me and all I done for him – all I worked to build up. He thinks it mighty clever to go working behind my back – the minute he gets the chance he's up on the hearthrug dictating his terms to me. He knows well enough I've counted on his coming after me. He's all I got since Richard went his ways – he's got me there. . . . He wants his price, he says – his price for mucking around with a bit of a muffle furnace in his play-hours – that's what it comes to.

Martin Ay – but he's happened on a thing worth a bit.

Rutherford Luck! Luck! What's he done for it? How long has he worked for it – tell me that – an hour here and a bit there – and he's got it! I've slaved my life long, and what have I got for it? Toil and weariness. That's what I got – bad luck on bad luck battering on me – seven years of it. And the worst bit I've had yet is that when it turns it's put into my son's hands to give me or not, if you please, as if he was a lord.

Martin He'll come roond – lads has their notions – we all want to have things for ourselves when we're young, all on us –

Rutherford Want – want – lad's talk! What business has he to want when there's Rutherfords' going to the dogs?

Martin That canna be, it canna – he'll have to see different.

Rutherford He won't see different.

Martin He'll learn.

Rutherford When it's too late. Look here, Martin, we can't go on – you know that as well as I do – leastways you've suspected it. Ten years more as things are'll see us out. Done with! Mr John's made this metal – a thing, I take your word for it, that's worth a fortune. And we're going to sit by and watch him fooling it away – selling it for a song to Miles or Jarvis, that we could break tomorrow if we had half a chance. And they'll make on it, make on it – while Rutherfords'll grub on as we've been grubbing for the last seven years. I'm speaking plain now – I'm saying what I wouldn't say to another living man. We can't go on. You've been with me through it all. You've seen me do it. You've seen the drag and the struggle of it – the days when I've nigh thrown up the sponge for very weariness – the bit o' brightness that made me go on – the times when I've stood up to the Board, sick in the heart of me, with nothing but my will to turn 'em this way or that. And at the end of it – I come up against this – a bit o' foolishness – just foolishness – and all that I done'll break on that – just that.

Martin Nay – nay –

Rutherford I'm getting old, they say – old – there's new ways in the trade, they say.

And in their hearts they see me out of it –
out o' the place I built afore they learnt
their letters, many of 'em –

Martin That'll never be.

Rutherford Why not – when you've got
but to put your hand in your pocket to save
the place and you don't do it. You're with
them – you're with the money-grubbing
little souls that can't see beyond the next
shilling they put in their pockets, that's
content to wring the old place dry, then
leave it to the rats – you're with a half-
broke puppy like Mr John that wants to
grab his bit for himself and clear out.
Twenty-five years . . . and you go snivelling
about what Mr John thinks of ye – what's
right for you to do. Everybody for himself –
his pocket or his soul, it's all one. And
Rutherfords loses her chance through the
lot o' ye. Blind fools!

Martin You blame me – you put me i' the
wrong. It's like as if I'd have to watch the
old place going down year by year, and
have it on my mind that I might ha' saved
her. But Mr John's got his rights.

Rutherford You think I'm getting this
metal for myself against Mr John?

Martin I'm loth to say it.

Rutherford Answer me –

Martin Mr John'll see it that way.

Rutherford Stealing like, out o' his pocket
into mine. When men steal, Martin, they
do it to gain something. If I steal this,
what'll I gain by it? If I make money,
what'll I buy with it? Pleasure mebbee?
Children to come after me – glad o' what I
done? Tell me anything in the wide world
that'd bring me joy, and I'll swear to you
never to touch it.

Martin If you think what you're saying it's
a weary life you got to face.

Rutherford If you give it to me, what'll
you gain by it? Not a farthing shall you
ever have from me – no more than I get
myself.

Martin And what'll Mr John get for it?

Rutherford Rutherford's – when I'm gone.
(*After a silence.*) He'll thank you in ten years
– he'll come to laugh at himself – him and
his price. He'll see the Big Thing one day
mebbee, like what I've done. He'll see that
it was no more his to keep than 'twas yours
to give nor mine to take. . . . It's
Rutherford's. . . . Will you give it to me?

Martin (*facing him*) If I thought that we'd
make a farthing out of it, either on us –

Rutherford Will ye give it me –

Martin *stands looking at him, then slowly begins
to feel in his pockets.*

Rutherford Got it – on you?

Martin (*taking out a pocket-book*) He'll never
forgi' me, Mr John won't – never i' this
world. . . . It should be somewheres. He'll
turn agin me – it'll be as if I stole it.

Rutherford Got it?

Martin Nay, I mun' ha' left it up hame.
Ay, I call to mind now – I locked it away to
keep it safe.

Rutherford Can ye no' remember it?
Think, man – think!

Martin Nay, I canna be sure. I canna call
the quantities to mind.

Rutherford (*violently*) Think – think – you
must know!

Martin (*wonderingly*) I can give it 'ee first
thing i' the morning.

Rutherford I want it tonight. . . . No, no –
leave it – you might get it wrong – better
make sure – bring it up in the morning.

Good night to 'ee – good night. And remember – I take your word to bring it – no going back, mind ye –

Martin Nay, nay. (*Turning to go.*) I doubt if Mr John'll ever see it in the way you do. If you could mebbe explain a bit when he hears tell of it – put in a word for me, belike –

Rutherford I'm to bed.

Martin I take shame to be doing it now.

Rutherford Off wi' ye – off wi' ye – wi' your conscience so delicate and tender. Keep your hands clean, or don't let any one see them dirty – it'll do as well.

Martin He worked it out along o' me. Every time it changed he come running to show me like a bairn wi' a new toy.

Rutherford It's for Rutherford's . . .

Martin Ay, for Rutherford's – Good night, sir.

He goes out.

After a pause, **Janet** *comes in to put things straight for the night. She goes into the hall and is heard putting the chain on the outer door – comes back, locking the inner door – then takes the whisky decanter from the tray and locks it in the sideboard, laying the key on the desk.*
Rutherford *stands on the hearthrug. As she takes up the tray he speaks.*

Rutherford How long has this been going on atween you and Martin?

She puts the tray down and stands staring at him with a white face.

Janet How long?

Rutherford Answer me.

Janet September – about when Mary and Tony came.

There is a long silence. When it becomes unbearable she speaks again.

What are you going to do? (*He makes no answer.*) You must tell me what you're going to do?

Rutherford Keep my hands off ye.

Janet You've had him here.

Rutherford That's my business.

Janet (*speaking in a low voice as if she were repeating a lesson*) It wasn't his fault. It was me. He didn't come after me. I went after him.

Rutherford Feel – proud o' yourself?

Janet You can't punish him for what isn't his fault. If you've got to punish anyone, it's me . . .

Rutherford How far's it gone?

Janet (*after a pause*) Right at first. I made up my mind that if you ever found out, I'd go right away, to put things straight. (*She goes on presently in the same toneless voice.*) He wanted to tell you at the first. But I knew it would be no use. And once we'd spoken – every time was just a little more. So we let it slide. . . . It was I said not to tell you.

Rutherford Martin . . . that I trusted as I trust myself.

Janet I'll give him up.

Rutherford You can't give him back to me. He was a straight man. What's the good of him now? You've dragged the man's heart out of him with your damned woman's ways.

She looks at him.

Janet You haven't turned him away – you couldn't do that!

Rutherford That's my business.

Janet You couldn't do that – not Martin. . . .

Rutherford Leave it – leave it . . . Martin's my servant, that I pay wages to. I made a name for my children – a name respected in all the countryside – and you go with a working-man. Tomorrow you leave my house. D'ye understand. I'll have no light ways under my roof. No one shall say I winked at it. You can bide the night. Tomorrow when I come in, I'm to find ye gone. . . . Your name shan't be spoke in my house . . . never again.

Janet Yes. (*She stands looking down at the table, then slowly moves to go, her feet dragging – stops for a moment and says in a final tone, almost with a sigh of relief.*) Then there'll be no need for anybody to know it was Martin –

Rutherford No need to know. Lord, you drive me crazy! With all Grantley telling the story – my name in every public-house.

Janet When I'm gone. (*Looking up.*) What did you say?

Rutherford It's all over the place by now. Richard's heard it – your own brother. . . . You've been running out o' night, I suppose. Somebody's seen.

Janet What's Dick heard?

Rutherford What men say about women like you. They got a word.

Janet The men. . . . O God!

Rutherford Ay – you say that now the thing's done – you'll whine and cry out now you done your worst agin me.

Janet Let me be.

Rutherford You're going to put things straight, are ye – you're going to walk out comfortable wi' your head up and your fine talk.

Janet I'm ready to stand by it.

Rutherford It's not you that's got to stand by it – it's me! What ha' you got to lose? Yourself, if you've a mind to. That's all. It's me that's to be the laughing-stock – the Master whose daughter goes wi' a working-man like any Jenny i' the place –

Janet Oh! You stand there! To drive me mad –

Rutherford That'll do – that'll do. I've heard enough. You've confessed, and there's an end.

Janet Confessed? As if I'd stolen something. (*Brokenly.*) You put it all on to me, every bit o' the wrong.

Rutherford Ah, you'll set to and throw the blame on Martin now. I thought we'd come to it.

Janet No, no. I've taken that. But . . . you make no excuse. . . . You think of this that I've done separate from all the rest – from all the years I done as you bid me, lived as you bid me.

Rutherford What's that to do wi' it? I'm your father! I work for 'ee. . . . I give 'ee food and clothes for your back! I got a right to be obeyed – I got a right to have my children live respectable in the station where I put them. You gone wrong. That's what you done. And you try to bring it up against me because I set you up i' the world. Go to bed!

Janet Oh, you've no pity. . . . (*She makes a movement to go, then turns again as if for a moment.*) I was thirty-six. Gone sour. Nobody'd ever come after me. Not even when I was young. You took care o' that. Half of my life was gone, well-nigh all of it that mattered. . . . What have I had of it, afore I go back to the dark? What have I had of it? Tell me that. Tell me!

Rutherford Where's the man as 'ud want you wi' your sulky ways?

Janet I've sat and sewed – gone for a walk – seen to the meals – every day – every day. . . . That's what you've given me to be my life – just that!

Rutherford Talk, talk, talk! Fine words to cover up the shame and disgrace you brought on me –

Janet On you?

Rutherford Where 'd you ha' been if I hadn't set you up?

Janet Down in the village – in amongst it, with the other women – in a cottage – happy mebbee.

Rutherford (*angrily*) I brought you up for a lady as idle as you please – you might ha' sat wi' your hands afore you from morn till night if ye'd had a mind to.

Janet Me a lady? What do ladies think about, sitting the day long with their hands before them? What have they in their idle hearts?

Rutherford What more did you want, in God's name?

Janet Oh, what more! The women down there know what I wanted . . . with their bairns wrapped in their shawls and their men to come home at night time. I've envied them – envied them their pain, their poorness – the very times they hadn't bread. Theirs isn't the dead empty house, the blank o' the moors; they got something to fight, something to be feared of. They got life, those women we send cans o' soup to out o' pity when their bairns are born. Me a lady! with work for a man in my hands, passion for a man in my heart! I'm common – common.

Rutherford It's a lie! I've risen up. You can't go back on it – my children can't go back.

Janet Who's risen – which of us?

Rutherford You say that because you've shamed yourself, and you're jealous o' them that keep decent like gentlefolk –

Janet Dick – that every one laughs at? John – with his manners?

Rutherford Whisht wi' your wicked tongue!

Janet Who's Mary? A little common work-girl – no real gentleman would ha' looked at. . . . You think you've made us different by keeping from the people here. We're just the same as they are! Ask the men that work for you – ask their wives that curtsey to us in the road. Do you think they don't know the difference? We're just the same as they are – common, every one of us. It's in our blood, in our hands and faces; and when we marry, we marry common –

Rutherford Marry! Common or not, nobody's married you that I can see –

Janet Leave that – don't you say it!

Rutherford It's the truth, more shame to 'ee.

Janet (*passionately*) Martin loves me honest. Don't you come near! Don't you touch that! . . . You think I'm sorry you've found out – you think you've done for me when you use shameful words on me and turn me out o' your house. You've let me out o' gaol! Whatever happens to me now, I shan't go on living as I lived here. Whatever Martin's done, he's taken me from you. You've ruined my life, you with your getting on. I've loved in wretchedness, all the joy I ever had made wicked by the fear o' you. . . . (*Wildly.*) Who are you? Who are you? A man – a man that's taken power to himself, power to gather people to him

and use them as he wills – a man that'd
take the blood of life itself and put it into
the Works – into Rutherford's. And what
ha' you got by it – what? You've got Dick,
that you've bullied till he's a fool – John,
that's waiting for the time when he can sell
what you've done – and you got me – me to
take your boots off at night – to well-nigh
wish you dead when I had to touch you.
. . . Now! . . . Now you know!

Act Three

It is about eleven o'clock on the following morning. **Janet** *is sitting at the table with a shawl about her shoulders talking in low tones to* **Mary**, *who is opposite.*

Janet (*after a pause*) You mean that you guessed?

Mary Yes.

Janet You knew all the time, and you didn't tell? Not even John?

Mary Why should I tell him?

Janet I would ha' told Martin if it had been you.

Mary Not John.

Janet It was good of you. You've always been better to me than I've been to you.

Mary What are you going to do?

Janet He says I'm to go. He's to come in and find me gone, and no one's to speak of me any more. Not John, nor Dick, nor Aunt Ann – I'm never to set foot in this room again. Never to lock up and give him the keys last thing. Never to sit the long afternoon through in the window, till the chimneys are bright in the dark. I've done what women are shamed for doing – and all the night I've barely slept for the hope in my heart.

Mary Hope?

Janet Of things coming. I had a dream – a dream that I was in a place wi' flowers, in the summer-time, white and thick like they never grow on the moor – but it was the moor – a place near Martin's cottage. And I dreamt that he came to me with the look he had when I was a little lass, with his head up and the lie gone out of his eyes. All the time I knew I was on my bed in my room here – but it was like as if sweetness poured into me, spreading and covering me like the water in the tarn when the rains are heavy in the fells.

Mary Is Mr Rutherford very angry?

Janet He won't never hear my name again. Oh, last night I said things to him, when he blamed me so – things he can't never forget. I was wild – mad with the bitterness of it. He made it all ugly with the things he said. I told him what I never looked to tell him, though I'd had it in my heart all these years. All the time I was speaking I was dead with shame that he should know, and I had to go on. But afterwards – it was as if I'd slipped a burden, and I was glad he knew, glad that Dick heard it in the street, glad that he sneaked of me behind my back – glad! For, when I'd got over the terror of it, it came to me that this was what we'd been making for ever since you came without knowing it, that we were to win through to happiness after all, Martin and I, and everything come right. Because I've doubted. Men's lives are different to ours. And sometimes, when we've stolen together, and afterwards I've seen his face and the sadness of it, I've wondered what I had to give him that could count against what he'd lost.

Mary But that's done with now.

Janet Yes! That's why I dreamt of him so last night. It was as if all that was best in me was in that dream – what I was as a bairn, and what I'm going to be. He couldn't help but love me. It was a message – I couldn't have thought of it by myself. It's something that's come to me, here. (*Putting her hands on her breast.*) Part of me.

Mary *looks at her with a new understanding. After a pause she speaks again, very gently.*

Mary Where are you going when Martin comes for you?

Janet I don't know yet. He'll say what to do.

Mary Have you got your things ready?

Janet (*as if she scarcely heard*) Yes.

Mary I could see to them for you.

Janet They're all ready. I put them together early in the box mother had. (*She breaks off, listening.*)

Mary Janet, if ever the time should be when you want help – and it does happen sometimes even to people who are very happy – remember that I'll come when you ask me – always.

Janet He's coming now! (*She sits listening, her eyes bright.* **Mary** *goes out quietly, closing the door.*)

Martin *comes in from the hall.*

Janet (*very tenderly*) Martin! (*He stands in the doorway, his cap in his hands, his head bent. He looks spent, broken, and at the sight of him the hope dies slowly out of her face.*)

Martin Is Mr John about?

Janet I don't know.

Martin I mun see 'n. I got summat to say to 'n.

Janet He's down at the Works mebbee –

Martin I canna seek him there – I got summat to say to 'n.

Janet You could give a message.

Martin Nay. It's summat that's got to be said to his face – like a man.

Janet Have you nothing to say to me, Martin – to my face like a man?

Martin What should there be to say betwixt you and me? It's all said long since.

Janet He's turned you away? (*He raises his eyes and looks at her for the first time.*)

Martin Ay. You've said it. What I've been trying to tell myself these three months past. Turned away I am, sure enough. Twenty-five year. And in a minute it's broke. Wi' two words.

Janet He'll call you back. He can't do without you, Martin. He's done it in anger like he was last night. He'll call you back.

Martin He never calls no one back. He's a just man, and he's in the right of it. Anger – there's no anger in a face that's twisting like a bairn's – white as if it was drained o' the blood. There's no anger in a man that stands still where he is, when he might ha' struck and killed and still been i' the right.

Janet *gets up slowly and goes to the fire.*

Janet Come and get warm by the fire. It's a bitter cold morning. Come and get warm.

He moves slowly across and sits on the settle. She kneels beside him, takes his hands and begins to rub them.

Janet (*as if he were a child*) Your hands are as cold, as cold – like frozen. It's all fresh and new to you now, my dear, the surprise of it. It'll pass – and by-and-by you'll forget it – be glad, mebbee. Did you get your breakfast?

Martin Ay.

Janet What have you been doing – since?

Martin Walking – walking. Up on the fell I been – trying to get it clear –

Janet On the fell, in such weather! That's why you're so white and weary. You should have come to me, my honey – you should ha' come straight to me. I would ha' helped you, my dear – out of my love for 'ee.

Martin There's no help.

Janet You say that now because your heart's cold with the trouble. But it'll warm again – it'll warm again. I'll warm it out of my own heart, Martin – my heart that can't be made cold, not if he killed me. Why, last night he was just the same with me as he's been with you. I know it all – there's nothing you feel that I don't know. We'll face it together, you and me, equal – and by-and-by it'll be different. What we done was for love – people give up everything for love, Martin; every day they say there's someone in the world that does it. Don't 'ee take on so – don't 'ee.

Martin Twenty-five year –

Janet Don't 'ee, my dear.

Martin (*brokenly*) I'd rather ha' died than he turn me away. I'd ha' lost everything in the world to know that I was true to 'n, like I was till you looked at me wi' the love in your face.

Janet Everything in the world. . . . I gave you joy – joy for the toil he gave you, softness for his hardness.

Martin (*without bitterness*) Ay, you were ready. And you gave the bitter with the sweet. Every time there was him to face, wi' a heart like lead.

Janet It was a power – a power that came, stronger than us both.

Martin You give me the word.

Janet You took away my strength. (*There is a silence. He sits looking dully at the fire.*) Anyone might think me light. It isn't true. I never had anyone but you, never. All my life I've been alone. When I was a little lass I wasn't allowed to play with the other bairns, and I used to make signs to tell them I wanted to. You'd never have known I loved you if I hadn't given you the word –

and all our happiness, all that's been between us, we'd never have had it – gone through our lives seeing each other, speaking words that didn't matter, and grown old and never known what was sleeping in our hearts under the dullness. I wasn't light. It was only that I couldn't be shamed for you.

Martin Nay, nay, it was a great love ye gave me – you in your grand hoose wi' your delicate ways. But it's broke me.

Janet But – it's just the same with us. Just the same as ever it was.

Martin Ay. But there's no mending, wi' the likes o' him.

Janet What's there to mend? What's there to mend except what's bound you like a slave all the years? You're free – free for the first time since you were a lad mebbee – to make a fresh start.

Martin A fresh start? Wi' treachery and a lyin' tongue behind me?

Janet With our love that nothing can break. Oh, my dear, I'll help 'ee. Morning, noon, and night I'll work for 'ee, comfort 'ee. We'll go away from it all, you and me together. We'll go to the south, where no one's heard tell of Rutherford's or any of us. I'll love 'ee so. I'll blind your eyes wi' love so that you can't look back.

Martin (*looking up*) Ay. There's that.

Janet We'll begin again. We'll be happy – happy. You and me, free in the world! All the time that's been'll be just like a dream that's past, a waiting time afore we found each other – the long winter afore the flowers come out white and thick on the moors –

Martin He'll be lookin' to me to right ye. He'll be lookin' for that.

Janet To right me?

Martin Whatever's been, they munna say his daughter wasn't made an honest woman of. He'll be lookin' for that.

There is a silence. She draws back slowly, dropping her hands.

Janet What's he to do with it?

He looks at her, not understanding.

Father – what's he to do with it?

Martin It's for him to say – the Master.

Janet Master!

Martin What's come to ye, lass?

Janet It's time you left off doing things because of him. You're a free man. He's not your master any more.

Martin What's wrong wi' ye?

Janet You'll right me because of him. You'll make an honest woman of me because he's looking for it. He can't make you do as he bids you now. He's turned you away. He's not your master any more. He's turned you away.

Martin Whisht – whisht. (*He sinks his head in his hands.*) Nay, but it's true. I'll never do his work again. But I done it too long to change – too long.

Janet He's done with you – that's how much he cares. I wouldn't ha' let you go, not if you'd wronged me.

Martin Twenty-five years ago he took me from nothing. Set me where I could work my way up – woke the lad's love in me till I would ha' died for him – willing. It's too long to change.

Janet (*passionately*) No – no.

Martin I'll never do his work no more; but it's like as if he'd be my master just the same – till I die –

Janet No, no, not that! You mustn't think like that! You think he's great because you've seen him at the Works with the men – everybody doing as he bids them. He isn't great – he's hard and cruel – cruel as death.

Martin What's took you to talk so wild?

Janet (*holding him*) Listen, Martin. Listen to me. You've worked all your life for him, ever since you were a little lad. Early and late you've been at the Works – working – working for him.

Martin Gladly!

Janet Now and then he gie you a kind word – when you were wearied out mebbe – and your thoughts might ha' turned to what other men's lives were, wi' time for rest and pleasure. You didn't see through him, you wi' your big heart, Martin. You were too near to see, like I was till Mary came. You worked gladly, mebbe – but all the time your life was going into Rutherford's – your manhood into the place he's built. He's had you, Martin – like he's had me, and all of us. We used to say he was hard and ill-tempered. Bad to do with in the house – we fell silent when he came in – we couldn't see for the little things – we couldn't see the years passing because of the days. And all the time it was our lives he was taking bit by bit – our lives that we'll never get back.

Martin What's got ye to talk so wild?

He moves from her as she talks and clings to him.

Janet Now's our chance at last! He's turned us both away, me as well as you. We two he's sent out into the world together. Free. He's done it himself, of his own will. It's ours to take, Martin – our happiness. We'll get it in spite of him. He'd kill it if he could.

Martin Whisht, whisht! You talk wild!

Janet Kill it, kill it! He's gone nigh to it as it is. (*As he makes a movement to rise.*) Martin, Martin, I love 'ee. I'm old – with the lines on my face – but it's him that's made me so. I'm bitter-tongued and sharp – it's him that's killed the sweetness in me, starved it till it died. He's taken what should have been yours to have your joy of. Stolen it – remember that – and say he's in the right! Say it when you wish me young and bonny. Say it as I shall when I look in your face for the love that can't wake for me.

Martin Bide still, bide still!

Janet I wouldn't ha' turned against you, not if you'd nigh killed me – and you set his love up against mine! Martin!

He gets up, not roughly, but very wearily, and moves away from her.

Martin It bain't the time, it bain't the time. I been a bad servant. Faithless. We can twist words like we done all along to make it seem different, but there it stands. Leave him, when you talk to me. Leave him. . . . Mebbee he's had his mind full of a big work when you've took a spite at him.

Janet Ah!

Martin Womenfolk has their fancies, and mebbee they don't know the harshness that's in the heart of every man that fights his way i' the world when he comes into the four walls of his bit hoose of a night and sees the littleness of it. (*Standing by the table.*) I'm a plain man with no book larning, and mebbee I don't see far. But I've watched the Master year in year out, and I never seed him do a thing, nor say a thing, that he warn't in the right of. And there's not a man among them that can say different. (*Taking up his cap.*) I'll be seekin' Mr John.

Janet (*speaks in a dull, toneless voice, kneeling where he left her*) He says I have to be gone by the time he comes in. Where am I to go to?

He turns to look at her with a puzzled face.

Martin Ay. There's that.

Janet Where am I to go?

Martin It would be best to go a bit away – where ye wouldna' be seen for a while.

Janet Where's a place – far enough?

Martin There's Horkesley – up the line. Or Hillgarth yonder. He's not likely to be knawed thereaboots.

Janet I haven't any money.

Martin *slowly counts out some coins on the table.*

Martin It'll be a hard life for you, and you not used to it. Work early and late – wi' a bairn mebbee. Bitter cold i' the winter mornings wi' the fire to light and the breakfast to get, and you not used to it; we mun just bide it, the pair on us. Make the best of it. I've saved two hundred pounds. There'll be summat to get along whilst I look for a job. Afterwards we mun just bide it.

There is a silence.

Janet (*without bitterness*) Take up your money.

Martin (*puzzled*) It's for you, lass.

Janet Take up your money. I'll have no need of it.

After a moment he picks it up and returns it to his pocket.

Janet (*still kneeling*) After all, you'd give the world to ha' been true to him – you'd give me, that you said was the world. He'd have you back if it wasn't for me. He needs you for the Works. If I was out of it there'd be no more reason – you'd go back, and people would think it all a mistake about you and me. Gossip. After a bit he'd forget and be the same. Because he needs you for the Works. Men forgive men easy where it's a woman, they say, and you could blame me, the pair of you. Me that gave you the word.

Mary *comes in hurriedly.*

Mary John's coming. He's coming across from the Works.

Martin *turns to face the door.* **Janet** *does not move.* **John** *comes in excited and nervous.*

John (*awkwardly*) Hullo! (*He looks at* **Janet** *and speaks to* **Martin**.) What are you here for?

Martin Mr John – I summat to say to you – summat I must say afore I go.

John You'd better keep quiet, I should think. Oh, I know! I've been with the Guv'nor, and he's told me plain enough. You'd better keep quiet.

Mary John, you must listen.

John I tell you I know! The less we talk about it the better; I should think you would see that – the whole beastly, disreputable business. I can't stay – I can't talk calmly, if you can – I'm better out of it. (*He makes for the door.* **Martin** *stops him.*)

Martin Mr John. . . . You been wi' the Master. What was it he told you – plain enough?

John (*significantly*) What was it!

Martin Did he tell you he'd got your metal?

John *looks at him.*

John Are you mad?

Martin I've give it him – I took it him this morning, and when he got it safe he turned me away. That's what I got to say.

John (*sharply*) I don't believe it! You can't have! You haven't got the quantities!

Martin The paper I took the last trial we made –

John (*his voice high-pitched with excitement*) Don't – don't play the fool.

Martin I'm speaking God's truth, and you'd best take it. Yesterday night he sent for me – and I give it him, because he asked me for it. He was i' the right, yesterday night – I don't call to mind how. And just now I give it him. That's what I got to say.

John *stands staring at him speechless.* **Martin**, *having said what he came to say, turns to go.* **Mary**, *suddenly realising what it all means, makes an involuntary movement to stop him.*

Mary Martin! You've given the receipt to Mr Rutherford! He's got it – he'll take the money from it! . . . You're sure of what you say, Martin? You haven't made a mistake?

Martin Mistake?

Mary You may have got it wrong – the quantities, or whatever it is. It all depends on that, doesn't it? The least slip would put it all wrong, wouldn't it?

Martin (*tired out and dull*) There's no mistake.

Mary (*with a despairing movement*) Oh! you don't know what you've done!

John (*almost in tears*) He knows well enough – you knew well enough. You're a thief – you're as bad as he is – you two behind my back. It was mine – the only chance I had. Damn him! damn him! You've done for yourself, that's one thing – you're done for! You'll not get anything out of it now, not a farthing. He's twisted you round his finger, making you think you'd have the pickings, has he? And then thrown you out into the street for a fool and worse. You're done for! . . . You've worked with me, seen it grow. I never thought but to trust you as I trusted myself – and you give it away thinking to make a bit behind my back! You'll not get a farthing now – not a farthing – you're done for.

Martin Hard words, Mr John, from you to me. But I done it, and I mun bide by it.

John Oh, clear out – don't talk to me. By heaven! I'll be even with him yet.

Martin I done it – but it bain't true what you think, that I looked to make a bit. I give it to him, but I had no thought o' gain by what I done. . . . It's past me – it's all past me – I canna call it to mind, nor see it plain. But I know one thing, that I never thought to make a penny. (*Suddenly remembering.*) It was for Rutherford's – that's what he said – I mind it now. He said, for Rutherford's – and I seed it yesterday night. It was as clear as day – yesterday night.

No one answers. After a moment he goes out.

As the outer door closes **John** *suddenly goes to* **Rutherford***'s desk and begins pulling out drawers as if searching for something.*

Mary (*watching him*) What are you doing?

John Where's the key, curse it!

Mary (*sharply*) You can't do that!

John Do what? I'm going to get even.

Mary Not money! You can't take his money!

John (*unlocking the cash box*) Just be quiet, will you? He's taken all I have. (*He empties the money out on to the desk; his hands shaking.*) Fifteen – twenty – twenty-three. And it's twenty-three thousand he owes me more like, that's he's stolen. Is there any more – a sixpence I've missed, that'll help to put us even? Twenty-three quid – curse him! And he stood and talked to me not an hour ago, and all the time he knew! He's mean, that's

what he is – mean and petty-minded. No one else could have done it – to go and get at Martin behind my back because he knew I was going to be one too many for him.

Mary (*imploringly*) Put it back! Oh, put it back!

John Oh, shut up, Mollie.

Mary Don't take it, John.

John I tell you it's mine, by right – you don't understand. . . . How am I to get along if I don't?

Mary You've not got to do this, John – for Tony's sake. I don't care what he's done to you – you've not got to do it.

John Don't make a tragedy out of nothing. It's plain common sense! (*Angrily.*) And don't look at me as if I were stealing. It's mine, I tell you. I only wish there were a few thousands – I'd take them!

Mary John, listen to me. I've never seriously asked you to do anything for me in my life. Just this once – I ask you to put that money back.

John My dear girl, don't be so foolish –

Mary (*compelling him to listen to her*) Listen! You're Tony's father! I can't help it if you think I'm making a tragedy out of what seems to you a simple thing. One day he'll know – someone'll tell him that you stole money – well then, that you took money that wasn't yours, because you thought you had the right to it. What will it be like for him? Try and realise – we've no right to live as we like – we've had our day together, you and I – but it's past, and we know it. He's what matters now – and we've got to live decently for him – keep straight for him –

John (*answering her like an angry child*) Then do it! I've had enough – I'm sick of it.

Janet, *who all this time has been kneeling where* **Martin** *left her, gets up suddenly, stumbling forward as if she were blind. The other two stop involuntarily and watch her as she makes for the door, dragging her shawl over her head. As the outer door shuts on her,* **Mary** *with a half-cry makes a movement to follow her.*

Mary Janet!

John Oh, let her be!

Mary (*facing the door*) Where's she going to?

John I'm not going to argue – I've done that too long – listening to first one and then another of you. What's come of it? You wouldn't let me go out and sell the thing while it was still mine to sell. I might have been a rich man if I'd been let to go my own way! You were always dragging me back, everything I did – with your talk. Tony – you're perpetually cramming him down my throat, till I'm sick of the very name of the poor little beggar. How much better off is he for your interfering? Give up this and give up that – I've lost everything I ever had by doing as you said. Anybody would have bought it, anybody! and made a fortune out of it – and there it is, lost! gone into Rutherford's, like everything else. Damn the place! damn it! Oh, let him wait! I'll be even with him. I came back once because I was a soft fool – this time I'll starve sooner.

Mary You're going away?

John Yes, I'm going for good and all.

She stands looking at him.

Mary Where are you going to?

John London – anywhere. Canada, probably – that's the place to strike out on your own –

Mary You mean to work then?

John (*impatiently*) Of course. We can't live for ever on twenty-three quid.

Mary What are you going to work at?

John Anything – as long as I show him –

Mary But what – what?

John Oh, there'll be something. Damn it, Mary, what right have you to catechise?

Mary Don't, please. I'm not catechising; I want to know. It's a question of living. What are you going to do when you've spent what you've got?

John (*trying not to look shamefaced as he makes the suggestion*) You could go back to Mason's for a bit – they'd be glad enough to have you.

Mary Go back?

John (*resentfully*) Well, I suppose you won't mind helping for a bit till I see my way. What was the screw you got?

Mary Twenty-five.

John That would help if the worst came to the worst.

Mary We lived on it before.

John We could put up at the same lodgings for a bit. They're cheap.

Mary Walton Street.

John (*loudly*) Anyway, I'm going to be even with him – I'll see him damned before I submit. I've put up with it long enough for your sake – I'm going to get a bit of my own back for once. After all, I'm his son – you can't count Dick; when I'm gone he'll begin to see what he's lost. Why, he may as well sell Rutherford's outright – with no one to come after him. He's worked for that – all his life! Lord! I'd give something to see his face when he comes in and asks for me!

Mary *makes no answer, as indeed there is none to*

make. She speaks again, not bitterly, but as one stating a fact.

Mary So that's your plan. (*There is a silence, in which he cannot meet her eyes. She repeats, without hope.*) John, once more – from my soul I ask you to do what I wish.

John (*impatiently*) What about?

Mary The money. To put it back. (*He makes a movement of desperate irritation.*) No, don't answer just for a moment. You don't know how much depends on this – for us both. Our future life – perhaps our last chance of happiness together – you don't know what it may decide.

John I tell you you don't understand. (*There is a blank silence. He moves uncomfortably.*) You can't see. What's twenty-three quid!

She makes a despairing movement.

Mary (*in a changed voice*) I'm afraid you'll find it rather a burden having me and Tony – while you're seeing your way, I mean.

John A burden? You? Why, you've just said you could help at Mason's –

Mary I can't go out all day and leave Tony.

John Old Mrs What's-'er-name would keep an eye on him.

Mary It would free you a good deal if we weren't with you.

John Of course if you won't do anything to help –

Mary (*after a pause*) How would it be if you went alone? Then – when you've seen your way – when you've made enough just to live decently – you could write and we could come to you. Somewhere that would do for Tony – wherever it may be.

John In a month or two.

Mary In a month or two.

John (*awkwardly*) Well, perhaps it would be better – as you suggest it. I really don't exactly see how I'm going to manage the two of you. . . . You mean – stay on here in the meantime.

Mary Yes – stay on here.

John But the Guv'nor – I'm afraid it'll be pretty rotten for you without me.

Mary That's all right.

John (*irritably*) All these stupid little details – we lose sight of the real issue. That's settled, then.

Mary Yes – settled. (*She moves, passing her hand over her eyes.*) How are you going?

John (*relieved*) What's the time now? Close on twelve!

Mary You're not thinking of going now – at once!

John There's the one o'clock train. I'll get old Smith to drive me to the Junction – it doesn't stop.

Mary There won't be time to pack your things.

John Send them after me.

Mary You've no food to take with you.

John That doesn't matter; I'll get some on the way.

Mary (*suddenly*) You can't go like this! We must talk – we can't end it all like this.

John I must – I didn't know it was so late – he'll be in to dinner. Cheer up, dear, it's only for a little while. I hate it too, but it wouldn't do for him to find me here. It would look – weak.

Mary No, no – you're right – you mustn't

meet – it would do no good. (*She stands undecided for a moment, then goes quickly into the hall and brings his overcoat.*) It's bitter cold. And it's an open trap, isn't it?

John I shall be all right. (*She helps him on with the coat.*) It won't be long – the time'll pass before you know where you are; it always does – I haven't time to see the kid – it's the only thing to be done – other fellows make their fortunes every day, why shouldn't I?

Mary (*as if he were a child*) Yes, yes, why shouldn't you?

John Something'll turn up – and I've got the devil's own luck at times – you'll see. I've never had a chance up to now. Some day you'll believe in me. (*He sees her face and stops short.*) Mollie –! (*Takes her in his arms. She breaks down, clinging to him.*)

Mary Oh, my dear – if I could!

John (*moved*) I will do it, Mollie – I swear I will. Something'll turn up, and it'll all come right – we'll be as happy as kings, you see if we aren't. Don't, dear, it's only for a little while. . . . Well then – will you come with me now?

Mary No, no, that can't be. Go, go – he'll be in directly. Go now.

She goes with him to the outer door. **Ann Rutherford** *comes in on her way through the room.*

Ann Who is it's got the door open on such a day? And the wind fit to freeze a body's bones! (*The outer door is heard closing.* **Mary** *comes in slowly, very pale.*) Come in, come in, for the Lord's sake. (*Looking at her.*) What be ye doing out there?

Mary He's gone.

Ann (*cross with the cold*) Gone, gone, this one and that – John? And what'll he be gone for? I never seed such doings, never!

Mary Shall I make up the fire?

Ann And you all been and let it down. Nay, nay, I'll do it myself. It'll not be up for ten minutes or more. Such doings. What'll he be gone for?

Mary He's had a quarrel with his father.

Ann (*putting logs on, half-whimpering*) A fine reason for making folks talk – bringing disgrace on the house, and all Grantley talking, and tomorrow Sunday – I never seed the like, never!

Mary It's no use crying.

Ann It's weel enough for you to talk – you bain't one of the family, a stranger like you. You don't know. When you've come up i' the world and are respected, there's nothing pleases folk better than to find something agin you. What am I to say when I'm asked after my nevvy? Tell me that. And him gone off without so much as a change to his back – it aren't respectable. And there's Janet not ten minutes since gone along the road wi' her shawl over her head like a common working lass. Where it's to end, I'm sure I can't tell.

Mary Perhaps it is ended.

Ann Perhaps half the work's left and the house upset. Susan'll be giving notice just now – her and her goings on. As if lasses weren't hard enough to get – and there's dinner and all –

Mary Do you want the table laid?

Ann It'd help – though you've no call to do it – you got your own troubles – the little lad'll be wanting you mebbee.

Mary He's still asleep. I'll leave the door open and then I shall hear him. (*She opens the door, listening for a moment before she comes back into the room.*)

Ann Janet'll be back mebbee afore you've

finished. Such doings – everything put wrong. I'll go and fetch the bread. (*She wanders out, talking as she goes.*)

Mary *takes the red cloth off the table, folds it, takes the white one from the drawer in the sideboard, and spreads it. As she is doing so* **Rutherford** *comes in. He stands looking at her for a moment, then comes to the fire.*

Rutherford (*as he passes her*) Dinner's late.

Mary (*going on with her work*) It'll be ready in a few minutes.

Rutherford It's gone twelve.

She makes no answer. He takes his pipe off the chimney-piece and begins to fill it. As he is putting his tobacco-pouch back into his pocket his eyes fall on the table; he stops short.

Rutherford You've laid a place short. (*Raising his voice.*) D'ye hear me, you've laid a –

She looks at him.

Mary No.

She goes to the sideboard and spreads a cloth there. He stands motionless staring at the table.

Rutherford Gone. Trying to frighten me, is he? Trying a bit o' bluff – he'll show me, eh? And all I got to do is sit quiet and wait for him to come back – that's all I got to do.

Mary (*quietly*) He won't come back.

Rutherford Won't he! He'll come back right enough when he feels the pinch – he'll come slinking back like a whipped puppy at nightfall, like he did afore. I know him – light – light-minded like his mother afore him. (*He comes to his desk and finds the open cash box.*) Who's been here? Who's been here? (*He stands staring at the box till the lid falls from his hand.*) Nay – he'll not come back, by God!

Mary (*hopelessly*) He thought he had the right – he believed he had the right after you'd taken what was his.

Rutherford I'd sooner have seen him in his grave.

Mary He couldn't see.

Rutherford Bill Henderson did that because he knowed no better. And my son knowed no better, though I made a gentleman of him. Set him up. I done with him – done with him.

He drops heavily into the arm-chair beside the table and sits staring before him. After a long silence he speaks again.

Rutherford Why haven't you gone too, and made an empty house of it?

Mary I'm not going.

Rutherford Not going, aren't you? Not till it pleases you, I take it – till he sends for you?

Mary He won't send for me.

Rutherford (*quickly*) Where's the little lad?

Mary Asleep upstairs. (*After a pause she speaks again in level tones.*) I've lived in your house for nearly three months. (*He turns to look at her.*) Until you came in just now you haven't spoken to me half-a-dozen times. Every slight that can be done without words you've put upon me. There's never a day passed but you've made me feel that I'd no right here, no place.

Rutherford You'll not die for a soft word from the likes o' me.

Mary Now that I've got to speak to you, I want to say that first – in case you should think I'm going to appeal to you, and in case I should be tempted to do it.

Rutherford What ha' ye got to ask of me?

Mary To ask – nothing. I've a bargain to make with you.

Rutherford (*half truculent*) Wi' me?

Mary You can listen – then you can take it or leave it.

Rutherford Thank ye kindly. And what's your idea of a bargain?

Mary A bargain is where one person has something to sell that another wants to buy. There's no love in it – only money – money that pays for life. I've got something to sell that you want to buy.

Rutherford What's that?

Mary My son. (*Their eyes meet in a long steady look. She goes on deliberately.*) You've lost everything you have in the world. John's gone – and Richard – and Janet. They won't come back. You're alone now and getting old, with no one to come after you. When you die Rutherford's will be sold – somebody'll buy it and give it a new name perhaps, and no one will even remember that you made it. That'll be the end of all your work. Just – nothing. You've thought of that. I've seen you thinking of it as I've sat by and watched you. And now it's come. . . . Will you listen?

Rutherford Ay.

She sits down at the other end of the table, facing him.

Mary It's for my boy. I want – a chance of life for him – his place in the world. John can't give him that, because he's made so. If I went to London and worked my hardest I'd get twenty-five shillings a week. We've failed. From you I can get what I want for my boy. I want – all the good common things: a good house, good food, warmth. He's a delicate little thing now, but he'll grow strong like other children. I want to undo the wrong we've done him,

John and I. If I can. Later on there'll be his schooling – I could never save enough for that. You can give me all this – you've got the power. Right or wrong, you've got the power. . . . That's the bargain. Give me what I ask, and in return I'll give you – him. On one condition. I'm to stay on here. I won't trouble you – you needn't speak to me or see me unless you want to. For ten years he's to be absolutely mine, to do what I like with. You mustn't interfere – you mustn't tell him to do things or frighten him. He's mine. For ten years more.

Rutherford And after that?

Mary He'll be yours.

Rutherford To train up. For Rutherford's? You'd trust your son to me?

Mary Yes.

Rutherford After all? After Dick, that I've bullied till he's a fool? John, that's wished me dead?

Mary In ten years you'll be an old man; you won't be able to make people afraid of you any more.

Rutherford Ah! Because o' that? And because I have the power?

Mary Yes. And there'll be money for his clothes – and you'll leave the Works to him when you die.

There is a silence. He sits motionless, looking at her.

Rutherford You've got a fair notion of business – for a woman.

Mary I've earned my living. I know all that that teaches a woman.

Rutherford It's taught you one thing – to have an eye to the main chance.

Mary You think I'm bargaining for myself?

Rutherford You get a bit out of it, don't you?

Mary What?

Rutherford A roof over your head – the shelter of a good name – your keep – things not so easy to come by, my son's wife, wi' a husband that goes off and leaves you to live on his father's charity. (*There is a pause.*)

Mary (*slowly*) There'll be a woman living in the house – year after year, with the fells closed round her. She'll sit and sew at the window and see the furnace flare in the dark; lock up, and give you the keys at night –

Rutherford You've got your bairn.

Mary Yes, I've got him! For ten years. (*They sit silent.*) Is it a bargain?

Rutherford Ay. (*She gets up with a movement of relief. As he speaks again she turns, facing him.*) You think me a hard man. So I am. But I'm wondering if I could ha' stood up as you're standing and done what you've done.

Mary I love my child. That makes me hard.

Rutherford I used to hope for my son once, like you do for yours now. When he was a bit of a lad I used to think o' the day when I'd take him round and show him what I had to hand on. I thought he'd come after me – glad o' what I'd done. I set my heart on that. And the end of it's just this – an empty house – we two strangers, driving our bargain here across the table.

Mary There's nothing else.

Rutherford You think I've used him badly? You think I've done a dirty thing about this metal?

Mary It was his.

Rutherford I've stolen it behind his back – and I'm going to make money out of it?

Mary I don't know – I don't know.

Rutherford It'll come to your son.

Mary Yes.

Rutherford Because I done that he'll have his chance, his place i' the world. What would ha' gone to the winds, scattered and useless, 'll be his. He'll come on, young and strong, when my work's done, and Rutherford's 'll stand up firm and safe out o' the fight and the bitterness – Rutherford's that his grandfather gave his life to build up.

Mary (*stopping him with a gesture*) Hush!

Rutherford What is it? (*They both listen.*) The little lad. He's waking!

Mary *runs out. The room is very silent as* **Rutherford** *sits sunk in his chair, thinking.*